LADS, CITIZENS AND ORDINARY KIDS

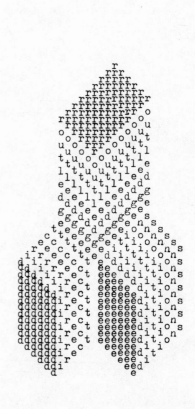

LADS, CITIZENS AND ORDINARY KIDS

Working-class youth life-styles in Belfast

RICHARD JENKINS
Research Unit on Ethnic Relations,
University of Aston in Birmingham

Routledge Direct Editions

ROUTLEDGE & KEGAN PAUL
London, Boston, Melbourne and Henley

First published in 1983
by Routledge & Kegan Paul plc
39 Store Street, London, WC1E 7DD,
9 Park Street, Boston, Mass. 02108, USA,
296 Beaconsfield Parade, Middle Park,
Melbourne 3206, Australia, and
Broadway House, Newtown Road,
Henley-on-Thames, Oxon RG9 1EN

Printed and bound in Great Britain by
Hartnoll's, Bodmin, Cornwall

Library of Congress Cataloging in Publication Data

Jenkins, Richard, 1952-
    Lads, citizens and ordinary kids.

    (Routledge direct editions)
    Bibliography p.
    Includes index.
    1. Youth - Northern Ireland - Belfast. 2. Labor and
laboring classes - Northern Ireland - Belfast. 3. Life
style. I. Title.
HQ799.G72B444 1983   305.2'35'094167   83-3339
ISBN 0-7100-9574-0

Dedicated to the memory of Milan Stuchlik

CONTENTS

ACKNOWLEDGMENTS

The research documented in this book was undertaken while working as a youth worker in Ballyhightown, in the first instance, and subsequently as a research student at Clare Hall, Cambridge. I am grateful to my original employer, the local Education and Library Board, and to the Department of Education, Northern Ireland, who awarded me a post-graduate scholarship. The Department of Social Anthropology, the University of Cambridge, funded the postal questionnaire of employers in Castleowen.

To Jack Goody I owe a huge debt of gratitude for his encouragement to do the research at all, and his subsequent supervision and good advice. The late Milan Stuchlik in Belfast, to whom the book is dedicated, was an inspiring teacher while I was an undergraduate, a supportive field supervisor and a useful critic during the writing up. Bob Blackburn, although he may not have realised it at the time, was an important source of ideas; Andy Ward and Tony Watts also gave useful critical advice. Janet Hall and Colin Duly patiently gave me much-needed advice and assistance with the computing.

With the 'viva' over, the task of transforming thesis into book was made much easier by the advice of the following: my examiners, Esther Goodey and Ray Pahl, my colleagues John Rex and John Solomos, and Philippa Brewster and David Stonestreet of Routledge & Kegan Paul. Different parts of the book have also benefited from being given as seminars at the Universities of Aston, Birmingham, Cambridge, Sussex, and the Queen's University of Belfast. All the typists who have had a hand in this work, Shelagh, Laraine, Rose, Christine and Joy, also earned my gratitude.

All anthropologists, however, must owe their major debt to the people among whom they have worked. I am no exception. In the interests of confidentiality, all proper names, of individuals and places, with any bearing on 'Ballyhightown', have been fictionalised in this book. In particular I must acknowledge the suuport, encouragement and tolerance of the following: the staff of the Youth Centre, the Principal and Staff of Ballyhightown Secondary School, local community workers, all the regulars at the Hillview Social Club, the Careers Officers from Gloucester House, all those connected with the local Church of Ireland, Methodist and Presbyterian churches, the Manager and staff of the local Social Security Office, the workers, trade unionists, employers and others I interviewed in the course of preparing Chapters 8 and 9, particularly those associated with 'TransInternational Electronics', the Director and staff of the Northern Ireland Training Executive and various Industrial Training Boards, and, most important of all, all the residents of Ballyhightown, young and old, who helped in one way or another but must remain anonymous. In addition, the following Northern Ireland government departments provided what assistance they could: the Departments of Education, Health and Social Services, and Manpower Services.

There is also a debt which is too great to be acknowledged, to Pearl, Nicky and Niel, who put up with my prolonged absences and preoccupation while I was at home. Pearl, as a sometime native of Ballyhightown, has been my most constant and constructive critic. Gabrielle and Mrs J. must also be mentioned: without their help it would not have been possible.

Finally it remains to recommend to the interested reader another work on Ballyhightown, 'Hightown Rules', published by the National Youth Bureau in 1982. Approaching the topic from very different perspectives, the two books are intended to complement each other.

Richard Jenkins
University of Aston in Birmingham

KEY TO ETHNOGRAPHIC QUOTATIONS

Unless otherwise specified, all speech acts quoted in this book are quoted either from field notes or written interviews.

(T)   Tape-recorded material

...   Pause in the conversation

...//...   Material edited out

( )   Explanatory information inserted

Chapter 1

INTRODUCTION

This book is an attempt to document and understand the passage
between adolescence and adulthood, between education and the labour
market, of the young men and women of a housing estate on the outskirts of Belfast. As such, it addresses itself to two separate
areas of academic debate: youth culture and the transition from
school to work on the one hand, and the Northern Ireland situation
on the other.

   In this introduction I shall attempt to put what I have to say
later into its proper theoretical context; although this is
primarily an ethnographic account, it would be misleading to pretend
that there is any such thing as theoretically innocent ethnography.
Without wishing to become bogged down in too much grand theory, I
shall begin by making explicit the theoretical scaffolding around
which the analysis is constructed.

YOUNG WORKERS

On examination of a number of accounts - both popular and academic -
concerned with the post-war 'social problem' of working-class youth,
it becomes apparent that two conflicting images of young workers in
modern industrial society are being mobilised. The literature on
the youth problem has been more than adequately summarised and
criticised elsewhere (Brake, 1980; Hebdige, 1979; Murdock and
McCron, 1976) and I do not intend to repeat these summaries here;
the contrasting images or models of youth implicit or explicit in
the literature are worthy of some discussion, however.

   In the first, young workers are seen to possess greater freedom
to determine their own destinies than any generation in recent
history. Better educated and less subject to the moral hegemony of
their elders, they are more powerful, both as consumers and at the
ballot box, than young people have ever been before. The second
image of youth has, for reasons which will perhaps be obvious,
achieved a measure of intellectual dominance in the 1970s. In
this, the disproportionate impact of rising unemployment upon the
young, the deskilling of many of those jobs which have traditionally
been accessible to working-class young people, and the resilience of

political and economic gerontocracy bespeak a very different reality
indeed. It is interesting that elements of both of these images
come together in the moral panics about the young which regularly
erupt onto the pages of the popular press.

This apparent paradox, that young workers are able to make
decisions about their own lives and act upon those decisions, whilst
simultaneously finding themselves constrained at almost every turn
by factors over which they have no control, was one of the earliest
and most abiding general impressions I formed during my time in
Ballyhightown. It remains basic to my understanding, arrived at
both during the fieldwork and as a result of my own youth in a
working-class neighbourhood, of the existential situation of the
young working class. Life is a paradox and for many of them it is
experienced as such. This is not, however, a situation which is
peculiar to either the young or the working class; given the position
of the young working class within the social and economic relations
of capitalist society, the irony of contradiction is perhaps most
marked in their case.

An imaginative attempt to mediate these contrasting images of
working-class youth within a unified theoretical paradigm has
characterised many of the most recent discussions of youth culture
and the relationship between class, education and the labour market.
Possibly the most important original work which has been done in
this vein is that associated with either the Centre for Contemporary
Cultural Studies, at Birmingham, or the Centre de sociologie
européenne, in Paris. Two names in particular stand out, although
the work of other authors is important as well: Pierre Bourdieu and
Paul Willis. As part of a loosely coherent school of analysis, I
shall characterise these authors as concerned with the analysis of
the cultural reproduction of society, in this case with the cultural
reproduction of capitalist society, although there is no reason why
such an analytical framework should not be equally useful in
understanding, for example, bureaucratic state socialism.

What, however, is meant by cultural reproduction? As I shall
use the phrase, and in agreement with Bourdieu (Bourdieu and
Passeron, 1977, p.10) and Willis (1981, p.49). it denotes the
manner in which cultural forms and social practices are continuous
with, generate, or tend to legitimate the relations of domination
in capitalist society.   In other words, I am concerned with the
process through which the working class may be said to learn,
accept, support and at times resist its own role and position in a
fundamentally unequal society.

There are many ways in which this basic problematic may be
operationalised in a particular research context, for example, Paul
Willis's 'how working-class kids get working-class jobs'. In this
book, however, I have chosen to tackle a slightly different topic:
what are the patterned differences, 'cultural' or otherwise, within
the (young) working class, and how are those distinctions produced
and reproduced? These linked questions are important for the
discussion of cultural reproduction in two respects. First, it
must be accepted that the maintenance of division within the working
class - however that class is defined - is a major constraint upon
the political mobilisation of that class as a class for itself.
Second, I shall be concerned to examine the degree to which these

divisions are produced and reproduced by the working class in their
own practice, and the degree to which they are the result of other
factors.

Although the analysis is situated firmly within the cultural
reproduction problematic, it is, however, intended to be rigorously
critical of some aspects of the existing studies within that paradigm.
In the sections which follow I shall, while acknowledging the gains
made by those studies, sketch out the basic outlines of my critique.

CULTURE AND THE REPRODUCTION OF DETERMINISM (1)

Underlying much of the discussion of cultural reproduction is the
essentially philosophical question of which model of mankind, the
passive or the active, is appropriate to sociological and political
debate. How can we explain the persistence of patterned social
inequality without falling back upon a deterministic model of social
process which allows no room for practice, in the sense of social
action?

A similar question is central to the project of Pierre Bourdieu,
who argues that sociology must 'escape from the ritual either/or
choice between objectivism and subjectivism' (1977a, p.4), insisting
that, 'rejection of mechanistic theories in no way implies that, in
accordance with another obligatory option ... we should reduce the
objective intentions and constituted significations of actions and
works to the conscious and deliberate intentions of their authors'
(ibid., p.73). In an attempt to mediate this theoretical contradiction, Bourdieu's theoretical scheme revolves around the notion of
habitus, 'a system of durable, transposable dispositions which
functions as the generative basis of structured, objectively unified
practices' (Bourdieu, 1979, p.vii).

The habitus is seen as the product of those 'objective' structures
which constitute the basic framework of social life, in Marxian
terms, the base or infrastructure. This production, however, is not
held in any sense to be a process of mechanistic determination; the
habitus is 'an acquired system of generative schemes objectively
adjusted to the particular conditions in which it is constituted'
(Bourdieu, 1977a, p.95), a constitution and adjustment which is
mediated by the subjective expectations which the actor has of the
objective reality of his/her position as a member of a class or
group (Bourdieu, 1979, pp.50-63; Bourdieu and Passeron, 1977,
pp.155-6). Although the concept of the habitus has not really
survived the appropriation of Bourdieu by anglophone sociology, the
vacuum left by its passing has been easily filled, however, by the
notion of culture. In the rest of this discussion I shall use
'culture' or 'subculture' as a gloss for Bourdieu's own terminology.

Another key concept in Bourdieu's sociology is misrecognition
('méconnaissance'), 'the process whereby power relations are
perceived not for what they objectively are but in a form which
renders them legitimate in the eye of the beholder' (Bourdieu and
Passeron, 1977, p.205). This becomes the cornerstone of his theory
of ideology. Building upon these foundations, Bourdieu's central
concern has been to understand the important role played by symbolic
modes of domination, in particular the education system, in the

generation and maintenance of systems of class-based power relations.
It is here that Marx and Weber meet in Bourdieu's thinking.

As Bourdieu defines it, an education system is a complex of
institutions and practices which serves to reproduce symbolic
violence, which underwrites and maintains the domination of one
group by another. This is achieved in the imposition, through the
pedagogic process, of the cultural arbitrary of that society, the
axiomatically legitimated dominant culture. Rooted in familial
primary socialisation, this imposition is brought to full consumation
through the experience of formal schooling.

Although the dominant culture is misrecognised as legitimate by
the subordinated classes, the members of these classes stand in a
different relationship to it than the dominant group(s), as a result
of differences in the class subculture (i.e. habitus) of each. The
culture or subculture of each group is generated by their contrasting
positions within the 'objective structures' of society, and their
differing subjective expectations of the objective probabilities
attaching to their respective class locations:

> the disposition to make use of the School and the predispositions
> to succeed in it depend, as we have seen, on the objective chances
> of using it and succeeding in it that are attached to the
> different social classes, these dispositions and predispositions
> in turn constituting one of the most important factors in the
> perpetuation of the structure of educational chances as an
> objectively graspable manifestation of the relationships between
> the educational system and the structure of class relations.
> Even the negative dispositions and predispositions leading to
> self-elimination, such as, for example, self-depreciation,
> devalorization of the School and its sanctions or resigned
> expectation of failure or exclusion may be understood as
> unconscious anticipation of the sanctions the School objectively
> has in store for the dominated classes. (ibid., pp.204-5)

The pedagogic process is legitimated by the coincident ideologies
of equality of opportunity, on the one hand, and achievement based
on meritocratic criteria alone, on the other. Bourdieu's main
thesis is that since what is being taught is the dominant cultural
arbitrary, excellence and scholastic achievement will naturally be
defined in terms of that arbitrary cultural paradigm. Those pupils
whose familial socialisation bestows upon them greater amounts of
cultural capital, i.e. familiarity with the cultural arbitrary, will
necessarily achieve more academically than those whose relationship
to the cultural arbitrary is more distant. Furthermore, the subculture of the subordinated class will, in legitimising their class
position, serve to inhibit their demands for access to the higher
reaches of the education system.

There is, therefore, a double-headed cultural reproduction of
the legitimacy of domination: as a legitimate educational process
based on notions of scholastic merit, and as a legitimate system of
class positions. Furthermore, because most members of the economic
elite also belong to the cultural elite, their dominance may be
legitimated as due to the possession of superior intellects. On
the other hand, because some members of the cultural elite are not
economically powerful, and vice versa, evidence is provided of the
inherent fairness of a meritocratic education system (Bourdieu,

1977b, pp.506-7). Thus are the existing power relations of society reproduced in their legitimate embodiment as the cultural arbitrary.

Looking at Bourdieu's work as a whole, there are a number of criticisms which must be made. Although he starts out by rejecting the 'false choice' between objectivism and subjectivism, the relationship which he eventually posits between 'objective' structures the habitus and practice becomes one of determination: structures produce culture, which generates practice, which reproduces the structures, and so on. Despite the stated project, the escape from 'reifying abstractions' and the production of 'relational concepts' (Bourdieu and Passeron, 1977, p.102), the notions of subjectivity and objectivity used throughout imply a causal model predicated upon a materialist determination in the last instance and the consequent reification of social structure in abstraction from practice. Thus the project fails in its own terms. (2)

This basic problem manifests itself very clearly in his formulation of the 'subjective expectation of objective probabilities', which provides the basis for the constitution of the habitus, and the relationship which this has to the 'misrecognition of objective power relations', which engenders the production and mobilisation of false knowledge. It is necessary to Bourdieu's model that the working class should understand and perceive a present and future somehow objectively constituted, while at the same time systematically mis-perceiving that present and future. The relationship between these contrasting modes of perception and knowledge is problematic and contradictory.

> The relation which the subjects have to their class condition
> and to the social determinisms which define it is part of the
> complete definition of their condition and the conditionings
> which it imposes. These determinisms do not need to be
> consciously perceived in order to force subjects to take their
> decisions in terms of them, in other words, in terms of the
> <u>objective future</u> of their social category (Bourdieu and Passeron,
> 1979, p.27).

In another publication, Bourdieu has elaborated upon the relationship between subjective dispositions and aspirations and their objective chances of fulfilment. His position is that, 'aspirations tend to become more realistic, more strictly tailored to the real possibilities, in proportion as the real possibilities become more realistic' (1979, p.51). The concept remains deterministic and tautological, however.

There is also another problem. In order to attempt the mediation of misrecognition and subjective expectations, Bourdieu is forced to posit that the former is a conscious process and the latter unconscious. Thus, of the two modes of knowledge referred to earlier, only one - misrecognised ideology - is readily available to the analyst via the speech acts and practices of actors. How the other, the 'real' generator of practice, is to be determined remains something of a puzzle (Bourdieu and Passeron, 1977, pp. 78, 226). The mystery is solved by a sleight of hand, however, when Bourdieu elides the distinction between folk models and knowledge and the models and knowledge of the analyst. This elision is latent rather than manifest most of the time, but on occasions the legerdemain is revealed.

> The objective future is that which the observer has to postulate
> in order to understand the present behaviour of social subjects,
> which does not mean that he places in the consciousness of the
> subject whom he observes the consciousness he has of their
> consciousness. For the objective future may not be a goal
> consciously pursued by the subjects and yet can still be the
> objective principle of all their conduct - because it is inscribed
> in those subjects' present situation and in their habitus,
> internalised objectivity, a permanent disposition acquired in a
> situation, under the influence of that situation ... they do not
> know that truth, but they enact it, or, if you will, they state
> it only in their actions. (Bourdieu, 1979, pp.92-3)

The 'objective probability' which the subordinated classes 'subjec-
tively perceive', albeit via their (collective?) unconscious, thus
turns out to be nothing more than the knowledge and calculations of
the researcher, a point to which I shall return later. Casting the
analyst in the role of deus ex machina, every move Bourdieu makes
helps to underline the determinism of his model.

Perhaps the most important piece of English empirical research
to concern itself with the problem of cultural reproduction is Paul
Willis's study of working-class schoolboys in a Midlands town
(Willis, 1977). Asking the question, 'why do working-class kids
get working-class jobs?', Willis's argument, put simply, is that
working-class kids are not in competition for 'middle-class' jobs.
They don't want them. An orientation towards manual labour is
produced in the milieu of the working-class counter-school culture
of the 'lads'. The rejection of middle-class cultural norms,
combined with strong anti-authoritarianism and the valorisation of
'masculine' manual labour, serves to legitimise the class position
of the 'lads' in their own eyes. In this sense, they 'choose' their
own future; this is their 'subjective expectation' of 'objective
probability'. Needless to say, it is an illusory choice.

> For a specific period in their lives, 'the lads' believe that
> they dwell in towers where grief can never come. That this
> period of impregnable confidence corresponds to the period when
> all the major decisions of their life are settled to their
> disadvantage is one of the central contradictions of working-
> class culture and social reproduction, and one in which the
> state school, and its processes, is deeply implicated....
> Ironically, as the shopfloor becomes a prison, education is
> seen retrospectively, and hopelessly, as the only escape.
> (ibid., p.107)

The decisions made by Willis's 'lads' should not, however, be
confused with the goal-oriented career choices of the occupational
choice literature (Ginzberg et al., 1951; Super, 1953). Within the
limited sphere of masculine waged labour the 'lads' are relatively
indifferent to the particular job they take: 'their general sense
of the similarity of all work as it faces them, is the form of a
cultural penetration of their real conditions of existence as
members of class (sic)' (Willis, 1977, p.136). Such subjective
perceptions of their 'objective' conditions of existence, 'penetra-
tions' in Willis's terminology, are, however, undermined and
subverted by their acceptance of, and participation in, the divisions
within the working class between male and female, black and white,

and mental and manual workers (ibid., p.145). Although the 'lads'
somehow 'penetrate' the opacity of their 'objective' domination
within the social relations and relations of production of capitalism,
they are inevitably drawn back into collusion in their own
subordination by their valorisation of manual labour. 'Lads' grow
up to be 'real men' (Willis, 1979).

This summary cannot do justice to either the ethnographic riches
of Willis's study or the imaginative power of his analysis; not
without reason has the book become something of a classic. What my
brief account has done, I hope, is demonstrate the homology between
Bourdieu's analysis and the model of cultural reproduction constructed
by Willis in 'Learning to Labour'. The misrecognition by the 'lads'
of their class condition, the ideological refraction of their
perception through the prisms of sexism, racism and workerism, is
the ultimate frustration of their knowledgeable 'penetration', their
'subjective expectation' of 'objective probability'.

There are, of course, other authors who have made important
contributions to the debate about cultural reproduction, or, more
generally, the social reproduction of capitalist society, however
that process is conceived of. In particular I refer to Althusser,
in his famous 'Ideological State Apparatuses' essay (1971, pp.121-73),
and Bowles and Gintis, in 'Schooling in Capitalist America' (1976).
I do not intend to discuss their work here because, in the first
place, their understanding of this process is more deterministic than
that of either Bourdieu or Willis. There seems no point in simply
rehearsing the same criticisms except in a stronger vein. In the
second, since these authors are arguably more interested in the
broader 'structural' topic of social reproduction, the patterned
historical process whereby the institutions of the state are
maintained, than in the more limited topic of cultural reproduction,
to do so in detail would be of limited relevance to this work. (3)

Returning to Bourdieu and Willis, there are several points of
substance to be made. First, they both overestimate the degree to
which the working class colludes in its own domination, although in
his more recent work Willis has placed greater stress on resistance
and negotiation by the working class within the dominant cultural
framework (1981, pp.53-7). In this context, Corrigan's study of
working-class schoolboys in Sunderland is of interest. There are
many points of substantive agreement between Willis and Corrigan,
e.g. the intrinsic lack of meaning which manual work holds for these
boys; one job is seen as much the same as another (Corrigan, 1979,
pp.76-8). The two authors differ, however, inasmuch as Corrigan
stresses the importance of the power relations of capitalist society,
exercised in the school and by the police and without the complete
legitimation of the working class.

It would be completely misleading, however, to ignore the
axiomatic acceptance by much of the working class of the taken-for-
granted legitimacy of their class position. One of the central
issues which must be grasped in the analysis of cultural reproduction
is the manner in which power may be mobilised and legitimated
simultaneously in consensus and legitimation, on the one hand, and
resistance, coercion and grudging accommodation, on the other.
Andrew Friedman, for example, in his study of industry in the
Midlands, correctly stresses the important role of worker resistance

in forcing through changes in workplace organisation and managerial practice (1977, pp.4-5). However, this resistance occurs within the framework of a de facto legitimation of the capitalist labour process: 'While worker resistance ... has grown and acquired institutional strength ... this resistance has rarely challenged the basic wage relation itself' (ibid., p.96).

This point is important for the investigation of divisions within the working class, inasmuch as it directs attention away from the rather lumpen model of that class implicit in Bourdieu and much of Willis, and towards the appreciation of political and cultural diversity; away from conformity to a situation in which a similar or predictable future is implicated and towards an appreciation of the differing social constructions of reality in which the working class participate. For example, as Angela McRobbie has pointed out, the ommission of girls from Willis's analysis - and other works in the cultural studies genre - is a major weakness (McRobbie, 1980), as is the lack of attention given to black youth. In my view, however, a more serious weakness lies in Willis's failure to account for the apparent lack of 'penetration' of the respectable 'ear 'oles' briefly mentioned in his work, as he himself has recently acknowledged (1981, p.62). Certainly, future discussions of young workers will, if they are to be taken seriously, have to direct their attention beyond the lumpen males who have been the focus of most studies to date.

All of these remarks come down to one thing at the end of the day: to date, most analyses of cultural reproduction have been fundamentally limited by their deterministic models of social reality and the practice of social agents. Clearly, whichever epistemology an author adopts will largely be a matter of conviction - at the paradigmatic level proof, like beauty, lying largely in the eye of the beholder - but if the object of the exercise is the restoration of a degree of autonomy to the practice of working-class people, within the framework of a class analysis (and this I take to be the project of the cultural reproduction problematic), then there is really no compromise possible with a deterministic materialist epistemology, regardless of how far removed the final instance of that determination might be. Notwithstanding what their original objectives might be, both Bourdieu and Willis are finally trapped by the determinacy of their philosophical framework and inevitably they reproduce that determinism within their own analyses.

TOWARDS AN ALTERNATIVE ANALYTICAL FRAMEWORK

It is one thing to highlight the problems inherent in a particular perspective, quite another to remedy those problems and propose a positive alternative. In this case, the task is that of providing an answer to the question, 'how are divisions within the working class produced and reproduced?', without either lapsing into the kind of determinism embraced by Bourdieu and Willis, or producing an a-theoretical, voluntaristic account which would ultimately be, at best, no more than descriptive. In order to establish a starting point for this task, it is necessary to examine some of the factors underlying that determinism.

There are two underlying theoretical difficulties which I am going to highlight. The first of these is the assumption that the social world can sensibly be divided into two distinct type of reality, the objective (or the material) and the subjective, the first of which causally determines, at no matter how many stages removed, what occurs in the latter. This is doubtless a crude characterisation of the various sub-themes of the objectivist epistemology but it is, I would insist, at the core of even the most subtle variations on the main theme, such as those developed by Bourdieu and Willis. It is the tension between this core epistemology and the attempt to nonetheless transcend determinism which leads to the problems in their work outlined above.

The second theoretical point which must be examined flows directly from the first, namely the view that it is useful to posit a 'level' of social reality commonly known as social structure which is both somehow more than the sum of its constituent parts, i.e. acting individuals, and plays an important part in determining the nature and behaviour of those constituent parts. The objectivist and social structural (not, it should be noted, necessarily structuralist) fallacies are inextricably linked. It is in the negation of these positions that we must construct an alternative. That such positions are those adopted by Bourdieu and Willis, as well as most other authors working in the cultural reproduction framework, is, I hope, adequately demonstrated in the previous section. Despite Stuart Hall's espousal of 'a general project - the elaboration of a non-reductionist theory of culture and social formations' (1980, pp.39-40), and the principled attempts made by the authors already discussed, and others such as Philip Corrigan (Corrigan and Willis, 1980) and Richard Johnson (1979), to write non-deterministic accounts of cultural processes, their reluctance to abandon even an emasculated materialist epistemology foredooms the project to eventual failure.

One contemporary theorist whose work may be helpful in resolving these questions is Anthony Giddens. Instead of risking entanglement in the objective/subjective dichotomy, Giddens seeks to develop a theory of structuration; 'to seek to explain how it comes about that structures are constituted through action, and reciprocally how action is constituted structurally' (1976, p.161). Thus, instead of positing a break between objective structures and sub-jective internalities which must be mediated, he advances the notion of the duality of structure; 'the essential recursiveness of social life, as constituted in social practices: structure is both the medium and the outcome of the reproduction of practices. Structure enters simultaneously into the constitution of the agent and social practices, and 'exists' in the generating moments of this constitu-tion' (1979, pp.4-5).

Social action, the practice of cognisant individuals, is thus correctly placed at the centre of the analytical stage. Contingent upon this central location of practice, Giddens takes it to be axiomatic that, 'every social actor knows a great deal about the conditions of reproduction of the society of which he or she is a member' (ibid., p.5). Accepting actors' accounts as of central importance raises the question, discussed in the previous section, of the distinction between folk models, the knowledge of research

subjects, and analytical models, the knowledge of the professional
social scientist. (4) An objectivist epistemology insists that
not only is there an objective reality, but that actors' accounts,
folk models, are necessarily 'false knowledge', and that objective
reality may only be apprehended in the analytical models of
'scientific' practice.

In this book I want to make a break with that epistemology,
insisting, with Milan Stuchlik, that,

> we are making an unwarranted division of the universe under
> consideration into two separate spheres: social reality itself
> and procedures for making generalised statements about it ...
> ascribing differential status to the observed people's activities,
> beliefs and knowledge, and to the anthropologists' activities,
> beliefs and knowledge.... Thus the agreement about culture
> being man-made becomes an empty concession, since the real
> meaning, or true contents, and in the last instance the very
> existence of the culture, is conceived of as being independent
> of those who are supposed to have made it. (Stuchlik, 1976, p.3)

This is, of course, no more than the earlier controversy within
anthropology, particularly in America, over the respective merits
of 'emic' or 'etic' explanations (Harris, 1968). I am not, however,
insisting that the only valid explanatory accounts are those couched
in wholly 'emic' terms, i.e. solely in the terms of the folk models
mobilised by actors. What I am saying is that analytical models
and folk models must be accorded epistemological equality, there
is no difference between the two in terms of objectivity or
subjectivity: they are both models of people and things in their
relationships with each other, formulated, however, by different
kinds of people in different situations. Both are essentially
oriented towards similar ends, the practical investment of perceived
reality with meaning.

Equality does not, however, mean that they are the same. It is
perfectly in line with my argument to accept that analytical models
will be both different from folk models and capable of making more
sense of social reality. This is so for a number of reasons:
analytical models may be capable of accommodating the contradictions
between conflicting folk models, social analysts may have access to
a broader or more general body of knowledge than their research
subjects, analytical models - inasmuch as they are consciously
formulated to this end - may be more explicitly communicative and
explanatory, etc. This is not, however, to accord greater
objectivity to analytical models: inasmuch as they are equally
socially constructed, both kinds of model are 'false knowledge'.
It would be closer to the spirit of this analysis to say that at
the end of the day the real problem becomes, and I have no space
to explore this here, the relationship between folk models and
analytical models (i.e. the folk models of social scientists,
political scientists, economists, etc.) in the production and
reproduction of social reality.

My point is perhaps best illustrated by returning to the
discussion of social structure. Following on from the above, it
becomes obvious that social structure is an analytical concept;
the equivalent folk model might well be the sociologically contro-
versial 'image of society' (Bulmer, 1975; Davis, 1979). The

essential point to be made is that looked at in this way, social
structure cannot produce the social reality to which it is held to
refer. At best, concepts of social structure might explain the
behaviour of sociologically-informed individuals or groups; generally
speaking, however, they make sense of society and cannot be used as
causal explanatory factors.

To return to Giddens, how does he develop his non-objective theory
of structure, structuration in his terminology? Because of his
stress upon action, space and time – as the constituting media of
action – are of central importance; his is an essentially diachronic,
dynamic model. This is perhaps best shown in his discussion of
institutions, which he defines as 'practices which are deeply
sedimented in time-space; that is, which are enduring and inclusive
"laterally" in the sense that they are widespread among the members
of a community or society' (1979, p.80). He then proceeds to draw
an important distinction between institutional analysis and the
analysis of strategic conduct, the two dimensions in which temporality
may be integrated into social theory. This is not new of course;
Nadel drew a similar distinction between structure as an 'infinitely
repetitive' pattern and as an 'event structure' (1957, pp.128, 132).

The crux of Giddens's argument and the argument of this book, is
that social structure can only be said to exist in the actions of
those people who reproduce and produce it, through the manipulation
of its constituent elements, rules and resources, in their everyday
transactions. His distinction between institutions and strategic
conduct is methodological; institutions do not exist, ontologically
speaking, in any sense separately from strategic conduct. A similar
approach is discernible in John Davis's advice to anthropologists
to look 'beyond the hyphen' when examining community-state relationships. Calling for an 'ethnography of the nation', Davis directs
the analyst to recognise that state administration consists not
simply of abstract macro-processes, but is constructed and worked
in the interaction of real people (1975, p.49).

Power is also important in Giddens's theory of structuration,
inasmuch as power relations help constitute the situational
definitions within which social interaction occurs. In this respect
his model is very close to Bourdieu's thinking: 'The reflexive
elaboration of frames of meaning is characteristically imbalanced
in relation to the possession of power .... 'What passes for social
reality' stands in immediate relation to the distribution of power'
(Giddens, 1976, p.113, original emphasis). As an example of what
is meant here, we may refer to labelling theory in recent criminology.
In this symbolic interactionist model of deviance, 'criminal identities
are as much, if not more, the product of the power of individual
agents within crucial institutions to inflict their situational
definitions of criminality upon significant others, as of the
criminal intentions or practices of those others (Becker, 1963;
Lemert, 1967). This perspective despite its shortcomings (Ditton,
1979), has, I would suggest, relevance far beyond the field of
criminology. As will become apparent in later chapters, one of the
main themes of this book is that divisions within the young working
class, as I describe them, can only be understood if they are seen
as partially produced and reproduced by the labelling decisions of
strategically placed individuals, drawing upon shared criteria of

attribution, in the institutions of education, social control and
the labour market. We are thus brought directly back to a
consideration of power as it is exercised within institutions.

   Although Giddens manages to avoid the epistemological tangle which
Bourdieu gets into over objectivity and subjectivity, his work raises
problems which are not dissimilar. The most serious of these is his
failure to resolve the ambiguities and epistemological difficulties
inherent in the concept of social structure. On the one hand, he
says that structure is produced in practice and reciprocally
constitutes the limits of enablement and constraint for subsequent
practice; on the other, however, we find him discussing 'contradiction'
as the 'opposition between structural principles', the implication
here being that such 'structural principles' exist at different
levels than the practice of social actors (1976, pp.118-26; 1979,
pp.141-5).

   It may, of course, be argued that the concept of social structure
is necessarily ambiguous, its most fruitful use lying in the careful
maintenance of the tension between its ambiguities: 'we profit not
from having defined a social structure, but from trying to define
it, not from having made the study but from making it' (Nadel,
op.cit., p.154). The maintenance of an equivocal attitude towards
the concept of social structure may therefore be defensible. The
theoretical attempt to 'have your cake and eat it', which is what
Bourdieu, Willis and - to some extent - Giddens are doing, is not.
Social structure may be conceptualised as, at best, a rather tricky
metaphor with which to order data in order that pattern emerges
from it, and which may subsequently provide a descriptive framework
for analysis. What it is not, however, is a superordinate or
determinate causal principle or principles, an expression of
'objective' reality, however depicted.

   In a very real sense, the problems surrounding the notion of
social structure lie at the heart of the cultural reproduction
problematic. Within this problematic, an account of social reality
must be generated which adequately comprehends the shared life-
worlds of research subjects while firmly situating those discourses
and practices within their wider social context. Such an account
must take as problematic that mixture of individual practice and
institutional, or other, constraint which constitutes the process
of the production and reproduction of social reality. In addition,
however, such an account of cultural reproduction must allow for
the description and analysis of the institutions and patterns of
events which may be loosely thought of as social structure - and
which are reproduced in practice - without reifying that concept
or equipping it with the attributes of determinacy. It is only in
the achievement of these two interlocking objectives that a non-
contradictory account of cultural reproduction becomes possible.
This book is an attempt to produce such an account, placing equal
emphasis upon individual practice, institutions and the reciprocal
significance each has for the other.

ETHNICITY AND CLASS IN NORTHERN IRELAND

The discussion so far in this chapter has been entirely concerned

with models of class society in general. In this respect, therefore,
a piece of research which has as its empirical focus a housing
estate in Belfast might be thought to require some justification or
special pleading, inasmuch as most research which has been done in
Northern Ireland has concentrated on ethnic or sectarian political
conflict, in one or other of its many manifestations. (5) This is
not to say, of course, that there has been no work done which is
primarily concerned with more 'conventional' social or economic
issues in Northern Ireland, issues such as urban development,
unemployment, poverty and education. There has, of course, been
research carried out in this vein. (6) However, as a generalisation,
it is true to say that, with the exception of technical or policy
documents produced by or for government agencies and a limited
amount of other work, most social research which has been done in
Northern Ireland, including that adopting a Marxist perspective, has
largely concentrated on the 'troubles', the politics of ethnic or
sectarian conflict and its resolution, at the expense of an examination of other dimensions of Northern Irish society. Most published
work on Northern Ireland starts with the present 'troubles' and then
proceeds to examine the interaction between the violence of politics
and the more mundane aspects of social life. Sectarianism and
ethnicity remain the main objects of academic attention.
    There is no doubt that this is as it should be. The political
situation in Northern Ireland is of interest and importance
precisely because of its urgent singularity. Moreover, in Ulster
sectarianism has so many ramifications and is so all-pervasive
that it would be foolish to pretend that it can be ignored in a
book such as this. The importance of the 'troubles' for the young
workers of Ballyhightown will be explored in Chapter 3. However,
Ulster's obvious differences from what is taken to be 'normal'
class society should not be allowed to mask the fact that in many
respects Belfast, for example, has much in common with similar
cities 'across the water' and has its roots in a generally similar
history. It therefore seems legitimate to generalise the arguments
of this book, at the level of underlying social process, to the
experience of young workers in capitalist society, particularly in
the rest of the United Kingdom. In so doing it is my hope that
some of the more mundane dimensions of day-to-day life in Northern
Ireland will thereby be restored to their proper place, alongside
the more obvious and spectacular facets of life in the Province
which constitute most of its public face. Thus, while accepting the
importance of the political situation, my starting point is different
from most other authors.
    There are two reasons for insisting that the similarities which
Northern Ireland has with its less-troubled neighbours be recognised.
In the first place, as I indicate wherever possible throughout later
chapters, there is a sufficiently good match between my own ethnography and the accounts of other researchers to suggest that the
young people of Ballyhightown are comparable, in some respects, to
their United Kingdom peers. Second, as even a superficial comparison
with the mainland demonstrates, the institutional context within
which these young people grow up exhibits some of the same constraining
features - increasing economic peripherality, declining traditional
industries and recently escalating unemployment - as many of the

older industrial regions of Great Britain. The specific history of
the north-east of Ireland has, of course - as is shown in Chapter 3,
generated a contemporary industrial pattern which is peculiar, in
some respects, to the region. In other respects, however, the
similarities are more marked than the differences.

Although there is therefore no reason to suppose that many of the
processes held to underlie the ethnographic pattern I shall outline
are peculiar to either Ballyhightown or, in most cases, Northern
Ireland, it is nonetheless important to briefly examine the degree
to which the experiences of protestant and catholic youth in Belfast
differ from each other and from their peers elsewhere. This is
impossible using my own data, which relates solely to protestant
youth in one area, so I shall rely instead on brief comparisons with
other research.

The life-style categories which I develop in Chapter 4 are along
a continuum from the 'rough' to the 'respectable' which has a long
history in the sociology of the English working class (Frankenberg,
1966). Recent sociolinguistic research in working-class districts
of Belfast suggests that this kind of broad distinction is similarly
useful in looking at both ethnic communities in Northern Ireland
(Milroy, 1980). Other research has also indicated that the
similarities between catholics and protestants occupying similar
class positions may be just as interesting and important as the
differences. For example, in response to survey questions concerning
attitudes to work, very few significant differences were recorded
in the answers solicited from catholics or protestants (Miller, 1978).
Still more recent research indicates that, with the exception of
explicitly political topics, gender was a more important indicator
of attitudes than ethnicity in a social psychological study of
catholic and protestant schoolchildren (McKernan and Russell, 1980).

However, the differences between the experiences of catholics and
protestants should not be underestimated either. Quite apart from
the different and conflictual relationship which many catholic
communities have with the institutions of state law and order, there
are three main areas of difference which are relevant to this study.
First, the job-search patterns of catholic youth are more circum-
scribed by the sectarian geography of Belfast than those of their
protestant peers; second, catholics may be discriminated against in
the job-search; and third, despite recent governmental encouragement
for the movement of employment into catholic west Belfast, they are
disadvantaged by the predominant location of industry in protestant
areas (Cormack, Osborne and Thompson, 1980). These are the specific
institutional constraints, of historical provenance, within which
catholic youth comes of age in Belfast.

Given the theoretical arguments advanced in the earlier sections
of this chapter, it is to be expected that these differences in
institutional context will generate important differences between
protestant and catholic youth. At the same time, however, evidence
of similarities and areas of experience in common should not be
ignored either. Without more detailed comparitive ethnography,
perhaps the safest conclusion is that, although there may be many
features in common between the life-styles of catholic and protestant
youth, these similarities will be offset to some extent by the
differences in the institutional contexts they inhabit, in particular
the labour market.

Although there is therefore a limit, albeit undefined in the absence of suitable comparitive research, to the generalisability of my analysis with respect to young catholic workers in Belfast, there is no reason to suspect that it cannot be generalised in broad terms to apply to white working-class youth in the rest of the United Kingdom. I say 'white' because it is arguable that protestants stand in a similar relationship to catholics in Northern Ireland as do whites to black ethnic minorities in Great Britain. (7) That, however, is another argument, and one which I cannot pursue here.

Chapter 2

AN ANTHROPOLOGIST COMES HOME

'Ballyhightown' is a large, post-war housing estate 'somewhere on the outskirts' of Belfast. The name is a pseudonym, as are all other proper names in this book. Between August 1976 and September 1977 I worked there as a youth worker, employed by the local education authority. With an office in Ballyhightown Youth Centre, a building I shared with three club-oriented youth workers, my brief was to work with school-leavers and the young unemployed in an outreach capacity.

During this period I kept a detailed field diary, although I did not know then that I would return to do research. I also established many personal relationships which were to stand me in good stead during the eight months further fieldwork I carried out as a research student. I returned to the estate for four periods of two months each, between April 1978 and June 1979. Most of the material used in this book was gathered during the second phase of my involvement with the estate.

FIELD RESEARCH AND PROBLEMS OF IDENTITY

There were several places in Ballyhightown which were particularly important focal points for the research. The first, perhaps obviously, was the Youth Centre, which I continued to frequent throughout the fieldwork. In addition, there were the Hillview Social Club, Ballyhightown Secondary School, the homes of a few close friends and the two flats in which I lived. Every bit as important were events: Saturday afternoon trips 'into town', watching the 'Blues' play at home or away, the never-to-be-forgotten minibus trip to Dublin to support Northern Ireland in their European Championship match against Eire, evenings spent drinking locally or in the Harp Bar in the city centre, local parties or evenings spent simply looking for something to do. These places and occasions were the basic framework within which questions were asked and notebooks filled.

This process was not without its problems, however, particularly during the period when I was no longer a youth worker. It proved difficult, for two reasons, to establish a new and clear-cut role

for myself. In the first place, I was still working, on a voluntary
basis and with an eye towards participant observation, in the Youth
Centre. In the second, I experienced some difficulty in explaining
to many people, both inside and outside the Centre, exactly what the
role of researcher was. I didn't appear to have a 'real' job and,
although I told them I was writing a thesis or a report about young
people from the estate, what they actually saw me do for most of the
time was hang about the Youth Centre or a couple of the local bars
and clubs. Telling them that I was a student didn't make matters
any clearer. In their experience, that meant either a student
teacher on teaching practice in a school or a student youth worker
on placement in the Centre; they knew that I was neither of those.
Some of the kids did appreciate my role and actively supported the
research, but very many more, particularly those with whom I had
only superficial regular contact, remained convinced that I was some
sort of youth worker.

I had several motives for continuing to work in the Youth Centre.
First, I intended to use the Centre's senior youth club and afternoon
sessions for the unemployed as venues for participant observation.
It was important, therefore, given the misunderstanding of my
research role by some of the kids, to have some sort of other role
in that context. Not being young enough or local enough to
participate as a club member, and given my personal history as a
Centre staff member, I settled for an identity somewhere between
that of observer and youth worker. In other words, while I tried
to get on with the club users in much the same way as I had
previously done, the staff didn't make the demands of me which they
would have done had I been there as a part-time worker. On balance,
this proved to be a successful enough compromise in practice.

Second, I actively participated in some senior youth club
activities in a more structured fashion, organising late-night
discussion groups on Sunday evenings, sometimes with invited
speakers, for a small group of senior members who had requested a
repeat of the previous year's successful discussion groups. This
provided me with an opportunity for recording their opinions on a
wide range of subjects, while at the same time relieving the Centre's
overworked staff of the responsibility for organising what, from
their point of view, was a desirable part of the club's programme.
Finally, there were personal reasons for continuing to participate
in the work of the Centre. I enjoyed it and it helped me to overcome,
to a limited extent, my feelings of being redundant at best and
parasitic at worst. Working in the Centre did not blunt the edge
of either of these self-criticisms; it did, however, enable me to
pursue the research without succumbing to them.

Thus, in the eyes of many of the young people - and adults -
living on the estate, I retained something of my previous role as
a youth worker. Viewed from the standpoint of doing research, this
situation had undoubted advantages. It was a role many people on
the estate were sympathetic towards and this may have led to me
being told things I might possibly not have discovered had my role
simply been that of researcher.

It is, however, also possible that my assumption of this identity
may have militated against the communication of information by
people who regarded the Youth Centre as an outpost of authority,

'them' as against 'us', in Ballyhightown. I suspect that this latter
disadvantage was, however, more than offset in practice by the
Centre's reputation locally as a rough and rowdy place, a place many
'respectable' young people 'wouldn't be seen dead in'. For example,
the only outright refusal I encountered during the formal interviewing
phase of the research was from one of the 'citizens', the 'respectable'
sample.

Role ambiguity of this sort poses ethical problems which I have
partially resolved by treating some of my data as confidential, only
to be used when suitable camouflage, the alteration of certain
details, does not undermine their usefulness. Furthermore, in some
cases in which I was knowingly privy to information which was
sensitive or confidential in a variety of respects, whether as a
youth worker or later, I have simply decided not to use it at all.
In most cases such information was not even recorded. (1) However,
given the richness of the data I do feel completely free to use,
these necessary limitations do not materially affect the quality
of the ethnographic account I shall present.

Ethical considerations of this nature are important in all research,
particularly when participant observation, however that is defined,
is involved. They have even greater urgency in Northern Ireland,
where political violence is an integral part of the social reality
being studied. In this situation responsibility and careful reporting
are of the greatest importance, if only to safeguard the researcher
and his/her informants. Therefore I make no reference to the
activities of any paramilitary organisation in Ballyhightown unless
they unavoidably impinge upon the topic under discussion, and then
not by name wherever possible. This is not to say that I did not
come into contact with them or did not establish a working modus
vivendi with those whom I believed to be members of such organisations.
Had I not done so, research in Ballyhightown would have been difficult,
at best. However, echoing Pitt-Rivers's sentiments concerning the
reporting of Anarchist activity in the Spanish village he studied
(1971, p.xiv), I cannot see that any point would be served in this
context by discussing something which was not the explicit focus
of the research. (2)

Remaining on the subject of the local problems of doing social
science fieldwork in Northern Ireland, it must be stressed that I
never attempted to become 'one of the lads'. However, I was equally
never an outsider in Ballyhightown in quite the sense that an
English, American, or even Belfast catholic, researcher might have
been. Although born in Liverpool, I grew up in Northern Ireland, a
protestant in a staunchly protestant rural town. As such, although
unfamiliar with many aspects of life in Ballyhightown peculiar to
the urban milieu, I was at home with the cultural milieu of Ulster
protestantism. In addition, I was accustomed to the kind of built
environment which Ballyhightown typifies; the housing estate in
Larne where I grew up, although less scarred by the present 'troubles',
was built by the Northern Ireland Housing Trust at about the same
time as Ballyhightown and to much the same design, albeit on a
smaller scale. Finally, my own network stretched into Ballyhightown
and Castleowen; a couple of the teachers in Ballyhightown Secondary
School had been at school with me, as had one of the civil servants
in the local social security office and one of the local employers

who returned my postal questionnaire. Another of these employers
had lived next door to my family at one time. In a more general
way, I regularly discovered that I had acquaintances in common with
people on the estate.

Whether or not this familiarity casts doubts upon my objectivity
as an observer must be for others to decide. What I can say, however,
is that it is precisely this familiarity which has made me careful
to distinguish between what was 'in my head' originally and what is
information deriving from observation or an informant's statements,
if such a crude distinction is possible. Thus, whenever, in
retrospect, I have had any difficulty in deciding whether particular
field-notes derive from observation and informants' statements, on
the one hand, or my own stock of folk-knowledge concerning Ulster
protestants, on the other, I have chosen to disregard them; the
fit between my knowledge and the perception of social reality of
the young people of Ballyhightown is unlikely to be as close as I
might sometimes fondly imagine. Among other things, this identity
of 'partial native' has made me particularly aware of the need to
distinguish between analytical models and folk models, as discussed
in Chapter 1.

THE NEGOTIATION OF RESEARCH ACCESS

In the above I broached some of the problems encountered in the
attempt to construct a credible research identity as a participant
observer in Belfast. Once this identity - such as it was - had
been established, there still remained the separate problem of
reaching my erstwhile research subjects and then persuading them to
participate in that research. In this section I shall draw attention
to some aspects of my role in Ballyhightown which affected the
access I had to particular sections of the estate's youth. There
are at least four problematic areas of the research in this respect.
(3)

First, there are the undoubted difficulties attached to being a
male researcher interested in investigating female social reality.
Such difficulties may appear to be obvious: it should not be
forgotten here that some women researchers appear to consider that
girls, particularly working-class girls, are more difficult to
investigate than their male peers. The barrier of reserve and
giggles seems to be inordinately hard to breach (McRobbie, 1978;
McRobbie and Garber, 1976). There is undoubtedly some truth in
this; given the distinction between the male public domain and the
privatised female world of domesticity, and the imbalance in power
and evaluation which accompanies it (Imray and Middleton, 1982),
it would be surprising if young men were not more accessible than
young women.

I would not wish to underestimate the difficulties involved in
doing research into young women, but such problems as I had seemed
to depend very much on the situation and the research strategy
adopted. For example, in undertaking the programme of formal
interviews, the results of which are documented in Chapters 5 and 6,
I did not feel my sex to be a major disadvantage. Given that the
Lads were, by definition, an all-male sample, the final composition

of the two other samples bear this out to some extent: 46 per cent
of the Ordinary Kids and 44 per cent of the Citizens were female. (4)
One aspect of the formal interviewing which may have been adversely
affected by the fact that I am male was the quality of rapport
between myself and the girl being interviewed. In general, it is
very difficult to comment on this in retrospect, except to say that
the interviews with the girls in the Ordinary Kids group did not seem
to differ markedly in this respect from those with the boys; they
were both very variable. The female Citizens, however, were quite
tricky to interview.

Inasmuch as participant observation is concerned, there are
certainly marked differences in the quality of the data with respect
to young men and young women. This is for at least two reasons. In
the first place, I was able to participate in male activities in a
way that I could never have done in the day-to-day life of the girls.
This is quite straightforward and unavoidable; no amount of good,
confidential relationships with individual girls can compensate for
this de facto exclusion from their shared group activities. The
second reason harks back to the distinction between the public and
private spheres mentioned earlier. The 'bedroom culture' of many
of these girls (Frith, 1978, p.66) is private and inaccessible;
the boys are simply more publicly available. Even in public, the
girls tend to be talked down by any males present; 'girl talk'
usually closes down at the approach of a man, be he a researcher
or otherwise.

The second problematic area, in research terms, also relates to
the dichotomy between the public and the private: my identity as
an ex-youth worker placed a limitation upon my research into family
backgrounds. As a youth worker, I had found it best only to contact
people's families at their specific request – or by chance, of
course. This was not due to any hostility on the part of either
the young people or their parents. The public sphere of the Youth
Centre was held to be a social arena distinct from the private
domestic world; by tacit agreement the most comfortable relationship
between the two was typically held to be one of insulation. While
carrying out the later fieldwork this separation remained important
for most of the kids, although there were important exceptions such
as Carol and Davy who are discussed in Chapter 7. While I do
present some material on the family, the focus of the research
remained firmly outside the household. The strength of the analysis,
that of doing 'insider' research, is also its weakness; I remained
very much limited to the spheres of action defined by the actors.

My close identification with the Youth Centre was also the source
of a third limitation upon my access to all sections of the young
people of the estate; my links with the Centre, a 'rough' place in
some eyes, made the 'respectable' Citizens more difficult to
interview, particularly the young women. More conscious of their
privacy than either the Lads or the Ordinary Kids, I had one
outright refusal, from a member of the Presbyterian Church's Girls'
Brigade company (although I did interview her sister). There were
two reasons for these difficulties apart from my past history in
the Youth Centre. First, whereas I was personally well known to
the members of the other samples, the reverse was true for the
Citizens. Second, I suspect it may have had something to do with

the greater privatisation of the respectable residents of Ballyhightown, as discussed in Chapter 4.

Finally, my work in the Youth Centre may have served to restrict my interviewing within the network of the Lads to those Lads who continued to use the Centre. This is also tied up with the constraints which resulted from the political situation in Northern Ireland. Although I appear to have successfully negotiated a tacit understanding with the various political groupings active on the estate, this most certainly does not mean that I ceased to be regarded with suspicion by some members of these groups. The fact that I finished the research without interference testifies to the fact that this suspicion never assumed 'terminal' proportions; nevertheless it existed and should not be underestimated. I remained an outsider, I did ask questions and some of those questions must have seemed pretty far removed from my stated area of interest, young people, education and work. It is therefore possible that some people, particularly those in the lads' network, steered clear of giving me an interview. I never encountered an outright refusal from any of the lads but it was easy enough to avoid being interviewed without seeming to do so. The implications of the possible self-selection by some of the lads will be discussed in Chapter 5, in the section on sampling.

Thus it is apparent that, in addition to the problems caused by the barriers of gender, my access to the young men and women of Ballyhightown was not uniformly adequate or open. Although there is a slight under-representation of women in the formally interviewed samples, the major deficiency in the research data from my point of view stems from the differences in the quality of the relationships I established with each particular section of the youth of Bally-hightown. This is mainly because of my particularly close identi-fication with the Youth Centre, which was clearly a mixed blessing. However, this kind of problem is by no means unique to my research. William Whyte, in his classic study of 'Cornerville', found that his friendship with Doc and his cronies in the Nortons militated against a similar relationship with the 'collegemen' of the Italian Community Club (Whyte, 1955, p.306). Similarly Ursula Sharma, in her research in two Indian villages found that

the social distance between the highest and the lowest castes is so great that one can establish relations of intimacy either with people at the upper end of the hierarchy, or with people in the lower echelons, but not with both. (Sharma, 1980, p.24)

The situation with respect to the different life-styles I describe in Ballyhightown is not radically different.

Given this imbalance in the quality of material available across the social spectrum within Ballyhightown, it is impossible to be precise as to the exact effect this has had on the conclusions I reach in this book. Hopefully the discussion in this section will serve to emphasise both the weaknesses and the strengths of the analysis, allowing the reader to form his or her own opinions as to the value of the particular research approach adopted.

A CHOICE OF METHODS

The title of this chapter implies that the account of Ballyhightown
I present in this book is in some sense specifically anthropological.
This, of course, begs the question of what the distinguishing
features of such an account are. Without wishing to bog the reader
down in an essentially futile beating of disciplinary boundaries,
there are two features of the anthropological tradition which I wish
to stress here: the construction of a holistic account of the social
reality being studied, and a concern with the day-to-day life of
the participants in that reality. An account of social reality must
be provided which adequately comprehends the life-worlds of research
subjects while firmly situating those worlds within their broader
social context. I take it to be axiomatic that this broader social
context includes the historical antecedents of the situation under
study. If an account is to be processual, as discussed in Chapter 1,
the analyst cannot afford to overlook the historical dimension.
   In order to construct a model of the lived reality of research
subjects, I can think of no more adequate research methodology than
participant observation. While accepting that, for the kinds of
reasons I have been at pains to point out above, the stress normally
falls more upon observation than participation, there is no doubt
that in the creative negotiation of interaction between researcher
and subject may lie a most potent destabilisation of the taken-for-
granted conventional wisdom of the social scientist. It is this
potential for surprise, the challenge to analytical models presented
by the knowledge and world view of research subjects, which should
be the great strength of participant observation. (5)
   However, it is equally important to understand the limitations
and weaknesses of participant observation as a research strategy.
While there may have once been a historical situation in which the
anthropologist working in an 'isolated' and 'primitive' community
could construct a holistic account on the basis of participant
observation fieldwork, it is hard to imagine a comparable situation
existing anywhere in the world today. Therefore, although this
book is a work of anthropology, in the sense outlined above, much
of the account could not have been written on the basis of data
deriving solely, or even mainly, from participant observation, the
research strategy most closely associated with social anthropology
(Lewis, 1976, pp.24-8).
   The inadequacies of the participant observer method for the
project of writing an anthropological account of complex society
are worth exploring in more detail. In the first place, anthropologists are as much participants in the power relations of the
societies they study as are their research subjects. What is more,
this is true whether the observer is a native of the society in
question or not. In many of the situations I discuss later, for
example the light engineering factory described in Chapter 9, I
simply was not empowered to observe directly much of what I have
written about. I could not participate in selection interviews at
TransInternational Electronics (in the good old days when they
were recruiting, that is), or in the 'chats' between the Personnel
Officer and the foremen, when the actual recruitment decisions
were made. My presence on these occasions would have been completely

inappropriate unless I had been prepared in some fashion to directly
associate my research with the interests of the company. Regardless
of my own feelings about such a course of action, this would have
immediately closed off other avenues of research.

The sources of information for this factory case-study were
formal interviews with officials of the company, the formal interviews
with young people that are the main data source for Chapters 5 and 6,
chance conversations, a pre-arranged, though highly informal,
discussion in a pub with an ex-senior foreman in the plant, other
discussions with past and present employees of the company and a
certain amount of documentary material, including newspaper cuttings
and material supplied by the firm themselves. Participant observation,
in any sense, had only a very small part to play, and then only
indirectly. The higher one searches within the hierarchies of power
of the modern state or industry, the less likely it is that one will
be permitted to engage in participant observation, and the more
rarely are enough decisions made in public to allow for the construction of an adequate account of what is going on by observation alone.

Power also has a bearing upon another limitation upon the use of
participant observation. The fact that society – and most certainly
capitalist society – is produced in the interaction of collectivities
who are often in overt or covert conflict with each other creates
very real problems for the would-be participant observer. It would
not, for example, be possible to construct an anthropological account,
along the lines suggested, of the relationship between criminals and
the police. One simply would not be trusted in both social worlds,
and trust is surely fundamental in participant observation. The
same arguably holds good for managers and workers. As I have
described earlier, even among the young people in Ballyhightown I
was looked at askance by some of the 'respectable' kids because of
my close identification with the Youth Centre. Due to the essential
'negotiatedness' of this kind of research, the researcher frequently
does not have the resources at his or her disposal to transcend
this problem: one negotiates an identity and this identity
necessarily colours the rest of the research. By its very nature
participant observation must lead to partial accounts.

In the above, I have returned to the distinction between the
public and the private discussed in the earlier sections of this
chapter. There are, however, two other constraints upon the use of
participant observation in urban, industrialised societies which
deserve a brief mention here: social scale and spatial scale.
There are very many more people, groups and institutions interlocked
in these societies than in the more traditionally anthropological
communities of the Third World or the European margins. Interaction
takes place over greater distances; not everything the researcher
is interested in is as routinely available within the confines of
manageable geographical areas. Furthermore, the time factor in
most research usually precludes over-indulgence in participant
observation, which is both labour-intensive and time-consuming,
on the scale which would be required to comprehend even a small
slice of an urban, industrial society, let alone a total view.
Participant observation on its own is no longer enough.

Finally, it is obvious that the choice of method also depends on
the uses to which the resultant data will be put. The questions to

be asked pre-empt, to some extent, the decision over the methodological options which may be open.   In this case, the use of formal
interviews, as detailed in Chapter 5, was determined by the desire
to build up a body of basic information on a fairly large number of
individuals from each of the life-styles identified.   Since the aim
was to compare the three life-styles, this information had to be
approximately comparable for each individual interviewed.   This
kind of coverage is impossible using participant observation and a
programme of interviewing using a formalised interview schedule was
the only realistic strategy available.

In Chapter 1, I argued the case for a social science paradigm which
allows us to construct a model of the institutional pattern of
society as produced and reproduced in the practice of real people.
In this chapter I have highlighted some of the problems I encountered
during my fieldwork and some of the inadequacies of the participant
observer strategy.   Essentially, my argument is that, unless we are
to remain limited to family studies, studies of small communities
and studies inside individual organisations, this research strategy
on its own is inadequate.   I am insisting that a methodologically
promiscuous approach is fundamental to the argument of Chapter 1,
although participant observation must remain central to that
approach.   Correspondingly, in the account presented in the rest of
the book I draw upon data deriving from a number of sources.
Wherever appropriate, I shall include further discussions of the
methodology upon which particular sections rest, in the hope that
this will better permit the reader to assess the relative contribution of each section to the overall argument of the book.

Chapter 3

BALLYHIGHTOWN

One of the things most apparent about Ballyhightown is the limited
relevance for this analysis of the concept of 'community'. At
least three Tenants' Associations have foundered due to lack of
support (although a fourth group was active in 1980), and the
annual Festival Week of 'community activities', inaugurated in
1976 and highly successful that year, was cancelled in 1979 due to
the disinterest shown by most local residents. The lack of communal
identity at the political and administrative level is exemplified
by the parliamentary constituency reorganisation proposed by the
Boundary Commission in 1979, two of the estate's local government
wards being placed in one of the new constituencies and two in
another. The lack of obvious 'community' has advantages for the
researcher, however. While the estate is an area with definite
physical boundaries, small enough to support the face-to-face
research typical of the community study (Frankenberg, 1966, p.15),
it would be almost impossible to lapse into the sociological
atomism documented by that approach's many critics (Boissevain,
1975; Ennew, 1980, pp.1-6). Most working residents leave the
estate every day to earn their living, few of them have lived there
for more than twenty years, and most of the decisions which affect
Ballyhightown are made by people who visit the estate rarely, if
indeed at all.

In this chapter, the area and its residents will be placed in
their proper context, the Northern Ireland state and the urban
economy of the greater Belfast area. In order that this context
be better understood, I shall first outline some of the historical
background.

NORTHERN IRELAND: THE BACKGROUND TO THE STUDY

The history of Northern Ireland begins with the Plantation of Ulster
by Scottish and English colonists in the seventeenth century (Beckett,
1966, pp.43-8). As a result of the Plantation, there developed a
series of marked differences between Ulster and the rest of the
island. In the south there developed an essentially rural and
agricultural society, based on commercially oriented tenant farmers;

on the western margins the remains of a subsistence-level peasant
economy clung to their small plots. In the north-east, however,
there eventually arose, by contrast, an urban and industrial
society, based on a small tenantry who were actively involved in
textile production (Cullen, 1969; Gibbon, 1975, pp.9-12).

The colonists had come from areas of England and Scotland with
traditions both of capitalist commodity farming and a domestic
textile industry. This, and access to English markets, provided the
foundation for industrial development in the north. The growth of
the textile industry in Ulster was so rapid that by the final
decades of the eighteenth century Belfast had established its independence of Dublin as a mercantile and financial centre. The
expansion of the industry, new technical developments and the boom
in cotton during the Napoleonic Wars, all combined to promote
mechanisation. By the 1830s, factory production was fast becoming
routine, with linen manufacture superseding cotton as the market
for the latter became more competitive (Crawford, 1972). In the
rest of Ireland, agriculture, either large-scale or subsistence,
was the major source of employment.

The mechanisation of textile production led to the development
of an engineering industry, originally based on the needs of local
mill owners for machinery and repairs. Although this development
was heavily dependent upon the mainland, particularly for technical
know-how and the entrepreneurs possessing such knowledge, those
enterprises which were established at this time were mainly local
firms, not accountable to external sources of control (Coe, 1969).

Alongside the mechanisation of the textile industry, its re-
location within factories and the emergence of a growing engineering
industry, went urbanisation. Whereas domestic industry and the
early small mills had been predominantly rural, the increasing
importance of large-scale manufacture with its need for easy
access to the sea for the import of raw materials and export of
finished goods, meant that Belfast and its hinterland became the
focus of industrial and commercial activity. This was so for three
reasons: the city's centrality within the commercially important
area east of the River Bann, its ready communication with the
smaller textile towns of the rest of the province through the
natural corridor of the Lagan valley, and its position as the major
deep-water port on the north-east seaboard. The city's importance
increased with the establishment of steamship services to Glasgow
and Liverpool from the 1820s onwards. From being smaller than either
Limerick or Waterford in 1800, Belfast had overtaken Dublin in both
size and commercial importance by 1891.

The industrial development of the Belfast area attracted many
immigrants from country areas, a trend which although already
apparent before the 1840s was encouraged by the depopulation of
rural areas in the wake of the Famine. Many were catholics from
the south and west of the province, attracted to Belfast by the
availability of work. The jobs they filled were largely unskilled,
in the textiles sector or as navvies. Skilled work, particularly
in engineering, was the prerogative of the protestant working man;
industry and commerce were controlled by the protestant bourgeoisie,
and hiring practices reflected the traditionally sanctioned
hierarchy of protestant and catholic (Baker, 1973, p.802). This

ethnic division of labour, although by now considerably diluted, remains apparent today (Fair Employment Agency, 1978).

However, there was also developing a clear division within the protestant working class between the unskilled (or, since mechanisation, deskilled) workers in the textile industry, who lived in houses in the Sandy Row or York Road areas built in the 1840s, and the skilled engineers of the shipyards, living in the later housing developments of the Shankill Road and Ballymacarret, which dated from the 1870s (Gibbon, 1975, pp.67-86). This distinction may still be discerned in the pattern of industrial location in Belfast. The tobacco factories of Gallaher's and Murray's, employing largely unskilled labour, are situated on York Road and Sandy Row, respectively, while the major non-marine engineering factories, Mackie's, the Sirocco Works and Short Brothers and Harland, are situated either in the Shankill area or in east Belfast, near the shipyards of Queen's Island.

With the increasing importance of shipbuilding and marine engineering from the mid-nineteenth century, the present industrial structure finally crystallised. This was due to a number of factors: the availability of a good deep-water harbour, the enthusiasm of the Harbour Commissioners in developing Queen's Island, and the increasing numbers of skilled men, such as boilermakers, in the local engineering industry (although many workers were brought in from outside, particularly from Clydeside). As the century drew to a close the area became an ever more important part of the national economy, particularly that region of it including the other great Irish Sea ports, Liverpool and Glasgow. Employers and men participated in national and regional industrial negotiations and disputes, and the commercial life of the city became more integrated with that of the rest of the kingdom, much local capital being invested on the mainland (Coe, op.cit., p.191; Lyons, 1973, pp.270-86).

However, Belfast differed from areas such as Glasgow and Merseyside in the narrow industrial foundations of its local economy. Although a thriving and locally-integrated industrial centre, it was heavily dependent for employment upon textiles and engineering. In the manufacturing sphere it remains dependent upon these two industries, as we can see in Table 3.1 The lack of diversity illustrated by this table is due to several factors. The province's reliance on external markets, particularly those of the Empire and overseas, led to a concentration upon commodities such as textiles, ships and marine engines, for which transport costs were not a competitive factor. This was further encouraged by the area's almost total lack of indigenous resources such as iron or coal and its physical distance from the important home markets of Britain. Due to the economies of scale available to producers on the mainland, there were many commodities which, despite the imposition of transport surcharges, could be more cheaply imported than locally produced. This further inhibited even small-scale industrial diversification, making local industry increasingly vulnerable to recessions in the world economy.

When the protestant Unionist Party took office in 1921 following the partition of Ireland, local manufacturers and workers were already beginning to feel the effects of the post-war recession:

TABLE 3.1   Population working in manufacturing, Northern Ireland,
June 1977 (thousands)

Industrial Sector (Standard Industrial Classification Orders) (a)	Employed (b)		Unemployed	
	Men	Women	Men	Women
Engineering (7-12)	36.2	7.5	2.3	1.0
Textiles (13, 15)	21.8	28.6	1.8	3.3
Other Manufacturing (3-6, 14, 16-19)	37.2	12.9	3.2	1.3

Source: 'DMS Gazette', No.3 (1979), Table 6.

(a) See: Central Statistical Office, 1968.
(b) Including self-employed workers.

'Unemployment rose from 18% in 1923 to 25% in 1926. Between 1930 and
1939 unemployment never fell below 20% and averaged about 25%.
Income per head declined to little more than half the average for the
United Kingdom' (Probert, 1978, p.52).
   These economic difficulties had their sequelae in increasing
labour unrest, particularly in Belfast (Farrell, 1976, p.27). In
contrast to the situation on the other side of the Irish Sea, however,
Ulster experienced no General Strike. In a local state whose leaders
had demonstrated that 'Ulster will fight and Ulster will be right'
in opposing Home Rule before the War, any combination between
protestant and catholic workers was seen as a threat, both to the
protestant ascendancy and the profits of local (protestant)
industrialists. Through their control of public and private employment, the Unionist establishment systematically undermined the
possibility of cross-sectarian labour organisation. Thus, in the
1920s and 1930s, due to political xenophobia and industrial
depression, the province withdrew into a reaffirmation of old ethnic
loyalties and conflicts. These conflicts were compounded by economic
decline and the negation of democratic politics in the administration
of government through the Unionist party machine (Bew, Gibbon and
Patterson, 1979, pp.75-101; Farrell, op.cit., pp.125-40).
   With the declaration of war in 1939, the situation changed; from
being a depressed and culturally archaic backwater of the Kingdom,
the province became strategically important in the Battle of the
Atlantic, and economically vital as an engineering centre and
agricultural producer. Northern Ireland's increasing incorporation
into the mainstream of UK life was affirmed by the many men who
joined up. The isolation of many of the rural areas began to break
down with the presence in the province of many thousands of American
and Commonwealth troops (Lyons, op.cit., pp.728-37).
   With the return of its de-mobbed sons in 1945, events served
further to indicate Northern Ireland's changed status, both internally
and in its relationship with the rest of the world. A number of
agreements between the Stormont government and the post-war Labour
government at Westminster concerning finance, social services and
education laid the foundations for local participation in the welfare
state. Although such reforms left untouched Unionist control of

local government, employment and housing, they did have two important
consequences. The first was the increasing importance of an educated
catholic middle class. The second was the re-emergence of that
liberalism which, with the late-nineteenth century demise of the
Liberal Party and Unionism's siege-mentality response to Nationalism,
had lain dormant in the conservative mainstream of Unionist politics.
These changes were accompanied by increasing demands from protestant
workers and the trade unions that there be no return to the 'bad old
days' of the 1930s.

One response to this pressure was the attempt to revitalise the
local economy by offering government subsidies to investors from
outside. There were several important features of this process of
neo-industrialisation. First, most of the new factories were located
in the already industrialised and predominantly protestant eastern
half of the province. Second, much of this industry was in the
traditional sectors of textiles, albeit now synthetic fibres, and
heavy or medium engineering. Exceptions to this were a number of
light electrical engineering companies, such as Pye and BSR, who
employed, in the main, unskilled female labour. Third, due to the
form which the government's incentives took, the receipt of subsidy
was not linked to the number of jobs created, as in other development
areas in the UK, but to the level of capital expenditure (Black,
1977, pp.59-71). This encouraged the setting-up of expensive plants
which did not necessarily employ large numbers of workers, for
example, the DuPont chemical plant near Londonderry. Fourth, most
of the new factories were simply export-oriented production
facilities, branches of external organisations whose policy-making
and research and development took place elsewhere, making them
vulnerable to closure during economic recession. Many of the jobs
created in these production facilities were of an unskilled nature.
Finally, some of these enterprises were very short-lived, remaining
open only as long as their attendant subsidy. Alongside the above
was the increasing penetration of external capital into the province
as local companies were taken over, a process which led in some
cases to their closure as the recession of the 1970s deepened. The
resultant pattern of eventual industrial control in the province
is shown in Table 3.2.

TABLE 3.2 Control of manufacturing industry in Northern Ireland

Locus of control	Size of firm (number of employees)		
	20-249	250-500	500+
Northern Ireland	461	11	9
Great Britain	192	28	18
North America	18	8	8
Elsewhere	19	4	5

Source: Review Team, 1976, p.77.

Despite the attraction of so much outside investment, an overall
decline in the numbers of people employed in engineering and textiles
has taken place since 1945. Accompanying this trend has been an
increase in the number employed in the service sector, many in part-

time jobs, and particularly women (Trewsdale and Trainor, 1979, pp.5-6; Workers' Research Unit, 1978, pp.2-4). Some of the changes in the pattern of employment in the province are summarised in Table 3.3.

TABLE 3.3 Employees in employment, Northern Ireland, 1959-79 (thousands)

	Engineering	Textiles	Construction	Services
June 1959	53.3	80.9	38.6	201.6
June 1964	50.6	72.8	42.4	222.3
June 1969	52.9	68.4	47.7	237.8
June 1974	51.9	61.0	39.3	284.4
June 1979 (a)	41.2	48.8	37.5	325.0

Source: 'DMS Gazette', No.1 (1978), Tables 1 and 2; No.3 (1979), Table 10.

(a) Provisional figures.

Full-time jobs in engineering and textiles have been decreasing in number and the number of service-sector jobs has risen. Expressed as a ratio, the relationship between the manufacturing and service sectors in 1979 was 1:2.3, as compared with 1:1.2 in 1959. This has serious implications for young workers on two accounts. First, textiles and engineering have traditionally been sources of unskilled work for girls and apprenticeships for boys, and second, many of those service jobs which have become available are either part-time, i.e. cleaners and 'home helps', or otherwise regarded as unsuitable for young people, i.e. many jobs in the flourishing security sector.

Thus, the decline of one area of employment for young workers has not been offset by the expansion of others. Furthermore, jobs in other areas of manufacturing have declined recently from their peak in the early 1970s, and the construction industry, a source of unskilled work for young men, is experiencing one of its worst recessions for the last twenty years.

There are two reasons for this pattern of recession. First, Ulster's sensitivity to the ups and downs of world markets means that local industry, despite state intervention aimed both at creating new jobs and protecting existing ones, has felt the full impact of the current depression in the 'developed' sectors of the capitalist world economy. Textiles and engineering industries which are suffering a global decline, have been affected by competition from cheap-labour economies such as Formosa and South Korea. This competitive disadvantage has been compounded by a dependence upon external markets and imported raw materials.

Second, it can of course be argued that the 'troubles' have added to the economic plight of the province by scaring away potential employers, deflecting public funds from areas in which they might most usefully be spent and inhibiting labour mobility and industrial redevelopment within the province (Review Team, op.cit.). There is undoubtedly some truth in this argument, but it must be modified in

at least two respects. First, the violence of the troubles has led
to the creation of jobs in some service sectors, particularly the
social services and the security industry, and second, the local
economy continued to expand after the start of the violence, reaching
its peak in terms of employment in the manufacturing industries in
the early 1970s, suggesting that already established industry had
adapted to the security situation rather than being depressed by it.

One important aspect of the local economy which has not yet been
discussed is the standard of living in comparison with the rest of
the United Kingdom. The situation may be summarised in three
phrases: average wages in Northern Ireland are lower, average prices
are higher, and social security benefits the same as in Britain.
The problem of poverty is compounded by high long-term unemployment
rates, much over-crowded or insanitary housing, and more single-
parent families than in the United Kingdom (Black et al., 1980;
Evason, 1976, 1978, 1980; Townsend, 1979, pp.549-59).

The importance of the economics of poverty should not be forgotten
when reading the ethnography in the following chapters. Youngsters
in Northern Ireland, when compared to their peers on the mainland,
tend to earn less money when working and pay higher prices for most
articles they buy. If they are out of work, their problem is worse.
Although benefits are calculated at the same rates which apply in
the rest of the country, the absence of any compensatory weighting
to allow for Ulster's higher cost of living means that, while life
on supplementary benefit in Britain means, at best, difficulty in
making ends meet, in Northern Ireland it means poverty, being
completely broke for most of the time.

The low-wage problem has dire consequences for certain categories
of worker, particularly unskilled workers with families. In this
situation it may be economically most 'rational' to remain
unemployed rather than take an unskilled, low-paid job and accept
a net loss of income. Due to the local ethnic division of labour,
catholic families are most affected by unemployment and low pay.
However, there are large numbers of protestant unskilled workers,
some of whom appear later in this book, who are increasingly
vulnerable in this respect. With the steady decline of traditional
employment, it is likely that the numbers of disadvantaged
protestant workers will swell (Byrne, 1981).

THE 'TROUBLES' (1)

In this section, I shall present a brief account of events since
1963, in order that the later account of the short history of
Ballyhightown may be placed in context. When Terence O'Neill became
Prime Minister at Stormont in 1963, it seemed to be the end of an
era for the Unionist Party. Traditional loyalism was in decline
and the six counties appeared to be on the road to tolerance and
modernity. However, 1964 saw the worst riots in Belfast since the
1930s, precipitated by the display of a Republican flag in Belfast
and inspired by a then obscure protestant cleric, Ian Paisley.
Fired by his eloquence extreme loyalist opinion grew ever more
militant, reacting strongly to the 1965 visit to Stormont of the
Irish Prime Minister and the processions the following year marking

the fiftieth anniversary of the Easter Rising. 1966 also saw the
first political murders in Belfast for a long time, appearing to
signal the resurgence of a newly-organised loyalist underground.

Catholic political action took a different course. The Irish
Republican Army (IRA) had stood down in 1962 following its abortive
border campaign; in 1967 the Northern Ireland Civil Rights Association
was formed out of the grievances of the catholic middle class, an
organisation which initially attracted many protestant fellow
travellers. As Civil Rights marches against unfair housing allocation
and local government discrimination gathered momentum throughout
1967 and 1968, they confronted the Unionist Party in the shape of
William Craig, then Minister of Home Affairs, who banned the marches
and called in the 'B Specials', a reserve paramilitary security
force manned exclusively by protestants. By 1969, O'Neill's liberal
faction was no longer dominant within the Unionist Party and in
April he resigned, leaving traditional Unionist politicians firmly
in control once again.

By August 1969, following violence in Derry which rapidly spread
to other parts of the province and left five people dead in Belfast,
the British Army was called in and the IRA began to regroup and
re-arm. Violence escalated as the Army became more deeply involved
in the policing of ever wider areas of the province and, inevitably
perhaps, they entered into open conflict with the IRA. As things
got worse ever more draconian responses were evoked from both
Stormont and Westminster, culminating in the reintroduction of
internment without trial in August 1971.

In the wake of the violence precipitated by internment, there
occurred the wholesale migration of families out of areas in which
they formed an ethnic minority and into safer areas. Some of this
movement was voluntary, but much of it was flight in the face of
intimidation. It has been estimated that between 8,000 and 15,000
families made this kind of move in the Belfast area in the early
years of the 'troubles' (Darby and Morris, 1974). Throughout the
early 1970s violent outrage matched violent outrage - Bloody Sunday
in 1972, the Provisional IRA's bombing campaign against civilian
targets, and the loyalist assassination campaign from 1973 onwards.
All contributed to an atmosphere of political uncertainty and
popular foreboding.

In 1972, following the imposition of direct rule from Westminster,
the local vigilante defence associations of working-class protestant
areas of Belfast amalgamated to form the Ulster Defence Association.
Created in response to the Provisionals' bombing campaign and the
perceived inability of the security forces to prevent it, the UDA
represented a new departure in Ulster politics. While it had, at
the beginning, overt links with and the support of senior Unionist
politicians such as Craig, it was, and remained, an essentially
working-class movement, capable of acting outside the political
arena of traditional Unionism.

In 1973, the Northern Ireland Assembly, an experiment in devolved
local government, met. That November the Executive, a 'power-sharing'
administration led by Brian Faulkner, previously a right-wing
Unionist, and including members of the Catholic opposition, the
Social Democratic and Labour Party, took office. They faced
resistance at every step, from both the Provisionals and a coalition

of Unionist interests led by Paisley, Craig and Harry West. In May 1974, the Ulster Workers' Council, an ad hoc organisation drawing its strongest support in the power stations and the shipyard, in collaboration with the UDA and the Unionist coalition, organised a general strike by protestant workers which led to the Executive resigning within a fortnight. In October 1974 this loyalist victory was decisively affirmed when the United Ulster Unionist Council took ten of the province's twelve Westminster seats at the General Election.

Since then there has been a political stalemate in the province, a state of affairs not relieved by the 1975 Constitutional Convention which, with a majority of loyalist members, returned a report demanding a return to the status quo of Unionist government from Stormont. This option is as unacceptable to all the parties at Westminster as it is to the Provisionals. As recent events have shown, it appears to be no longer acceptable to the UDA either (New Ulster Political Research Group, 1979). Direct rule by a Secretary of State responsible to the Westminster government has continued. Local government, following its reorganisation in 1973, is largely administered through executive boards, responsible either for education or health and social services and appointed by the Secretary of State. Local councils are largely ineffectual bodies with little power and most public service functions, such as public works and housing, are the responsibility of central government agencies like the Housing Executive or the Department of the Environment (NI).

Within this political limbo, the institutions of direct rule have apparently been taken for granted. There still seems little likelihood of a new political solution materialising, despite the recent initiatives of the Secretary of State. One thing which is becoming apparent, however, is the changed political role of the protestant working class. Despite the violence of the H-Block hunger strike protests there has been, as yet, no return to mass Loyalist political violence. The growing awareness of many loyalists of their identity as working-class is apparent to this author. Whether or not this incipient class consciousness will result in a weakening of their solidarity with the protestant middle class and rural loyalists cannot be speculated upon. However, a return to the old class-alliance of Unionist politics is unlikely, as loyalist politicians discovered to their cost when they attempted to repeat the success of the 1974 strike with the United Unionist Action Council's stoppage in May 1977. Lacking the support of a majority of the protestant workforce or the whole-hearted backing of the para-military organisations, the action was a resounding failure.

The failure of the 1977 stoppage was as obvious in Ballyhightown as elsewhere and since that time ambiguity and uncertainty have characterised local loyalist politics. In Figure 4.1 in the following chapter I identify a continuum of political identities between loyalism and unionism which approximately matches the distinction between the 'rough' and the 'respectable'. This necessary simplification should not, however, conceal the overarching ethnic loyalties which unite the protestant working class and remain potentially important for political mobilisation.

THE ESTATE AND ITS DEVELOPMENT (2)

On the outskirts of Belfast, between the city and the hills, lies
Ballyhightown, approximately three square miles of public housing
providing homes for about 14,000 people. In many ways it is a 'no
man's land', stretching as it does between the suburbs of Belfast
proper and the residential villages of Castleowen, the borough
within which it lies, its borders marked on all sides by major roads.
Although it is of Belfast, inasmuch as its residents tend to identify
with and orientate themselves towards the city in their working
lives and leisure activities, it is administratively part of Castleowen. To all intents, and for some official purposes such as the
supply of gas or the payment of electricity bills, the estate is
part of the Belfast urban area.
     The first ground was broken at the beginning of the 1950s and
work then proceeded in phases until the completion of the 'top end'
and the high-rise flats in the late 1960s. Planned as a dormitory
development to accommodate the overflow from a rapidly growing
Belfast, Ballyhightown was originally something of a model estate,
in which the 'respectable' working class (in the context of the
official attitudes of the time, mainly protestants) could live
respectable lives in modern and healthy surroundings.
     The blocks of flats at Ballyhightown are of great interest
     from an architectural point of view, and they add much to the
     character of the district. The tall, finely proportioned blocks
     rise above the surrounding houses, providing variety and contrast
     in the urban scene and emphasise important parts of the neighbour-
     hood such as the shopping centre. (3)
Even during the period of my fieldwork, long after Ballyhightown's
character had changed for the worse in many people's eyes, it was
still seen in contrast to what had been left behind in Belfast.
     I remember, after we'd been living here for a couple of years,
     going back up the Oldpark where we used to live ... and, I mean,
     you'd wonder how you ever lived there. Tiny wee houses with
     little rooms and windows and the damp coming in everywhere.

     I can remember before I used to live here, when we used to come
     up ... I thought all snobs must live here. It was lovely in
     them days, or at least it looked it to me.
However, with changes in government policy during the 1960s, the
estate's function changed from overspill accommodation to housing
families from slum clearance areas. This meant an influx of people
from some of the city's most deprived and 'roughest' areas. Due
to the phased building of the estate, the newcomers, significantly
both protestant and catholic, were concentrated in the north and
west of the estate, the 'top end'. By the early 1970s, it may be
estimated that approximately a third of the residents were catholics,
living mostly in the recently built, most densely packed areas at
the northern end.
     When the troubles broke out it seemed for a time as if the
relatively peaceful co-existence of catholic and protestant on the
estate would continue. Relations between the two groups steadily
deteriorated, however, and although accounts differ as to what
actually happened and why, by 1973 only a few catholic families,

probably less than thirty out of over a thousand, remained in Ballyhightown. Some people who were involved agree that there was an
organised campaign of intimidation; others, equally deeply implicated,
offer a different explanation.

> There were a few people who were put out, but we knew who they
> were, IRA men ...//... but a lot of them saw that as a general
> threat to themselves and packed up and left ... and a lot of them
> just wanted a new house elsewhere. It wasn't what you'd call a
> general policy of intimidation, it was a sort of snowball effect.

Regardless of which account one believes, the estate was gradually
caught up in the violence that spread throughout working-class areas
of Belfast. With few exceptions, those catholics whose windows
weren't broken pre-empted the possibility and left. This violent
affirmation of ethnic boundaries was neither peculiar to Ballyhightown nor historically particularly novel (Baker, op.cit.). It must
also be understood in its local context, however. The intimidation
in Ballyhightown and the earlier formation of a local Defence
Association in the summer of 1971 were, at least partly, a response
to the presence of an IRA unit in the district, whose activities
culminated in 1972 in the shooting of an Ulster Defence Regiment
member and the shooting by the police of a catholic resident of
Ballyhightown who opened fire on one of their patrols with a machine
gun.

These remarks are not to be read as a mitigation of intimidation,
which fell like the rain on the just and the unjust alike. However,
when talking about Ballyhightown, which is practically synonymous
in Belfast with intimidation and loyalist violence, it is necessary
to point to reasons, both immediate and historic, for these events.
It is not enough to blame it on 'a load of bully boys', as did one
prominent local trade unionist whom I interviewed.

Following this exodus the estate's character began to change
rapidly. Many of the houses so hurriedly vacated were damaged, in
understandable anger, by their fleeing tenants; plumbing was
smashed and electrical wiring ripped out. These houses were then
occupied by protestant families in flight from other troubled parts
of the city. As squatters, the new occupants were not entitled to
have repairs carried out by the Housing Executive and much of the
housing stock, particularly at the top end of the estate, deteriorated.
By the time the tenancies were legitimised, much damage had been
done and boarded-up houses began to be a familiar sight.

Further factors also affected the condition of the housing stock.
Some of the flat blocks praised so fulsomely in the quotation at
the beginning of this section were four-storey structures containing
eight one-bedroomed maisonettes, heated by under-floor electric
central heating and originally very popular as first homes for young
couples. Because of the undesirability of the estate to upwardly-
mobile couples due to its newly-acquired 'bad name' (particularly
the top end), the availability of similar accommodation in nearby
estates with better reputations, the availability within Ballyhightown of flats in the newer multi-storey blocks in the centre of the
estate (more respectable and better insulated, socially, against
their surroundings), and the rising costs of using electric central
heating, many of these small blocks of flats, particularly at the
top end of the estate, fell into disuse. They were boarded up and

served to make a bad situation worse. To complete the cycle of stigmatisation, there is much local anecdotal evidence that the top end is being used as a 'sink' by the Housing Executive, 'problem' tenants being dumped there or refused transfers to elsewhere.

Another, although perhaps less obvious, consequence of the troubled years of the early 1970s, was the partial dislocation of accepted norms of right and wrong behaviour, particularly for many adolescents. There would appear to be two reasons for this. First, at this time there appeared within the local network of 'rough kids' a large number of young people who were intimately acquainted with the previous three or four years of violence in the inner city and who had been further unsettled by the flight to the suburbs. Second, and more significant, was the development within the estate of a milieu of incipient lawlessness. This was the result of two connected circumstances: the prominent role of the local 'lads', the KAI (about whom I shall have more to say in Chapter 4), in the worst of the intimidation, and the seeming disinterest for a couple of years of the local police, who appear not to have cared about what went on inside the estate, so long as that was where it stayed.

Having sown the seeds of minor anarchy by discouraging police operations in the estate and, at best, turning a blind eye to the activities of the KAI, local paramilitary groups were eventually driven to respond to the resultant boom in juvenile crime by primitive 'community policing': beatings and, in extremis, 'knee-cappings'. It might be claimed that they met with some degree of success in discouraging burglary, for example, but they began to drift into disrepute among their own supporters. This, combined with increasing police activity on the estate, led to a suspension of summary punishments. They were not suspended completely, however; in the autumn of 1979, 'Tailor' Burton, one of the 'lads', who will be discussed later, was kneecapped for alleged rape. The legacy of this policy is the alienation of the paramilitary organisations from many of the young people of Ballyhightown.

This brief account brings us to August 1976 when I first arrived in Ballyhightown. The estate had then, as it still has, a reputa-tion as a very 'rough' area. In my home town, for example, twenty miles from Belfast and a staunchly loyalist place, Ballyhightown is seen as a violent district, to be avoided if at all possible. This was certainly my view until I got to know the place better.

I shall now discuss two further aspects of the estate which are important to this account: the local employment situation and the differences between the top and bottom ends of the estate. Un-employment, while not as severe as in areas of west Belfast, for example, was bad and is getting worse. Statistics for the estate are not available and such estimates as I could make would not be reliable, so I shall confine myself to saying that the unemployment rate is certainly much higher than that for the Belfast travel-to-work area, as defined by the Northern Ireland Department of Manpower Services. In July 1979 this figure was, according to the DMS's monthly press notice, 10.5 per cent: 11.6 per cent for males and 9.1 per cent for females.

Employment-wise, one of the biggest problems for the estate's residents is the decline of immediately local employment. Although most people work away from Ballyhightown, the provision of work nearby is important and has become more so since the troubles began, particularly for young workers, many of whom are loath to work in Belfast itself, particularly in republican or 'troubled' areas. In fact, although the estate was originally designed to mainly accommodate people who worked in Belfast, it was an explicit aim of the planners to provide work locally as well; Castleowen was seen as one of the centres of an industrial development zone stretching ten miles or so beyond the city boundaries. In addition to the existing mills and factories of Castleowen's older villages of Craigabann, Craigowen and Glasnacree, some of which are as old as the mechanisa- tion of textile production in the province, the Stormont Ministry of Commerce developed two industrial estates in the area in the 1950s and 1960s, one of which is on the borders of Ballyhightown. In 1979 there were only two factories still in production here, the other six lying empty and bricked up. One of these has been re- opened by an American company; one of the two still open in 1979 has since closed, however. On the other industrial estate, a mile- and-a-half away at Priorville, two factories, both American-owned, are still active. Although one of these hired more workers to fulfil a new order while I was there, the other, TransInternational Electronics, was operating well below its maximum manning levels, having made over a thousand workers redundant in the early 1970s. They have announced further lay-offs since I left Northern Ireland.

In the last ten years much new employment, most of it in distributive industries, i.e. warehouses, transport firms and wholesalers, has been sited in Castleowen, in the newest and largest industrial estate at Dunbeg, some miles from Ballyhightown on the other side of Glasnacree. Many of these companies have moved out from Belfast, bringing their existing workforce with them and hence are not 'new jobs'. During the 1970s and since, the dominant trend in employment opportunities for Ballyhightown's residents has been contraction, particularly in manufacturing industry. There has been, however, an increase in service sector employment, much of which is, as argued above, not always available to or suitable for young workers (see Table 3.4).

Looking at immediately local manufacturing employment there were, according to my files of local newspaper cuttings, over 370 jobs lost between January 1977 and February 1980, with the definite creation of only thirty new jobs by way of compensation. A new supermarket complex opened in November 1978, but many of the jobs thus created were part-time. Add to these widespread redundancies in firms in Belfast and elsewhere and the picture becomes even more gloomy. Table 3.4, illustrating the overall trend in employment in Castleowen, reflects two things: the growth of service sector employment and the trend for easily mobile concerns in transport, distribution and small-scale manufacturing to move out of central Belfast to the trading estates on the city's periphery. As discussed above, this does not necessarily mean the provision of new jobs, particularly for young workers. Furthermore, in interpreting these figures it should be borne in mind both that the economic climate has worsened since June 1978 and the population of Castleowen has increased dramatically since the 1971 Census. (4).

Finally, the difference between the top and bottom ends of the estate remains important in the eyes of both residents and outsiders.

TABLE 3.4   Employees in employment, Castleowen, 1971 and 1978

Industrial sector (Standard Industrial Classification Orders)	April 1971 (a)		June 1978 (b)	
	Male	Female	Male	Female
Manufacturing (3-12)	2141	1713	1768	1564
Other manufacturing (13-19)	1230	598	2798	422
Total manufacturing (3-19)	3371	2311	4566	1986
Construction (20)	1387	68	1664	68
Distributive trades (23)	727	563	1038	1081
Other services (21, 24-27)	1779	2379	3389	4266
Totals	7264	5321	10657	7401

Source: (a) 1971 Census, Economic Activity Tables.
          (b) Statistics Branch, Department of Manpower Services,
              Belfast.

It is also reflected in official statistics. The data from the
most comprehensive discussion of urban deprivation in Belfast,
'Belfast Areas of Special Social Need' (Project Team, 1976), since
they are available at local government ward level, can be used to
illustrate some dimensions of this distinction. In order to preserve
the estate's precarious anonymity, I have chosen not to provide
detailed citations from the Report for the data I use below.
     Taking the four wards which make up the estate, Ward A is the
'bottom end', Ward B is intermediate and Wards C and D are the 'top
end'. Looking at adult male unemployment, in 1975 Wards A and D
had lower rates than B and C; once again in 1975, Ward D had the
highest level of juvenile male unemployment and Ward C the lowest.
If we examine the number of households receiving Family Income
Supplement in 1975, Wards B and D had the greatest numbers of low-
wage families.
     Educationally speaking, there also appear to be important
differences between the Wards; the statistics for 'retarded readers',
as a percentage of all eleven-year-olds in 1975, reveal much higher
concentrations in Wards B and D. The 1974 data relating to
'educationally sub-normal' children indicate higher rates of incidence
in Wards A and D.
     These figures must be interpreted with caution, however. First,
they were collected by different official agencies, at different
times, for different purposes and using different techniques. Second,
the method of aggregation and presentation in the report utilises
such broad catagories that the actual value for any index for any
ward may vary within a very wide band. The picture is further
complicated by the fact that Wards A and C include small tracts
of owner-occupied property. Nevertheless, bearing these reservations
in mind and accepting these statistics at face value as indicating
genuine social and economic deprivation, it may be concluded with
confidence that the top end of the estate, particularly Ward D,
differs from the bottom end in being more deprived in a number of
important respects.

Official statistics thus bear out to some extent the local folk
model of the estate as being divided by an invisible line separating
the top from the bottom. I have documented this folk model in more
detail elsewhere (Jenkins, 1982c) and it is well illustrated in the
quotation below from a resident of the estate, in a 'Belfast
Telegraph' article about Ballyhightown's decline.

The place has settled down in the past years or so. I know that
it has a bad image, but I can speak for the lower and middle part
and I have found the average person to be honest and hard working

The folk model finds frequent expression in the view that only those
houses on the 'main drive' or at the bottom of the estate receive
regular maintenance or adequate redecoration from the Housing
Executive. It is one of the dominant themes which structures the
experience of life in Ballyhightown.

In this chapter I have provided some of the necessary background
against which the analysis in the rest of the book must be set.
However, in so doing it has been my intention to do more than simply
provide depth and context. I have also tried to demonstrate some
of the ways in which stratified divisions within the working class
in Northern Ireland have been generated over time.

Looking at the macro-economic level, for example, it is clear
that the Plantation and the later development of capitalist industry
in the province provided the conditions under which two ethnically
stratified segments of the working class came into being. Within
the dominant protestant working class, it is equally clear how the
development of textile production and engineering not only created
the broad distinction between the skilled and the unskilled, but
also, to some degree, served to reproduce that distinction in
residential patterns. This homology between occupational level and
residence was, of course, nothing like perfect; it was simply an
overall identifiable pattern. A much more definite pattern 'on the
ground' was (and is) the more-or-less rigid residential segregation
between protestants and catholics (Baker, op.cit; Boal, 1981).

Coming to unemployment, it is equally apparent that factors such
as the narrowness of the industrial base and changes in demand have
been crucial factors in producing long-term high levels of unemployment in Northern Ireland. Furthermore, the post-war governmental
industrial development strategies can be seen to have had the effects
of reinforcing the ethnic division of unemployment, producing mainly
unskilled production jobs, and creating jobs which were very
vulnerable to international recession. This latter is well
illustrated by the fact that, with the demise of British Enkalon's
plant at Antrim in 1982 and the previous closures of the Courtaulds
and ICI plants at Carrickfergus, virtually all of the 'new' jobs in
synthetic fibres have vanished. In reading the Chapters which follow
it is important to bear in mind the impoverished opportunity
structure which faces the young people of Ballyhightown.

Finally, looking at the estate itself, it can be seen how the
division into the top and the bottom has been produced by the
intimidation of the early 1970s, the housing policies which preceded
it in the final phase of the estate's development, the inadequacies
of the Housing Executive's response to that intimidation, and housing

allocation decisions which tend to reproduce the distinction between the rough and the respectable, the desirable and the undesirable, in residential patterns.   This latter is a process which has also been documented elsewhere (Baldwin and Bottoms, 1976; Gill, 1977).

I have tried to show how some of the differences within the Northern Irish working class have developed historically, in what has been a condensed and, therefore, necessarily superficial discussion.   In the context of Ballyhightown the most important of these divisions are between the top and bottom of the estate, the rough and the respectable, the unskilled and the skilled and the unemployed and the employed.   In the Chapters which follow I shall explore how these divisions come together and find expression in the lived experience of the young people of Ballyhightown.

Chapter 4

LIFE-STYLES

Much of the recent sociology of youth is written within the framework of the 'new left' sociology of culture, as discussed in Chapter 1. Without wishing to expand my critique of theories of cultural reproduction, I shall, if possible, avoid talking about subcultures here, preferring the term life-style, as used by Hannerz (1969), Pryce (1979), Stewart, Prandy and Blackburn (1980), and, indeed, Bourdieu (1980). This is for two reasons. First, the notion of life-style directs our attention away from the cultural realm of meaning and towards the emphasis on practice suggested in Chapter 1. Second, the concept of subculture tends to exclude from considera-tion the large areas of commonality between subcultures, however defined, and implies a determinate and often deviant relationship to a notional dominant culture. Recent work (Cohen, 1980; Hebdige, 1979; Robins and Cohen, 1978) has explicitly theorised subcultures as the deviant or stylistically bizarre misrecognised working-class resistance to modernising capitalism. Once again, the notion of 'false knowledge' enters the analysis.

Thus, in order to distance myself from the subcultural tradition, I prefer the term life-style to denote observable patterns of social practices distinguishing groups of people who may be said, on the grounds of shared language or ethnicity, for example, to belong to the same cultural group. This concept derives ultimately from Weber's discussion of status groups (1968, pp.306-7); however, following Giddens (1981a, p.111), I would insist that since class is a socially constructed complex of practices, there will be differences between the practices of members of different classes, however defined. Furthermore, since classes are not lumpen phenomena, the same must hold good for the patterned or stratified divisions within classes. There are, therefore, life-style differ-ences both within and between classes; it is partly in this differ-entiation that a class-stratified society is socially constructed (cf. Stewart, Prandy and Blackburn, op.cit., pp.27-36). Used in this manner the life-style model may be a strategic concept in analysing the manner in which class distinctions are actively produced and reproduced in practice. Furthermore, this notion may also allow the discussion of changing youth life-styles (i.e. subcultures) to be integrated with a discussion of more stable,

generalised class life-styles (Clarke et al., 1976; Murdock and
McCron, 1976).

Basing my account on their models of themselves, I shall describe
three life-styles adopted by young people in Ballyhightown: the
lads, the ordinary kids and the citizens. I do not, however, claim
to present a comprehensive picture of all the estate's youth. There
must have been a few kids, neither members of the Centre's clubs nor
the church organisations, who were not readily visible and were
overlooked. I do not think, however, that this minor absence
detracts too much from the usefulness of the ethnography.

This tripartite scheme appears to have much in common with
Willmott's classification of Bethnal Green's young men into 'rebels',
'working class' and 'middle class' (1969, pp.172-6). Ashton and
Field, in their study of young workers (1976), similarly distinguish
between those with 'extended careers', those with 'short-term
careers' and the 'careerless', their extended career respondents
coming mainly from lower middle-class homes and the short-term
career pupils from the 'respectable' working class. While accepting
the descriptive validity of both these accounts, I question the
attribution to some of their subjects of a middle-class identity.
It seems more likely that the three life-styles I identify, for
example, are integral parts of the wider canvas of working-class
life and probably always have been (Bell and Newby, 1971, p.202).
The 'rebels', or the lads, reflect not rebellion against working-
class values but an exaggeration of the 'traditional' working-class
valorisation of masculinity (Willis, 1977, 1979). Similarly the
'middle-class' kids, the citizens, are the apotheosis of the
respectable working-class ideals of sobriety, independence and
self-advancement. This is not to deny the similarities between the
citizens and the lower middle class; I am simply insisting that
working-class life must be viewed in the first instance as (more or
less) autonomous, rather than derivitive, and that the boundaries
between classes here are, at best, imprecise (cf. Rosser and Harris,
1965, pp.82-9). The 'respectable' working class may be equipped
for social mobility and a middle-class destination, but if so it is
largely on indigenous working-class principles and practices that
they draw.

The model I present is also at odds with the simpler, bi-polar
model of the young working class developed by Hargreaves (1967),
Lacey (1970) and Willis (op.cit.). These studies were all done
within single schools; given the inherent stratification of our
education system, this immediately produces a narrowed social
spectrum, resulting in a correspondingly foreshortened model of
internal class divisions. In addition, the inclusion of girls in
my study demands a category which while not 'rough' is certainly
not 'respectable'; all of the studies just referred to are limited
to boys.

AN INTRODUCTION TO KAILAND

Driving along the main road at the top of the estate, the motorist
sees this message painted on the gable end of a house: YOU ARE NOW
ENTERING KAILAND. These three letters, KAI, are sprayed, written

and painted all over the estate. The motif is a recurrent theme in local songs and tattoos, symbolising the solidarity experienced by some of the estate's kids, the 'rough' lads.

We come from the 'Town and we hate the Micks,
We beat their ballicks in with our sticks,
We'll fight the Fenians 'til we die,
We are the 'Hightown Kai-ai.

It starts with a K and it ends with an I,
There's an A in the middle and they call us Kai,
A Tartan gang with a Tartan scarf,
We are the 'Hightown Kai-ai.

The name itself derives originally from a Scandinavian footballer, Kai Johansen, who played for Glasgow Rangers, scoring the winning goal in a famous Scottish Cup Final against Celtic. It has also been used by protestant gangs in Glasgow, who paint it on walls to defy their catholic rivals (Patrick, 1973, p.119). This may have been how it found its way to Ballyhightown; there is much coming and going between Belfast and Glasgow during the 'mad month' of July, when bands from Northern Ireland travel to Scotland to participate in the Orange marches and there is a reciprocal influx of Scottish bands into Belfast. There is also much local interest in Scottish football, some people from Ballyhightown regularly spending weekends in Glasgow supporting 'the 'Gers', especially if they are at home to Celtic. Mackers, for example, met the girl he was 'seeing' throughout the winter of 1978-9 on the train from Glasgow to Stranraer, while on his way home from such a weekend. She was from the Tigers' Bay area of Belfast.

However, it is just as likely that the magic of the word was conjured up locally. I have heard several different accounts of how so-and-so was playing football one day, pretending to be Johansen, 'King Kai', and the name stuck. Another informant insists that it was the name given by Jonty Bryans to his gang. Once the name had acquired its magic, however, it soon acquired other meanings: 'Kill All Irish', 'Kill All Informers' and 'Kill All Intruders'. This bloodthirsty bravado should certainly not be taken too seriously, but it does, none the less, vividly articulate some of the central concerns of Ulster loyalism: 'Substantively a "frontier" culture ... which continued to stress encirclement' (Gibbon, 1975, p.36).

The Kai motif was further incorporated into the local milieu by the naming of one of the estate's flute bands. 'The Sons of Kai' band was formed in the spring of 1972 and still functions today, although it has changed its name twice in an attempt to evade the ban placed on it by many District Orange Lodges because of its reputation for fighting and drunkenness. Spring 1972 was a time when violence in the estate was at its peak; in the middle of much of that violence was the Kai, a loose collective noun for the young people who were on the streets at the time.

There was a gang of us, sometimes there would have been as many as two hundred of us, all young fellas, going around. This was at the time of the paint pots ... people getting crosses painted on their doors and windows. There was one time we lifted someone's garden fence and bucked it through their front window

and I can remember another time putting one of those wee Tan-
Sads (i.e. a pushchair) through a window, only that was a mistake,
they were prods.

Which came first, the flute band or the general usage, is impossible
to say. However, the Kai does not ever seem to have been an organised
gang, with a leader, officers and internal organisation. (1) Not an
institution in any concrete sense, it is more a diffuse symbol
denoting membership in a particular Ballyhightown network. It
identifies the lads when outside the estate, at football matches,
for example, and inside it, as distinct from 'snobs', 'licks' or
the citizens. As such, it remains as potent an ideology today as
ever.   Although one hears girls singing the Kai songs and there is
the occasional girl with a self-inflicted Kai tattoo, the prevailing
ethos of the Kai is male. In Ballyhightown it symbolises both
militant loyalism and the masculine domain of the lads, revolving
around the pub and the bookies. A flute band as opposed to an
accordion band, a world which some of the girls and women view very
cynically. Here is Susan Steenson, describing the Friday night disco
held in a local pub: 'The last of the 'Hightown Kai making their
last stand.' She is talking about men like Alfie Wright or Bobby
Bothwell who, although married with children, still go out for 'a
rake with the boys', trying to 'get my hole' or 'touch for a wee
doll'.

Why, it may be asked, is there no female life-style equivalent
to the lads? Among other reasons (cf. Brake, 1980, pp.137-54), the
following factors are important: first, the ideology of respectability for girls in Ballyhightown, particularly as this relates to
marriage prospects; second, their atomistic 'bedroom culture',
which precludes the peer-group solidarity upon which the lads'
life-style is based; third, there is the relative subservience of
the girls to the social demands of their boyfriends; fourth, most
girls' time is taken up to some extent in housework; and fifth, the
distinction between the public domain of men and the private world
of women inhibits the creation of a 'rough' female life-style. This
is not to say that there are no 'rough' women or girls, there are.
The role of women, as wives and mothers, in the reproduction of
'rough' working-class life-styles is a question I shall return to
in the last chapter.

Apart from the pubs, the social clubs and the bookies, another
important institution in the lads' world is the Youth Centre. Owned
and run by the local Education and Library Board, it stands in the
centre of the estate at The Square. Opened in the late 1960s, it
has been a long-standing focus for the lads in their spare time,
particularly since the local cinema was burned down several years
ago. This importance is as much in the absence of alternatives as
anything else, particularly for the lads, who are less geographically
mobile than other kids from the estate. Feuds, both real and
imagined, with lads from other areas, both protestant and catholic,
are a major constraint on mobility, but factors such as the lack of
money or transport also contribute to this situation. So they fall
back on the resources of the estate: drinking, backing horses, or
hanging around the Centre if they are unemployed or have taken a
day off work. Within the security of the known network it is easier
to make limited funds stretch; money can be 'tapped' from mates and

there is usually someone around to buy a drink.

There are, nonetheless, recognised limits to the lads' reciprocity and tolerance of their indigent peers. In the conversation below, Mitch has been complaining about how pissed off he is, out of work and without enough money for a pint.

Browner   Why don't you be like me? I have always money. That's 'cos I only go out drinking once or maybe twice a week.

Mitch   That's all right for you. At least you have someone to spend your fucking time with.

Browner   (Shrugging) Whose fault's that? Why don't you go out tomorrow and get yourself a job?

Mitch   I have to go to Gloucester House (i.e. the Job Centre in Belfast) tomorrow anyway, I'll see what they have.

Browner   That's no fucking good. You'll need to do more than that.... Anyway, are you a proper plasterer? I mean ... you'd think a plasterer could get a job whenever he wanted, for fuck's sake.

Mitch   No, ... that's a bit of a problem.

Browner   If you hadn't fucked about so much you'd have been out of your time a year ago and you wouldn't be stuck now ...//... If you don't watch yourself you'll leave it for a week, then it'll be a month and you won't have nothing, for fuck's sake (pulls out his trouser pockets to illustrate the point), and we'll all be walking round with heaps of money and all. And then you'll wish you got a job.

This conversation illustrates two principles which are important for an understanding of the lads' social world. First, employment outcomes are interpreted as the result of each individual's actions, which in turn reflect upon his character. Unemployment is seen as the result of personal failure, even though the lads know that there are not enough jobs to go round. Second, there is a limit to the lads' tolerance of and support for the network's unemployed members. They will lend money to, or buy drinks for, their mates who are laid off or out of work, recognising that, as for most of them in the past, it might be their turn tomorrow. However, they also recognise a fine, if situationally imprecise, line between being hard up and scrounging.

In the light of this it is not surprising to find that those lads who are unemployed for long periods form a distinct group, the 'brue-men', the brue being the local word for the Social Security Office. This is no more than might be expected in the light of their availability as company for each other during the day. However, their distinctiveness as a small group is emphasised by the fact that they spend much of their time together in the evenings and at weekends. (2) Ironically, perhaps, they appear to regard unemployment as a virtue, in contrast to 'working like a mug', as is illustrated by the following situation.

One Friday towards the end of May 1979, the Centre was not open, as it normally would be, for the unemployed to use, since the staff were in Glasnacree, organising the senior club's stall at the following day's Round Table Charity Fair. Some of the regulars, Alfie Wright, Robbo and Ivan Green, were annoyed by this and sent Jimmy, the Centre Warden, a note asking why the Centre was closed, more as 'a bit of banter' than anything else. Jimmy sent them a reply advising them that perhaps they should solve their problem by going out and getting a job; he had to work for his living and had no time for leisure activities. The lads' written reply to this is reproduced below.

GENERAL UNEMPLOYED AND LAYABOUTS' UNION

Dear Jimmy/John/Marjorie (i.e. the Centre staff)

I would like to thank you for your letter dated 29/5/79 and having carefully read it would like to point out one of our regulations

Rule (1) Paragraph (1)
"MEMBERS OF THE ABOVE MENTIONED UNION MAY NOT SEEK HEALTHY GAINFUL AND FULL TIME EMPLOYMENT. THE PUNISHMENT FOR ANYONE DOING SO IS INSTANT DISMISSAL."

Now that you have been made aware of this rule we would be very grateful if you would reconsider our request for the Centre to be made available for our members on Friday afternoons.

If you, the workers, require some more free time to yourselves, please feel free to leave your present employment and join us. We will make you very welcome.

We remain,

       Yours,

Alfie Wright	(Chairman)
Ivan Green	(Treasurer)
Billy Robinson	(Secretary)
Robert Drummond	(Committee Member)

This good-humoured exchange clearly illustrates the brue-men's image of themselves as failures and the role of their own ironic ideology of idleness in mitigating that failure for them. In addition, their own equality, both economically and socially, means that they can 'tap' off each other. Thus, whenever Alfie got his share of his wife's Child Benefit it went towards buying the boys a drink or some cigarettes in the middle of the week. He, in turn, could rely on Ivan to see him right at other times.

We should beware, however, of attributing cohesion or stability to either the group or the brue-man ideology. These lads still subscribe to a 'protestant ethic'; a few weeks after the letter was written, its main instigator, Alfie, did start work. Even more telling, it was as a Council street-cleaner, a job regarded as less than desirable by the lads, even though some of them have done it at one time or another. Although it pays well and involves working on one's own in the open air away from direct supervision, it is dirty and regarded as a menial occupation, one step down from emptying

the dustbins. Alfie got the job through the good offices of his
father, who works for the Council.

The brue-men should, therefore, not be regarded as a coherent
group; they are an ad hoc response to the problems of long-term
unemployment, a fluid coterie whose membership changes as its members
find work and some of the other lads lose it. Of the four who signed
the letter, three are also in the Kai band, Alfie, Ivan and Robert,
and two, Alfie and Billy, play for the Centre's football team. Thus
they are also involved, together, in the networks of other informal
institutions. Furthermore, Robert's signature on the letter is
misleading since he is not a regular at the Centre's afternoon
sessions for the unemployed.

BOYS AND GIRLS

The lads are not the majority of the Youth Centre's users. There is
a wide network of young people who use various of the Centre's
facilities and of which the lads form a part. These other young
people, not as self-consciously 'hard' as most of the lads, remain
quite distinct from the citizens, the church-going 'respectable'
youngsters I shall discuss later. I shall refer to them as the
ordinary kids of the Youth Centre network. Lacking the self-
conscious identity of the citizens and the lads, this is how they
described themselves when I asked, simply as 'ordinary kids'.

A major difference between the lads and the ordinary kids is the
role of women among the latter. Although the sexes maintain
separate spheres of interaction and friendship, male and female
inhabit one more or less unified social universe. The world of the
lads, however, is male-oriented and -dominated, women usually
intruding as mothers or sex objects. The relationship between the
sexes among the rest of the crowd who use the Youth Centre, although
closer, is none the less not equal. Boys expect to continue going
out with their mates, while their girlfriends are expected to remain
at home on these nights, perhaps occasionally going out for a 'hen-
party'. Here Carol Monteith recounts a telephone conversation with
Jenny, her fiancé's mate's fiancée, and an old friend of hers.
> We were talking about how when we got engaged *we* gave up all our
> friends and now when they go out with their friends we're just
> stuck in the house with no one to go out with. And it's all
> very well saying, why not go out with Jenny?, but all Smith's
> got to do is click his fingers and she's away. You couldn't
> depend on her. And it's no good going out on your own.
Distinct though they are, the difference between the lads and the
young men of the ordinary kids is one of degree; the latter still
risk experiencing their mates' censure, expressed in public sarcasm
and name-calling (such as, 'Look who's turning citizen', for
example), if they pay their girl-friends too much court or appear
to forsake the company of 'the boys' too often. Being 'one of the
boys' remains important.

Underlying this difference between the sexes is a basic sexist
morality. It may be all right for a young man to be promiscuous
and 'have a bit on the side', it is in fact something to boast about
in the company of men, but a young woman who is believed to enter

into too many sexual relationships too quickly becomes known as a
'scrab' or a 'wee ride' (cf. Cowie and Lees, 1981). This dual
standard, on the part of both sexes, extends to any girl who sets
up in her own flat without a public male consort; she risks acquiring
a reputation for promiscuity, whether deserved or not.

These sexual mores are accepted by most young people in Ballyhightown, regardless of their sex or life-style; they are one of the
foundations of working-class protestant life in Ulster. A woman's
place is ideally in the home and high standards of morality and
respectability are demanded of her. (3) Due largely to economic
necessity women have always gone out to work, in the textile mills,
for example, but the domestic domain remains the world of women.
Upon marriage, women are ideally supposed to devote themselves to
the 'real' work of reproducing the family, keeping house and managing
the primary socialisation of the children. The return to wage-labour
usually comes when the children are of school age; it is a necessity
if the marriage breaks up.

Marriage itself tends to be early; the sentiment is often
expressed that, 'eighteen's a nice age for a wee girl to get married
and twenty-one for a fella'. This ideal folk model is borne out by
the data for Ballyhightown marriages summarised in Table 4.1. From

TABLE 4.1   Marriages in Ballyhightown, 1976-8

| Age | Bride's Occupation (a) | | | | Groom's Occupation (a) | | | |
(years)	U	SM	WC	O	U	SM	WC	O
16-17	11	–	4	2	–	–	–	–
18-19	29	4	14	2	15	13	3	–
20-21	13	6	13	2	14	25	4	4
22-25	6	2	11	1	4	17	7	5
26+	6	2	5	1	7	8	5	3
Total:	65	14	47	8	40	63	19	12

Source: Registers of Marriages, Ballyhightown Church of Ireland,
Methodist and Presbyterian Churches.

(a)   U = Unskilled, SM = Skilled manual, WC = White collar, O = Other
(see Appendix Two)

this table it also appears that earlier marriage, for both sexes, is
associated with lower-status occupations. Without pursuing the
matter in great detail, this pattern is probably related to the
differences between the Youth Centre network and the churchgoing
network which I shall discuss later. Among the latter, there is a
tendency to aspire to higher-status jobs and to marry later, both
strategies being related to a general goal of upward social mobility,
particularly as reflected in the move off the estate into a 'bought'
house.

It is obvious, of course, that these figures must also reflect
to some extent the occupational distribution of young people on the
estate. For males, skilled manual work remains the largest occupational group, followed by unskilled work, while for females, white-

collar work and unskilled work are of more or less equal significance.
(4)

CRIME AND PUNISHMENT

Returning to the lads and the ordinary kids, another difference
between them is their involvement in crime. With few exceptions,
the lads have got criminal records and many have spent time in prison.
This is not so for the ordinary kids, who tend, once again with
exceptions, to have been free from serious entanglement with the law.
One of the reasons for this difference lies simply in the fact that
the lads are the 'rough' end of the Centre network. Since one of
the diagnostic features of 'roughness', both in the eyes of the
Ballyhightown residents, and, therefore, in my eyes as well, is
criminality, the problem is at least partially one of definition.
There is more to it, however; there are reasons why this particular
group of young people is more in conflict with the agencies of law
and order than other groups. In Ballyhightown I can identify at
least five factors at work. First, the incipient lawlessness of the
early 1970s led to an undoubted increase in juvenile crime, particularly among the lads. Although violence on the estate has since
abated, juvenile crime remains a problem. (5) Second, there is the
influence of a small number of adults from the estate, with the
appropriate contacts in Belfast and elsewhere, who 'fence' stolen
goods. Third, the combination of a sense of masculinity with heavy
social drinking leads almost inevitably to the acquisition of a
criminal record, particularly for offences such as assault and
drunk and disorderly. Fourth, there is the importance to the lads
of 'having a rake', doing an impromptu something on the spur of the
moment 'for a laugh'; joyriding in a car or 'borrowing' a park bench
for someone's living room. Anything to pass the time (cf. Corrigan,
1979, pp.119-41; Downes, 1966). Finally, it should not be forgotten
that the local police know the lads and know where to come if they
are looking for suspects. Once labelled with this kind of reputation
it may be very hard to stay out of trouble, regardless of guilt or
innocence.
This is as far as I shall go with this topic. It seems to me
that the significance of the last three factors, in particular,
cannot be underestimated. For example, Browner, who had been drinking
all one Saturday afternoon with 'Whippet' McIlwaine from the nearby
estate of Ballysloe, tells of the ensuing fight. He had had a row
with McIlwaine over a year before, but thought it had been long since
forgotten:
> He fucking judassed me, so he did, the bastard. He'd been drinking
> with us all day, like, wine and all, outside, and I didn't drink
> no more of it, so I didn't ... and then he comes to me and he
> says, 'There's a fella wants to see you outside, Browner', and I
> says, 'Who is it?', and he says, 'Come on outside and you'll see'.
> So I goes outside, and I wasn't expecting nothing like and I says
> to him, 'Where is he then?', and he says, 'Here', and I turned
> around and he whacked me one.... Look here, what the bastard done
> to my eye (showing me). So I says to him then, 'Right McIlwaine,
> you bastard, just you and me, right outside the gates', you know,

right outside the grounds of the Hillview like.... So I took him
outside, on the street, like, and I kicked the bastard's cunt in,
so I did.... D'you see when I get the bastard, see if I even see
him walking down the street, I'll fucking judas him, so I will.
I'll jump on the bastard's back.

SOLIDARITY AND STYLE

There are of course other differences between the lads and the
ordinary kids; the lads are more likely to be tattooed and are less
interested in up-to-date fashion styles, sticking to denims and
leather jackets while tapered trousers and winkle-pickers were
fashionable. They appear to prefer the more basic atmosphere of
the estate's social clubs to drinking in pubs. This may reflect
more than simple preference; the social clubs, run by locals, not
by businessmen from outside the estate, are more easily approached
with an apology if they have had a particularly rowdy night for
which they might be barred. Apart from anything else, the drink is
cheaper in the social clubs.

'ROUGH'		'RESPECTABLE'
←———————Youth Centre Network———————→		←———————Church Network———————→
The lads	Ordinary kids	Citizens
Social clubs, pubs, perhaps local discos.	Pubs, discos.	Perhaps non-local discos.
Youth Centre afternoon sessions.	Youth Centre senior youth club.	Church youth clubs, Boys' Brigade, Girls' Brigade.
Denims, leather jackets, tattoos.	Fashionable clothes, occasionally tattoos.	Sober clothes, but 'up to date'.
Kai Band, loyalism.	Kai and other flute bands, accordion bands, loyalism.	Boys' Brigade band, Unionism.
Local orientation.	(Intermediate.)	Upwardly mobile out of Ballyhightown.
Criminal records.	Usually no criminal records.	'Good living'.
Marry early, sex before marriage.	(Intermediate.)	Marry later, usually no sex before marriage.
PUBLIC		PRIVATE

FIGURE 4.1 Working-class youth life-styles in Ballyhightown

The overall differences between the lads, the ordinary kids and the citizens are schematically presented in Figure 4.1. Three things should be borne in mind in interpreting this summary ethnography. First, although the lads are a group in that they identify themselves as such and are so seen by other people, the ordinary kids of the Centre network do not constitute such a group. They are more a loose network of friendship groups and male-female alliances. As a group, it only exists in two places, the membership records of the Centre (and perhaps not even there, since many of the Centre's users in this age-group are not actually members of the senior youth club), and this analysis. Second, the social boundaries between the lads and the ordinary kids are fluid. There are those individuals who, when travelling with the Kai Band become, briefly, one of the lads; at other times they are part of a friendship group within the wider Centre network. Similarly, there is a process, usually involving a 'steady' girl, in which boys go from being one of the lads to respectability, if not 'citizenship'. This is illustrated by the case study of Davy and Carol in Chapter 7.

Finally, the characteristics which I attribute to one life-style or another in Figure 4.1 are not necessarily all exhibited by any specific individual to whom I might ascribe a place within this scheme. It is simply a rough and ready guide to the impressionistic picture of the youth life-styles of Ballyhightown which I built up during my research. As such, I would expect no individual to fulfil all the criteria for membership in any of those categories. Rather the reverse, in fact; I should expect real people to display some divergence from this ideal typical model.

THE CITIZENS

Coming now to the citizens, they, too, are best viewed as a loose network of small friendship groups and couples. Similarly, there is no fixed boundary which separates the citizens from the ordinary kids, the church from the Youth Centre networks. Having said this, however, as individuals, and in their small groups, many of them are acutely conscious that although they are 'respectable' they live in an estate which in their eyes, and the eyes of many other people, is anything but.

Ballyhightown is an overcrowded estate – it's so sort of concrete in the middle. There's certain areas that's clean and respectable, but not to a great extent.

It was good, but it's not now.... The Housing Executive should be more particular about who they let in. They shove all the people from the Shankill down in here.

These views of the estate came from members of the Citizens sample (which is described fully in the next chapter), in response to the question, 'What is your opinion of Ballyhightown as a place to live?'. On the basis of these comments, which could be matched by similar comments from some of the lads or the ordinary kids, the citizens' identity as a life-style would be difficult to establish. However, the pattern of responses to this question from all three samples, the Lads, the Ordinary Kids and the Citizens, demonstrates some of the differences between the three life-styles (Table 4.2).

TABLE 4.2 Attitudes towards Ballyhightown: Lads, Citizens and Ordinary Kids

	Positive liking	Acceptance	Dislike of parts of the estate	Complete dislike	Total
Lads	2 (14%)	10 (71%)	–	2 (14%)	14 (100%)
Ordinary Kids (a)	8 (15%)	22 (42%)	2 (4%)	21 (40%)	53 (100%)
Citizens	1 (6%)	5 (28%)	2 (28%)	7 (39%)	18 (100%)

(a) One member of this sample, who lives outside the estate, gave no response.

One important factor contributing to the distinctiveness of the citizens is their possession of a clearer image than the ordinary kids, and possibly the lads also, of their 'way of life', which they feel they must consciously defend and strive to maintain. Witness the testimony of Mrs McCullough, a stalwart of the local Methodist church, discussing her daughter's boyfriend. He had spent some time in prison for theft and came from a broken home, in Mrs McCullough's view, 'a bad background'.

> My husband took him to one side and warned him off. He told him that our Wilma wasn't going to go his way and that if he wanted to continue seeing her he'd have to go her way.... He's very quiet now, they just sit in the house or go out for walks.

This self-consciously defensive stance has three consequences for the citizens which are relevant here. First, members of the church network tend to live more private lives than most of their neighbours. As families, they 'keep themselves to themselves'; mothers keep an eye on precisely who their children play with and where. Second, the citizens will often maximise their links with people outside the estate. For example, those children who do not satisfy the selection criteria for grammar schools (6) will, instead of being sent to Ballyhightown Secondary School, often attend Woodlands Secondary instead. This school is situated right on the southern border of Ballyhightown, at the 'bottom end', and attracts children from a wide catchment area, including many areas of private housing. The school's headmaster consciously cultivates an academic and 'respectable' reputation and in the eyes of many parents Woodlands is a better school than Ballyhightown: 'The children get more discipline there and they have to learn their lessons.' The citizens' greater geographical mobility is further encouraged by their relatively greater prosperity and lack of involvement in the territorial feuding which constrains the lads and, occasionally, some of the ordinary kids. Finally, many of the citizens aspire to occupational and geographic mobility. They want to 'make something of themselves', to get out of Ballyhightown and buy their own house. Not all aspire to these goals, of course, and with respect to the latter not all of them will be able to afford it.

This has not been an easy chapter to write.   In outlining the life-styles of the kids of Ballyhightown, I have been forced to do violence to the complexity of life on the estate and the variations within these life-styles.   Lack of space has forced me to leave much unsaid, concerning both the differences between life-styles and the areas of experience they may have in common.   That the ethnography is presented largely from the standpoint of the lads and the ordinary kids accurately reflects the nature of my involvement with the young people of Ballyhightown.   In Chapters 5 and 6 I shall examine the contrasts between life-styles in greater detail.

Chapter 5

GROWING UP

In the last chapter I described three life-styles adopted by the youth of Ballyhightown, using their own models of the contrasts between different groups of kids as the basis for my account. In this chapter I shall describe how I drew samples of individuals from those life-styles in order to compare them more rigorously and construct a more detailed analytical model of the differences between them. The samples are simple crude quota samples: a more exacting random sampling procedure would have been difficult in Ballyhightown. The response rate would probably have been low and such an exercise might have raised problems in this setting. I felt very much confined to those young people I already knew, or could be satisfactorily introduced to.

Having earlier criticised some of the presumptions of objectivist social science, however, I do not intend to fall into the same trap here. In the presentation of the statistical data gathered in the formal interviews there is no suggestion that I am illustrating the 'objective structure' of the relationships between these young people. The quantitative material is not intended to 'estimate the limits within which some characteristic measured in the sample is likely to fall in the parent population', but 'to make relationships among data within the sample explicit' (Mitchell, 1967, p.35). Having identified these relationships and patterns, their interpretation will rest mainly on data from participant observation.

INTERVIEWING THE SAMPLES

Coming to the ordinary kids first, the sampling procedure used was simply to interview as many of the post-school-leaving regular users of the Youth Centre, and their friends, as I could. The interviewing was done either in an office in the Centre or the interviewee's home. Since my involvement with the Centre began in 1976, by the time of the research I knew many young adults who had been past-users of the Centre. These were included in the sample as a means of accumulating longer employment histories than I would have obtained from younger interviewees, and in order to gather data about courtship and marriage patterns. Some further details about the samples is presented in Appendix 1, as are some details of the life-style affiliation of individuals named in the ethnography.

At the end of the fieldwork period I extracted a sample of the lads from this larger sample, since, as part of the Centre network, they were included within it. The procedure for doing this was as follows: taking as my starting point Jonty Bryans, the alleged founder of the original Kai, I constructed, from my field notes and memory, an egocentric network of the lads with whom he regularly interacted, 25 individuals in all. This is only a very partial network for Jonty, since there are many other people, in Ballyhightown and elsewhere, who are at least as close to him as those I have included. This is simply that section of Jonty's immediate network which was publicly apparent to me during the fieldwork.

Having thus established which lads I was interested in, I abstracted from the original Youth Centre sample every individual who was also represented in my diagram of Jonty's network. As a result, I arrived at two samples, one of the ordinary kids, 54 in total, 29 boys and 25 girls, and one of the lads, 14 in number. I shall refer to these samples as the Lads and the Ordinary Kids, to distinguish them from the more general usage, for which no capital letters are used.

The eleven members of Jonty's network not interviewed represent the older core of the network and there are probably a number of reasons for their non-availability to me for interview, including the possibility of deliberate avoidance, as discussed in Chapter 2. The most likely reason for their absence from the final sample is their non-use of the Youth Centre, itself a function of age. Thus the Lads sample should be seen as the younger section of the lads' network, that part which continues to patronise the Centre. The implications of this bias towards the younger lads should not be too great, however. First, it is arguably advantageous inasmuch as it makes this sample more comparable, age-wise, with the other samples. Second, looking at my field-notes there is no reason to suspect that the members of the Lads sample are different in any fundamental way from their older peers in the lads network, except with respect to wives and families and this, once again, is a function of the passage of time. However, in the absence of detailed data concerning the older lads the reader must take these assertions at face-value.

The third sample is of the citizens of the church-going network and I shall refer to it as the Citizens. Because I only possessed a limited knowledge of this side of life on the estate, I decided that the best sampling procedure would be, in effect, to allow a member or members of that network to do the sampling for me. I also hoped that this would enable me to operationalise the folk-model of respectability held by members of that network. To this end, I approached the ministers of the three local churches, the Church of Ireland, Methodist and Presbyterian, who put me in contact with the leaders of the church youth organisations: the Boys' Brigade and Girls' Brigade in the case of the Church of Ireland and Presbyterian churches, and the Methodist Youth Club. In the event, as mentioned in Chapter 2, I did not interview any members of the Church of Ireland Girls' Brigade company.

I asked the leaders of the various organisations if they could

choose four or five members of their organisations for me: in the
case of the Methodist Youth Club, which is open to both sexes, I
requested a group of four or five girls and four or five boys. It
was made clear to the youth leaders that I wanted young people who
in their view epitomised the virtues of 'respectability', 'steadiness',
etc. Ideally, I would have interviewed between 24 and 30 young
people, more or less evenly distributed between the sexes. The
problems of being in the right place at the right time, combined with
the non-availability of the Church of Ireland Girls' Brigade company,
reduced the eventual total to 18, 10 boys and 8 girls.

The Ordinary Kids and the Citizens are roughly comparable in
terms of their mean ages at time of interview. For the Citizens
the mean ages are 19.2 years for the males and 18.7 years for the
females; for the Ordinary Kids the corresponding figures are 19.3
years and 18.1 years, respectively. The Lads, however, are slightly
older, 20.7 years on average. (1) This might be a result of the
sampling procedure, of course, focussing as it does on Jonty Bryan's
network, few of whom were under 20 in early 1979. This is not the
case, however: this particular network of lads was simply the only
one publicly visible to me in the post-school-leaving age bracket.
The next comparable group were in their early teens, the Outlaws,
a network centred around a few boys, with one dominant individual
as a focal point. They are not an organised gang but, young as
they are, have some longevity as a group, having been active as
the Outlaws since at least late 1976. (2) This life-style developmental cycle is similar to the pattern described by Parker in his
study of Liverpool (1974, p.47), with the important difference that
the cycle appears to be slightly longer in Ballyhightown, perhaps
because the estate's greater insularity, itself a product of the
'troubles', has encouraged the development of longer-lasting patterns
of interaction. The higher mean age of the Lads is a reflection
of the pattern of interaction within the 'rough' male life-style
of Ballyhightown. Finally, there are several individuals within
the Ordinary Kids whose life-styles are similar to the lads in
some respects; since they do not participate in the lads' network,
however, they have not been included in the Lads sample. Similarly,
there are several individuals, girls, in the Ordinary Kids sample
who resemble the citizens in many respects; since the focus of their
life-style remains the Youth Centre, however, they remain with the
Ordinary Kids.

The interviewing was carried out using a standard interview
schedule administered by me. (3) The data thus gathered was either
put onto index cards or stored in the computer; the cross-tabulations
were done using the SPSS package available through the University of
Cambridge Computing Service. One problem with this data is that
much of it is retrospective; there was, however, no readily available
alternative source of data if employment histories, for example,
were to be gathered. Wherever possible this kind of data has been
cross-checked with data from other interviewees or sources.

FAMILY BACKGROUNDS

It is accepted sociological wisdom that the family as an arena

of socialisation is one of the major institutions of social and
cultural reproduction. However, how to examine the role of the
family in the reproduction of the three life-styles was not immediately
apparent, particularly given the relative poverty of the data on this
topic as mentioned in Chapter 2. Eventually, I decided that the role
of the family in this respect might be reflected in different reproductive strategies, as indicated by different family sizes, or in
father's occupation, indicating differing occupational goals and
career strategies.

Looking at family size, there is little difference between the
samples. The families of the Lads have a mean number of 3.5 children,
the Ordinary Kids 4.2 children, and the Citizens 3.9 children. There
is, therefore, nothing to suggest that this is an important factor
differentiating the life-styles.

TABLE 5.1 Father's occupation: Lads, Ordinary Kids and Citizens

Father's occupation	Lads	Ordinary Kids	Citizens
Unskilled	4 (31%)	28 (53%)	6 (33%)
Skilled manual	8 (61%)	24 (45%)	7 (39%)
White collar	-	1 (2%)	5 (28%)
Other	1 (8%)	-	-
Total	13 (a) (100%)	53 (a) (100%)	18 (100%)

(a) Two not known, because of father's early death in both cases.
     For details of this occupational classification, see Appendix
     2.

Coming to father's occupation (Table 5.1), the Lads are more
likely to have fathers in skilled manual occupations, while the
Citizens are more likely to have fathers who are white collar workers.
Despite this, more of the Citizens have a father in either unskilled
or skilled manual occupations than in white collar occupations. If
we look at the occupations of sample members (Table 5.2), the pattern

TABLE 5.2 Occupation: Lads, Ordinary Kids and Citizens

Occupation	Lads	Ordinary Kids	Citizens
Unskilled	13 (93%)	27 (50%)	1 (6%)
Skilled manual	1 (7%)	19 (35%)	8 (47%)
White collar	-	7 (13%)	7 (41%)
Other	-	1 (2%)	1 (6%)
Total	14 (100%)	54 (100%)	17 (100%) (a)

(a) One Citizen, aged seventeen, is still at grammar school.

is clearer; the majority of the Lads are in unskilled occupations,
half the Ordinary Kids are unskilled, most of the rest being in
skilled manual jobs, and most of the Citizens are either skilled
manual or white collar workers. If cultural reproduction entails
the inter-generational transmission of occupational orientations,
in the broad sense implied by the crude occupational classification
I am using (see Appendix 2), then it may be useful to look at the
relationship between parental occupations and the occupations of the
sample members in more detail.

Before doing so, however, some reservations must be introduced
about using this data. First, looking at father's occupation only
ignores the significance of mother's occupation for daughters
(Garnsey, 1978). However, examination of the interview data produces
too many responses such as 'housewife' to the question on maternal
occupation to have made a consideration of maternal occupations
comparatively useful. Furthermore, many interviewees, when pressed,
appeared not to know their mother's pre-marital or pre-parental
occupation. Second, the failure to distinguish between females and
males will certainly obscure patterns of inter-generational occupational mobility. However, in the absence of comprehensive data
about maternal occupations there is no point in disaggregating the
occupational data by sex. Third, there is the possibility that
many fathers are not in their original occupations; these original
occupations might have an effect upon the kind of occupation chosen
by their children (cf. Stewart, Prandy and Blackburn, 1980, pp.33-6).
Once again, however, many respondents, asked to identify their
father's original occupation, appeared not to know.

If we do, however, compare occupation with father's occupation,
the actual relationship, if any, between the two is different for
each sample. Among the Ordinary Kids there has been some inter-
generational movement upwards, although there appears to be some
equivalence between occupation and fathers' occupation. For the
Citizens, the relationship is different: the pattern is an obvious
one of upward mobility. With the Lads, the trend is more marked,
although in the other direction. Thus, although it appears that
the paternal occupational status quo is being reproduced by the
Ordinary Kids, both the Lads and the Citizens display inter-generational occupational mobility, downward in one case and upward in
the other.

That the maintenance of the status quo by the Ordinary Kids is
something of an analytical artefact can be shown by disaggregating
the data for this sample: 33 per cent are in higher status
occupational categories than their fathers, 41 per cent in the same
category and 24 per cent lower down the occupational hierarchy.
Thus, despite the apparent reproduction of paternal occupational
status by the Ordinary Kids, less than half are in the same occupational category as their fathers. Looking at the Citizens, 50 per
cent of sample members exhibit upward mobility, 39 per cent are on
an approximate par with their fathers and 6 per cent are downwardly
mobile. For the Lads, the equivalent figures are 7 per cent, 21 per
cent and 64 per cent, respectively. The patterns of inter-generational mobility within the samples are quite apparent.

The above were taken to indicate possible familial strategies
with respect to children and their careers. However, other factors,

related to family histories, not self-conscious strategies, may be
important. One of these is the presence of both parents in the home.
The differences between the samples in this respect are striking.
Only 7 of the Lads (50 per cent) have both parents living at home,
compared to 43 of the Ordinary Kids (80 per cent) and 15 of the
Citizens (83 per cent); 3 of the Lads (21 per cent) have divorced
or separated parents, as against 4 of the Ordinary Kids (7 per cent)
and one Citizen (6 per cent). Finally, the figures for sample members
with one or both parents deceased are 4 of the Lads (29 per cent),
7 of the Ordinary Kids (13 per cent) and 2 Citizens (11 per cent.

   The pattern is clear; the interpretation, however, is not. First,
the high number of single-parent families or 'broken homes' might
appear to partly explain the differences between the Lads and the
other two samples. However, this does not explain the differences
between the Ordinary Kids and the Citizens; I am wary of placing too
much weight upon this explanation of life-style differences. Second,
even accepting this as an explanatory factor, the Lads' higher score
with respect to both 'broken homes' and deceased parents implies
that there may be more than one reason behind this pattern; its
interpretation is problematic in the absence of more detailed
qualitative data.

   One conclusion can be drawn with some certainty. In the reproduction of life-styles, either the family does not play a uniform
role in the process (it is unclear, for example, how the Lads'
families – with or without both parents at home – might systematically
produce the pattern of downward mobility), or its efforts are modified
by other factors. This is not to say that the family does not play
a role in cultural reproduction; its role in this process is, however,
not straightforward and must be understood in the context of other
factors.

EDUCATION, SCHOOLS AND TEACHERS

The other complex of institutions which social scientists typically
implicate in cultural reproduction is the education system.
Fortunately, it is easier than in the case of the family to trace
the young person's educational career. The hierarchical nature of
the school system and the institution of certificated educational
achievement make it possible to gather relatively precise information
about each individual's experience of formal education.

   First there is the kind of post-primary school attended: 51 of
the Ordinary Kids (94 per cent) attended secondary school and the
remaining 3 grammar school (6 per cent), 13 of the Lads (93 per cent)
attended secondary school and one (7 per cent) grammar school, and
13 of the Citizens (72 per cent) attended secondary school while
5 (28 per cent) went to grammar school. I do not see this as
reflecting intellectual ability, as nominally assessed in selection
tests and assessments, since I have no data about the performance
of sample members in this kind of test.

   If we look at the length of time spent at school, the pattern
is as follows. None of the Lads, 6 of the Ordinary Kids (11 per
cent) and one Citizen (6 per cent) left school one year early; all
of the Lads, 47 of the Ordinary Kids (87 per cent) and 8 Citizens

(44 per cent) left at the statutory school-leaving age. Only one
of the Ordinary Kids (2 per cent) stayed on past the fifth year,
compared to 9 (50 per cent) of the Citizens. These data presuppose
that the distribution of those young people whose sixteenth birthday
fell between the end of the summer holidays and the end of August,
making them eligible to leave school a year early, is the same across
all of the samples.

   More of the Citizens might have been expected to have stayed on
at school, if only because more of them attended grammar schools.
However, of the 9 Citizens remaining at school over the age of
sixteen, 6 did so in a secondary school, 1 left grammar school to
spend two years in the College of Business Studies and another left
grammar school to attend the local Technical College. Only one
Citizen stayed at grammar school over the age of sixteen, the
remaining two grammar school pupils leaving at the end of their
fifth year. The one Citizen who left school at the end of his
fourth year, left to take up a prized apprenticeship with the
Northern Ireland Electricity Service.

   I left to get a job, although I was staying on to do 'O' levels.
   If I had've waited I wouldn't have got a trade.... My father
   works in it and he pointed out the advert in the paper and he
   went and found out about it. But he didn't speak for me.
Coming to those Citizens who attended secondary schools, 6 went
to Ballyhightown Secondary, 4 to Woodlands and 2 girls attended a
school several miles away. The latter is an all-girls school which
their parents thought was 'less rough' than anything in the local
area. It would be unwise, however, to infer much selection of
secondary schools from these data: the four Citizens who attended
the higher-status Woodlands Secondary all lived within the school's
catchment area.

   Schools attended may reflect the distinction between the 'top'
and 'bottom' ends of the estate, however. Of the thirteen secondary
school pupils in the Lads sample, 12 went to Ballyhightown Secondary
School at the 'top' end. There is an indeterminate 'middle of the
estate', and the 'main drive' which goes through the top and middle
of the estate is generally understood to be more desirable than the
streets leading off it. Of the ten Citizens who live neither in
the 'bottom end' proper nor just outside the estate, six live on the
'main drive' and one in the insulated atmosphere of the multi-
storey flats. Of the other three, only two live in the 'top end'
proper. Of the Lads, apart from Robbo who now lives in Priorville,
all live in the 'middle-to-top-end' of the estate. Thus the
distinction between the 'top' and 'bottom' ends of Ballyhightown
is reflected in the composition of the Lads and Citizens samples.
The Ordinary Kids exhibit a much less segregated residential pattern.

   The differences between the samples with respect to certificated
educational achievement reveal a pattern of qualitatively differential
involvement with school: the Citizens do much better, in conventional
terms, than the rest (Table 5.3). The Lads might have been expected
to do poorly, given their attitudes to school discussed in Chapter 4.
What is so startling is the large number of Ordinary Kids who left
school without any formal qualifications: 36 members of this sample,
67 per cent, left school without any certificated evidence of
educational achievement.

TABLE 5.3 Formal educational achievement: Lads, Ordinary Kids and Citizens

	No. of CSE subjects				No. of GCE 'O' levels			
	0	1-3	4-6	7+	0	1-3	4-6	7+
Lads	14	-	-	-	13	1	-	-
Ordinary kids	38	3	13	-	47	5	2	-
Citizens	7	4	5	2	5	5	5	3

The scale of this non-achievement suggests that any explanation based on the distribution of innate ability must be rejected, leaving two possible explanations. Either the schools are failing in their pedagogic task or the Lads and the Ordinary Kids are resisting the schools' efforts. The first possibility is incorrectly put, however; it is more correct to say that the education system fails in this respect only if its task is taken to be the education of every pupil to the highest level of formal educational achievement possible. Clearly the hierarchical organisation of the school system contradicts such a possibility. As the headmaster of Ballyhightown Secondary School told me, 'You have to fail an exam to get here'. Seventy-three per cent of the Ordinary Kids went to Ballyhightown Secondary School and the view of that school as at the bottom of the system, both as a secondary school and as situated in a 'bad' area, is widespread among staff and pupils.

The inequalities of the educational hierarchy are reproduced within the school by the streaming system, descending from those who are encouraged to do 'O' levels to the remedial classes. Even at the age of eleven, after less than a year in the school, the implications of which class one is in are obvious.

I do not no what I want to be after I leave school because I have not decied what to be yet I don't think I will get a job because I am in J6 and that is a stupid class and I will never get a job I no I won't. (4)

However, a stratified education system, nationally and within the school, does not in itself explain why 67 per cent of the Ordinary Kids 'fail' educationally. Given the streaming system in Ballyhightown Secondary School, which at the time of the research allocated less than 20 per cent of the pupils to non-examination streams, and the stated aim of the headmaster that, regardless of this streaming, all pupils except those with identifiable learning difficulties should be encouraged to take at least one CSE subject, greater numbers of the Ordinary Kids might be expected to have at least one or two CSEs.

One explanation which must be considered is that teachers, themselves socialised into the conventional competitive model of education, make decisions about individual pupils, which are communicated to pupils either explicitly or implicitly in a cumulative labelling process, the partial outcome of which is the construction of a graded hierarchy of success and failure. (5) Just as not everyone can be allowed to fail, not everyone can

TABLE 5.4   Attitudes to school: Lads, Ordinary Kids and Citizens

| | Attitudes towards school | | | |
	Positive	Equivocal	Negative	Total
Lads	1 (7%)	9 (64%)	4 (29%)	14 (100%)
Ordinary Kids	18 (33%)	18 (33%)	18 (33%)	54 (100%)
Citizens	12 (67%)	4 (22%)	2 (11%)	18 (100%)

succeed if the value of education and the professional teacher's
position within it is to be maintained. There is no conspiracy,
simply a taken-for-granted model of ability and meritocratic
achievement which serves to legitimise both success and failure
(Bourdieu, 1977a). Inasmuch as the different life-styles of pupils
are visible (see Figure 4.1) they are bound to feed in, as descriptive
folk-models, to this decision-making process.

To turn to the sample members' attitudes to school; the answers
to the question, 'What was your attitude towards school while you
were there?', are summarised in Table 5.4. The difference between
the samples are obvious, the most surprising result perhaps being
the preponderance of equivocal answers from the Lads. These answers,
however, only indicate attitudes, at best: first, they are retrospective, second, they may be a product of the interview situation,
some kids probably telling me what they thought I wanted to hear, and
finally, it is difficult to fit all the answers into a simple three-
celled coding. Bearing this in mind, consider the data on self-
reported truancy, or 'beaking', arising from the same interview
question (Table 5.5).

TABLE 5.5. Self-reported truancy: Lads, Ordinary Kids and Citizens

	Beaked 'a lot'	Beaked 'sometimes'	Beaked rarely/ never	No informa- tion given
Lads	5 (38%)	2 (14%)	1 (7%)	6 (43%)
Ordinary Kids	17 (31%)	15 (28%)	14 (26%)	8 (15%)
Citizens	–	1 (6%)	14 (78%)	3 (17%)

It is obvious from Table 5.5 that, in the case of the Lads, in
particular, their statements about school are belied by the vote
which they cast with their feet while at school. From personal
knowledge and school records, I can further modify this picture;
several of those, particularly the Lads, included in the 'no
information given' column, were chronic truants; the data under-
estimates the degree of truancy. However, they are probably more
accurate than the official figures. (6) As Blacko and Mackers tell
us, there are many ways of taking time off without being entered as
absent in the register.

I fucking hated it. Every fucking second of it. I didn't beak
a lot ... couldn't be annoyed with it. I was in every day to

get marked off. I was in more than I was out. I used to get
marked off and then go out. (7)

I was a runner, you know, running around the school and taking
messages and all. I did what I liked, I went and came and
nobody said anything. I used to come in at eleven o'clock or
that and go and get the attendance book for my class and tick my
name off in it. The secretary, she never said anything, she
thought I'd been sent to fetch it or something.

Despite these misgivings about some of the data, it may be
concluded that there is a relationship between life-style and
experience of education. The citizens tend to stay at school longer,
acquire more certification, regard school more positively and truant
less than the lads and the ordinary kids. The lads and, to a lesser
extent, the ordinary kids, dislike or are apathetic towards school,
do less well in examinations (if they sit them at all) and truant
much more frequently. This difference is due partly to the resent-
ment of some of the lads and ordinary kids towards the apparent
power of the school, and their attempts to negate this through
beaking and non-co-operation. For example, Mac Sutherland is
described as follows in his fourth year internal reports at Ballyhightown Secondary: 'specialises in dumb insolence', 'impossible
to penetrate barrier of indifference and "us" and "them" mentality'.
Comments such as these could be duplicated for most of the lads.
Education is viewed partly as an overt struggle for control by both
teachers and pupils, particularly those pupils whose control is most
often at issue.

R.J.   What did you think of Ballyhightown Secondary?
             Be honest ...//...
Gary Brown Some of the fuck ... the rules they made in it.
             Fucking stupid. Rubbish ...//... You must wear
             school uniform, tie ... walk on the left-hand side
             like the fucking primary. Real fucking stupid.
R.J.   And what about the education you actually received?
Gary Brown The education? Fuck! ... You didn't really fucking
             learn much.   (T)

However, the difference between lads and citizens is not simply that
one is pro- and the other anti-school. Without wishing to deny that
anti-intellectualism is a potent ideology in Ballyhightown, there
are three other factors which are also important in producing the
differential academic achievement of the three life-styles. First,
the fear of failure, even within the modest academic hierarchies
of the secondary school, encourages conservatism. Many of the lads
or the ordinary kids have never attempted examinations because they
'knew' they would fail, having been told often enough that they
were stupid. Better not to take the examination and salvage some
self-respect than to risk public failure. (8)

Audrey Duff I was supposed to do cookery and typing but I didn't
             bother doing it ... I dropped out of it about three
             weeks before the exams.
R.J.   Why?
Audrey Duff 'Cos I didn't wanna do it.... You should see all
             the rest of the ones in typing and ... they're dead
             fast and all ...//...

Tania Barr   That's the thing that puts me off, you know, the
other ones ...//... That's why I wouldn't do exams.
I'm not doing exams and be made an idiot out of.
I'm not going to <u>pass</u> them, like ...//... I'd hate
that because in our house, sure if you don't pass ...
'Ah, you're stupid, you're stupid'.

Audrey Duff   I know, that's why I didn't do it.   (T)

Allied to the fear of failure, paradoxically, the fear of
success, as something which will distance them from their mates.
Wilkey's school file, for example, contains the following information:
'His attitude is peculiar, wanted to borrow books before exam, then
later asked for marks to be reduced so that he could be kept from
exam classes'. This was during his third year and might be explained
as the fear of failure. However, conversations with Wilkey have
convinced me that his unwillingness to be singled out as 'somebody
special' stemmed from his fear of isolation from his mates and 'getting
a death' for being a 'snob or a lick'. (9)

Similarly, one afternoon I was sitting with some friends when
their eldest daughter, in her third year at Ballyhightown Secondary,
arrived home. Heather was doing well at school and her ambition was
to train as a teacher. The conversation turned to her education and
which examinations she would take at the end of fifth year. Under
pressure from her teachers and her parents to take 'O' levels in as
many subjects as possible, Heather's major concern was about the
reaction of her peers: 'It's wick, but ... Mr Williamson stood up
and said how well I'd done and all in front of the whole class. And
it's wick, all the rest call you a snob and all, so they do'.

Finally, there is another factor; quite simply there are things
which many of these kids would rather do than go to school or do
homework. As Davy Douglas explained, remembering his school days,
'I wasn't there a lot. I liked it, but I never went. Beaking off
was like an adventure - you thought you were getting off with
something.' Obviously part of the adventure of beaking lies in
flouting the authority of the home and the school. This is also
part of the deterrent, if Mandy McAuley's experience is representative.

I enjoyed school. I never beaked. I was too scared. If my ma
or da had've got me they'd've killed me so I never went on the
beak ... I sometimes took the afternoon or morning or something
off, towards the end of term or when we'd no classes. But I
was too scared to beak.

However, while the delights of beaking are partly those of resistance
to authority, it is also a valued activity in itself, encompassing
the company of mates, watching afternoon television, sex, having
adventures 'up the hill', or perhaps a bit of breaking and entering.
The attraction of extra-school or non-school activities may also
combine with fear of isolation from the peer group. Johnny McAndrew
is one of the Ordinary Kids who went to grammar school; however,
he left at the end of his fourth year.

I was getting grand results for the first two or three years, but
it got me down. Too many homeworks, it was getting me down and
I left. I didn't even stay for no 'O' levels. I mean ... I was
staying in swotting six or seven hours a night and my mates were
out running around. If I'd have swotted then I'd have been as
good as any of them, so I would.

To summarise, there are marked differences in the samples' experiences of education, particularly between the Citizens on the one hand, and the Lads and the Ordinary Kids on the other. While some of these differences may be due to differences in their dispositions towards education, other factors, such as the hierarchical organisation of the school system, the decisions made by teachers within that organisation and the influence of the peer group, have a part to play as well. Furthermore, while it is likely that which school is attended is important, differences between life-styles within the school are important as well.

Finally, another contrast in the educational experience of the youth of Ballyhightown is that between male and female; that this is a general phenomenon has been well documented (Deem, 1980; Spender, 1982). Looking at the samples, the differences in formal achievement are minor: for the Citizens the contrast is very small, the girls doing slightly better; of those Ordinary Kids who did sit examinations, the boys are more likely to have '0' levels and the girls CSEs. However, the numbers involved either way are very small.

More important than certificated educational success is the nature of the curriculum; like girls elsewhere (McCabe, 1981), the girls in Ballyhightown tend to do 'feminine' subjects such as shorthand, typing, domestic science, English and religious education. The boys, however, pursue the 'masculine' interests of metalwork, woodwork, technical drawing, maths and physics. The curriculum reflects and reproduces the sexual division of labour of the home and the labour market. This is so regardless of the life-style and is a source of irritation to some girls, who find that they cannot, for example, do both woodwork and typing, because of the organisation of the curriculum in Ballyhightown Secondary School. Once again the institutional organisation of schooling is revealed as an important factor in cultural reproduction, although this time with respect to gender distinctions. Similarly, the difference between the grammar schools and the secondary schools, apart from notional excellence, is the distinction between the academic (female: middle-class) and the practical or technical (male: working-class). This difference is reflected in the Citizens sample: 38 per cent of the girls attended grammar schools, compared to 20 per cent of the boys.

CRIMINAL RECORDS

One of the clearest differences between the three life-styles lies in their involvement with crime: only 2 of the lads (14 per cent) reported no criminal convictions, compared to 35 of the Ordinary Kids (65 per cent) and all of the Citizens. Furthermore, 5 of the Lads (36 per cent) reported more than five convictions, as against only 3 (6 per cent) of the Ordinary Kids. A similar pattern emerges from the data on self-reported periods in detention: (10)   36 per cent of the Lads have never been in prison, compared to 91 per cent of the Ordinary Kids and all of the Citizens. The Citizens, therefore, appear to have a completely clean record.

Once this data is broken down by sex a different pattern emerges: none of the girls in the Ordinary Kids sample have criminal records or have ever been detained. The reasons for the non-criminality of

the girls are probably similar to the reasons for the absence of a
female life-style equivalent to the Lads as discussed in Chapter 4.
(11) Looking at the boys, the differences between the Lads and the
Ordinary Kids remain marked: 34 per cent of the male Ordinary Kids
have apparently never been in trouble with the law, while only 14 per
cent of the Lads have a similar record. Furthermore, calculating
the mean number of convictions for those Ordinary Kids and Lads who
admitted to a criminal record, we arrive at figures of 4.00 for the
Lads and 2.36 for the Ordinary Kids.

I am certain that the figure for the Lads is too low; at least
two of the Lads, Browner and Tailor, omitted to tell me about
convictions which I knew about anyway. This was probably for two
reasons. First, there is some confusion about exactly how many
convictions they have: cases may drag on over several hearings, a
number of charges may have been heard at once, sentences may run
concurrently and the passage of time renders memory uncertain.
Second, they both 'forgot' an indecent assault case on which they
were convicted with two of the Ordinary Kids, who did list it during
their interviews.

Offsetting this deficit are the confessions of Robbo, who
dramatised his life-history by adding certain incidents, such as
the possession of a Luger, which never happened. I can say this
with confidence because I was around at the time of the supposed
offences, which would have been impossible to keep quiet in Ballyhightown. In addition, one of his mates took me aside a couple of
days later and told me that Robbo had 'told me a fairy story'.
Having edited Robbo's interview of the most obvious flights of
fancy, there still remains what appears to be an exaggerated number
of convictions. Hopefully, in the overall figures his imagination
will compensate for the modesty displayed by Browner and Tailor.

The difference between the two samples might, of course, be due
to age differences, the slightly older Lads having had longer
criminal careers. This may be true, although the difference is
slight: the average age of those Ordinary Kids with convictions
is 19.7 years, that of the convicted Lads 20.7 years. However, on
closer inspection, of the seven Lads who were twenty-one or older
in June 1979, only one, Robbo, had been in trouble in the previous
two years. Thus it seems reasonable to dismiss the difference in
the age-structure of the samples as contributing to the greater
apparent delinquency of the Lads.

There is one further difference between the Lads and the Ordinary
Kids, the nature of the offences for which they have been convicted.
The tentative conclusion to be drawn is that, while both sets of
young men have in the past participated in the essentially juvenile
activities of breaking and entering or petty theft, the Lads appear
to be more likely to appear in court for offences such as drunk and
disorderly or assault, 46 per cent of their total convictions being
for this type of offence, compared to 29 per cent for the Ordinary
Kids. This might almost be expected in the light of the discussion
in Chapter 4. The combination of a milieu of aggressive public
masculinity with regular heavy drinking and a criminal reputation
in the eyes of the local law is probably sufficient explanation.

In this chapter I have compared three samples which should,
hopefully, represent to some extent the three life-styles described

in Chapter 4. It has been shown that the samples differ in important
ways with respect to family background, inter-generational mobility,
education and criminal records. In the next chapter I shall take
these comparisons several stages further before drawing the threads
of the analysis more tightly together.

Chapter 6

COMING OF AGE

The experiences of school and petty criminality discussed in the previous chapter are aspects of adolescence, central features of the juvenile phase of the life cycle. The passage from youth to adulthood in Ballyhightown, as elsewhere, is intimately bound up with two different areas of experience: the labour market and courtship. However, it is not that school or crime suddenly become unimportant; from, at the latest, the age of fifteen, most working-class girls and boys in areas such as Ballyhightown find their lives increasingly structured by concerns arising within either or both of the social arenas of work (and unemployment) or courtship (and marriage). It is within these arenas that the complex and often painful transition into adult life is made. In this chapter I shall outline the differences between the life-style samples in these respects.

WORK AND UNEMPLOYMENT

In the earlier discussion of family background I looked at the occupational composition of the three samples. It is clear that the norm for the Lads is an unskilled occupation; half the Ordinary Kids, but only 6 per cent of the Citizens, had unskilled jobs. None of the Lads, 13 per cent of the Ordinary Kids and 41 per cent of the Citizens were white-collar workers; 7 per cent of the Lads, 35 per cent of the Ordinary Kids and 47 per cent of the Citizens were in skilled manual work. The pattern of differences is obvious (Table 5.2).

There are other ways to look at the experience of work, however. Comparing the samples with respect to the proportion of their working life, i.e. the period since quitting full-time education, spent in full-time employment (Table 6.1), it becomes apparent that there are substantial differences between them. The Citizens have, on average, spent less, if any, time unemployed than the Ordinary Kids, who have suffered unemployment less than the Lads.

This pattern is probably related to the occupational composition of the samples: taking the samples as a whole, of the 41 sample members in unskilled occupations, 16 (39 per cent) had worked for

TABLE 6.1 Working life spent in full-time employment: Lads,
Ordinary Kids and Citizens

| | Proportion of working life spent in employment | | | | |
	0-25%	26-50%	51-75%	76-100%	Total
Lads	2 (14%)	4 (27%)	4 (27%)	4 (27%)	14 (100%)
Ordinary Kids	5 (9%)	6 (11%)	10 (19%)	33 (61%)	54 (100%)
Citizens	-	-	2 (12%)	15 (88%)	17(a) (100%)

(a) One of the Citizens was still in full-time education.

half of their working lives or less, compared to none of the skilled
manual and only one (7 per cent) of the white-collar respondents.
Similarly, while only 15 (37 per cent) of the unskilled interviewees
had been in work for more than 75 per cent of that period, the
corresponding figures for the skilled manual and white-collar sample
members are 26 (93 per cent) and 9 (64 per cent), respectively.
Unemployment is, as we might expect, a feature of the unskilled
working life (Sinfield, 1981, pp.126-9).

Another way of looking at the samples' experiences of the labour
market is to compare them with respect to the number of jobs they
have had since leaving school. It is quite possible that there are
individuals whose employment histories reveal considerable job-
changing without their having been unemployed for long periods.
Once again there are considerable differences between the samples,
the Ordinary Kids occupying an intermediate position between the
Lads and the Citizens. Eleven of the Lads (79 per cent) have had
more than five jobs, compared to 9 (17 per cent) of the Ordinary
Kids and none of the Citizens; at the other end of the spectrum,
16 (94 per cent) of the Citizens and 32 (59 per cent) of the
Ordinary Kids have had only one or two jobs, compared to only one
(7 per cent) of the Lads. This pattern is also probably related
to the samples' occupational composition, as can be seen from
Table 6.2.

TABLE 6.2 Occupation by number of jobs since leaving school:
Lads, Ordinary Kids and Citizens

| Occupation | Number of jobs since leaving school | | | |
	1-2	3-4	5+	Total
Unskilled	16 (39%)	8 (20%)	17 (42%)	41 (100%)
Skilled manual	20 (71%)	5 (18%)	3 (11%)	28 (100%)
White collar	12 (86%)	2 (14%)	-	14 (100%)
Others	1 (50%)	1 (50%)	-	2 (100%)

At this point it might be objected that part of the difference
between, for example, the Citizens and the Lads reflects the higher
average age of the Lads, who have, therefore, spent longer in the

labour market. However, most of the Lads have spent periods out of
the market in detention; a comparison of the distribution of job
totals by age does not show the number of jobs increasing by age
for the Citizens (Table 6.3).

TABLE 6.3 Number of jobs since leaving school by age: Lads and
Citizens

Age	Number of jobs since leaving school				
	1	2	3-4	5-6	7+
18 yrs or under	- [1]	- [5]	- -	- -	- -
19-20 years	- [5]	(1)[1]	(1)[1]	(2)-	(3)-
21-22 years	- [2]	- [2]	- -	(3)-	(2)-
23 yrs or over	- -	- -	- -	- -	(1)-

O = Lads; □ = Citizens

The three samples have, therefore, been shown to differ markedly
in their experience of the labour market. This is so with respect
to both the kinds of work they do and their experiences of unemployment and job-changing. The absence of the Lads from white-collar
occupations might be expected, given the 'feminine' nature of many
routine white-collar occupations (Hakim, 1979, pp.27-9) or the
educational requirements often required to fill white collar jobs.
However, the differences between the Ordinary Kids and the Citizens
cannot be explained by the invocation of sexual differences, although
educational factors, as we shall see, are important.

Of the 7 Citizens who are in white-collar jobs, 6 are female: of
the 7 Ordinary Kids, 5 are female. The sexual division of labour
indicated by this (and Table 4.1) is broadly confirmed in Table 6.4,

TABLE 6.4 Occupation by gender: Lads, Ordinary Kids and Citizens

Occupation	Female	Male
Unskilled	17 (52%)	24 (46%)
Skilled manual	4 (12%)	24 (46%)
White collar	11 (33%)	3 (6%)
Others	1 (3%)	1 (2%)
Total	33 (100%)	52 (100%)

although for the males of my samples unskilled and skilled manual
work are equally important, unlike Table 4.1, in which skilled
manual work is the most important male occupation. (1) Gender is
also important within the samples: 67 per cent of the female
Ordinary Kids are unskilled workers, compared to 34 per cent of the
males (of whom 59 per cent are in skilled manual jobs): of the
female Citizens, 75 per cent are in white collar occupations; 66 per

cent of the males are in skilled manual work and only 11 per cent in unskilled jobs.

The proportion of working life spent in employment and the number of jobs held since leaving school also vary with life-style, as indicated by sample membership. The Citizens have, on average, spent more time employed in fewer jobs than the Ordinary Kids, who have spent less time unemployed and changed jobs fewer times than the Lads. Thus, if we define labour market continuity as a function of both the proportion of the individual's working life spent in full-time employment *and* the amount of job-changing experienced by each individual, (2) it is clear that the Citizens exhibit greater continuity than the Ordinary Kids, who, in their turn, have more continuity in employment than the Lads.

Given this difference between the samples, it is apparent from the above discussion and Table 6.2 that differences in labour market continuity reflect the distribution of occupations between the samples. Thus, it appears that labour market continuity is a function both of life-style and of differences in the organisation of occupations. Before proceeding to discuss the relationship between labour market continuity and occupation, however, I shall examine the data concerning education and employment. Not surprisingly, perhaps, those respondents in unskilled occupations tend to possess few or no educational qualifications and are more likely to have taken the opportunity to leave school a year early. Those in white collar occupations are most likely to have four or more GCE 'O' levels (Table 6.5).

TABLE 6.5 Occupation by formal educational achievement: Lads, Ordinary Kids and Citizens

Occupation	Number of CSE subjects			Number of GCE 'O' levels		
	0	1-3	4+	0	1-3	4+
Unskilled	38	2	1	38	3	-
Skilled manual	15	3	10	20	6	2
White collar	5	2	7	6	1	7
Others	-	-	2	1	1	-

To look at it from another perspective, out of all the jobs the sample members have had, 27 per cent of the white-collar jobs were filled by individuals with no formal qualifications, as against 43 per cent of the skilled manual jobs and 87 per cent of the unskilled. Looking at occupation and time spent in post-primary education, the pattern is also unambiguous: of the seven sample members who left school at the end of the fourth year, five are in unskilled and two in skilled manual work. By contrast, of the nine who stayed on past the school-leaving age, six are in white-collar jobs, two in skilled manual jobs, and one in an unskilled occupation (cf. Stewart, Prandy and Blackburn, 1980, pp.216-23).

In looking at the data on the relationship between education and employment, it is clear that although formal qualifications do make a difference they are clearly not the only factor affecting

labour market outcomes. The fact that, for example, 15 (54 per cent)
of the sample members in skilled manual occupations possessed no
certificated qualifications upon leaving school indicates that
formal 'cultural capital' (Bourdieu, 1977b) is not uniformly
influential in its effect upon occupational careers. This is in
broad agreement with other studies (Ashton and Maguire, 1980, 1981;
Manpower Services Commission, 1978, pp.46-7; Reid, 1980, 1981;
Sawdon et al., 1981, pp.56-61).

Since labour market continuity appears to be related to life-
style, as reflected in sample membership, and to occupation, I shall
now examine some of the ways in which occupation and work organisation may affect it. First, there is the nature of recruitment into
employment. On the basis of interviews with young workers it is
difficult to examine this topic; to do so requires that respondents
were privy to decisions concerning whether or not to hire them.
One item of information which has some relevance, however, is the
data from the question, 'How did you get the job?', in the part of
the interview devoted to employment history (Table 6.6).

TABLE 6.6 Methods of obtaining jobs: Lads, Ordinary Kids and
Citizens

Method of obtaining job	Lads	Ordinary Kids	Citizens
Via official agency	13 (15%)	32 (22%)	4 (14%)
Via 'personal contacts'	36 (41%)	70 (48%)	15 (54%)
Via other channels (a)	39 (44%)	45 (31%)	9 (32%)
Total number of jobs	88 (100%)	147 (100%)	28 (100%)

(a) Typically 'just an interview' resulting from answering a news-
    paper advertisement or asking at the gate.

It must be borne in mind in interpreting Table 6.6 that the data
represent the applicant's perception of what happened in the
recruitment process. It is obvious that there will be many occasions
when the applicant will not know why they, and not someone else, was
chosen. Furthermore, the value of personal contacts may be over-
emphasised, if the mediator exaggerates the influence that he or she
can bring to bear. There are also several cases in which, although
an official agency was mentioned, the respondent further specified
that 'so-and-so got me started'. Bearing this in mind, however,
and given that many jobs, particularly white collar jobs, have
minimum educational requirements, it seems likely that within the
limits set by such initial screening requirements the power of
informal networks in recruitment is considerable. (3) It is
interesting that the Lads, whose jobs are typically unskilled, rely
least of all upon 'not what you know, but who you know'. One
inference which may be drawn from this is that the unskilled end
of the labour market is more casually organised and less constrained
by patronage and gate-keeping than other areas. This view receives
support from the Lads' relatively greater dependence upon job-getting
methods such as 'walking around asking at the gate' (Table 6.6).

TABLE 6.7   Reasons for leaving jobs: Lads, Ordinary Kids and Citizens

Reason for leaving	Lads	Ordinary Kids	Citizens
Left voluntarily:			
Personal dissatis- faction.	16 (20%)	28 (25%)	2 (18%)
To go to another job	14 (18%)	22 (20%)	7 (64%)
Left involuntarily:			
Redundant, 'paid off' (a)	18 (23%)	20 (18%)	2 (18%)
Sacked (misconduct)	24 (30%)	23 (21%)	–
Medical reasons (b)	1 (1%)	6 (5%)	–
Other reasons (c)	5 (6%)	10 (9%)	–
Not known:	1 (1%)	2 (2%)	–
Total	79 (100%)	111 (100%)	11 (100%)

(a) This includes temporary jobs, fixed-term job creation schemes
    or training places, etc.
(b) This includes four pregnancies.
(c) This includes six prison sentences.

Coming now to sample members' reasons for quitting jobs, it is much easier to base the account upon respondents' statements. They may not know why they were hired, but they will probably have a fuller knowledge of the reasons why they left a job. The data summarised in Tables 6.7 and 6.8 derive from individual work histories compiled on the basis of interviews and field notes.

Table 6.8 reveals that the occupational category within which most coming and going takes place is the unskilled. This data thus supports the earlier finding that unskilled workers are more likely to suffer from unemployment and have more jobs than skilled manual or white-collar workers. Similarly, this data underlines the conclusion that the Lads have less continuity in the labour market than the other samples. They have left jobs an average of 5.6 times, the Ordinary Kids 2.1 times and the Citizens 0.6 times each.

The most important question is whether this is due to the Lads' cultural orientations towards employment or exogenous factors rooted in the kind of work they typically do. That unskilled jobs do differ from other jobs in their characteristic hiring and firing patterns may be inferred from Table 6.8. However, it is also important to examine as comprehensively as possible the role which the Lads' own models of work play in their instability in employment. There are two aspects to this question: first, do the Lads share in a general valorisation of skilled manual work, i.e. are they failed aspirants to skilled manual work or have they consistently chosen the occupations they were in in June 1979, and second, does

TABLE 6.8 Reasons for leaving jobs by occupation: Lads, Ordinary Kids and Citizens

Reason for leaving	Unskilled	Occupation Skilled manual	White-collar	Other
Left voluntarily: Personal dissatisfaction	35 (22%)	8 (24%)	3 (37%)	–
To go to another job	30 (19%)	9 (27%)	4 (50%)	–
Left involuntarily: Redundant, 'paid off' (a)	33 (21%)	7 (21%)	–	–
Sacked (misconduct)	40 (25%)	7 (21%)	–	–
Medical reasons (a)	6 (4%)	–	1 (12%)	–
Other reasons (a)	12 (8%)	2 (6%)	–	1 (100%)
Not known:	3 (2%)	–	–	–
Total	159 (100%)	33 (100%)	8 (100%)	1 (100%)

(a) See Table 6.7 for the explanation of these headings.

their lack of continuity in employment reflect their attitudes to work in general?

It has already been shown that, by comparison with their fathers' present occupations, the Lads' largely unskilled status constitutes downward occupational mobility. It is, however, possible that their present unskilled status indicates a shared orientation towards unskilled work. That this is not the case is suggested by their job histories: although eight of the Lads (57 per cent) started work in unskilled jobs and have continued in similar jobs since, two others started out in unskilled jobs, briefly entered apprenticeships, and left these to re-enter unskilled work, where they have since remained, two started apprenticeships (although one only lasted one day) but eventually ended up as labourers, and one started work as a trainee accountant (Alfie Wright, the only one of the Lads to have gone to grammar school) but ended up in a succession of unskilled jobs. The last of the Lads, Eddy Stewart, had a variety of unskilled jobs but eventually found himself an apprenticeship, which he hung on to and completed, despite a serious industrial injury and three months spent in prison.

Thus, out of this small sample, 43 per cent cast doubt upon the idea that the Lads share an orientation towards unskilled work, either manual or non-manual. That they do not, in fact, valorise unskilled work in itself is further indicated by three themes which emerged from the many discussions about work I had with them.

First, unskilled work (typically unskilled manual work) is seen mainly as a source of high wages upon leaving school, as opposed to apprenticeships or white collar jobs which, in the immediate post-

school years, are less well paid: to quote Tinker, 'I don't think
I would do an apprenticeship, the money's not very good at the start
of it. There's more money at the labouring'. When asked for their
occupational preferences, and the reasons for those preferences, the
answers summarised in Table 6.9 were given. The totals are not
related to the numbers in the samples, respondents being allowed to
give more than one answer.

TABLE 6.9   Reasons for occupational preferences: Lads, Ordinary Kids
and Citizens

Reason for preference	Lads	Ordinary Kids	Citizens
Wages	15 (48%)	37 (39%)	2 (7%)
'Kind of work'	10 (32%)	23 (24%)	13 (48%)
Amount of travelling	3 (10%)	12 (13%)	2 (7%)
Prospects for advancement	3 (10%)	23 (24%)	10 (37%)
Total	31 (100%)	95 (100%)	27 (100%)

The differences between the samples are marked.   The Ordinary Kids
are most interested in wages, followed by the kind of work they
would be asked to do and the prospects of advancement in the job,
while the Lads' dominant concern is with wages, followed by the kind
of work.   The Citizens, however, are most interested in the kind of
work and the prospects for advancement, in that order.   Given these
preferences unskilled work is an obvious choice for the individual
who wants the rewards of work today, sooner than relying upon the
'prospects for advancement' to deliver them at some time in the
future.

Given that unskilled work may be seen as a route to relatively
high wages now, the kind of work involved is not, however, unimportant
to the Lads.   Basically they distinguish between jobs which they like
doing, typically outdoor jobs which offer the chance to 'be your
own boss', (4) 'message jobs', which involve being publicly at
someone's beck and call, dirty jobs and boring jobs. (5)   Being a
bin-man or a street cleaner involves the worst of the first two
undesirable worlds, as Wilkey discovered: 'I was up in the Club
last night.   It was wick, we got a terrible death.   Everywhere you
looked it was, "Hey ... my bin didn't get emptied".'   None the less,
Wilkey and Tinker stayed 'on the bins' for a while, little relishing
the prospect of unemployment.   Eventually they had the satisfaction
of seeing Ernie Thompson, one of their worst tormentors, working
alongside them.

Labouring on building sites is a job which, although valued by
the Lads for its outdoor setting and relatively high wages, involves
being treated as a 'message'.   Some jobs, such as office boy, they
see as a complete waste of time because of this.   It may also be one
of the reasons why some of the Lads steer clear of apprenticeships.
First-year apprentices are believed to be treated as 'gets' ('get
this and get that') or 'gophers' ('go for this and go for that'):

Craig McComb, one of the Ordinary Kids, and an apprentice plumber,
suffered intense teasing about being an apprentice tea-boy. Some of
the tales told by apprentices reinforce this folk model of apprenticeships. I was talking to Billy Turner about why he had taken the day
off work.

Billy   It's the fella in work. You know ... the tradesman.
            You know, you've got to work with a tradesman? You
            should've seen what the bastard made me do yesterday.
            There was this wall they built and they done it wrong,
            so they did ...

R.J.   Did you have to knock it down then?

Billy   No ... they knocked it down, like. D'you know what the
            fuckers made me do? I had to clean all the bastarding
            bricks. I had to sit down and scrape all the mortar
            off them, for fuck's sake ...//... Fuck them.

There are other unskilled jobs, for example in Craigowen Meats,
which are popular with the Lads because of their relatively high
wages. The work itself is universally regarded with horror, however.

R.J.   What kind of stuff d'you do on the killing floor?

Billy

Bradshaw   Take out their bellies and all ... just rip 'em.

R.J.   Do they get killed actually there?

Billy   Aye ... killed downstairs, then they come up the stairs
            on them, you know ... big things.

R.J.   Aye.

Billy   They come down the line then and people do the jobs on
            them.

Paul

Williams   ... a big pulley and all ...

Billy   ... for all the size of them ...//... A big belly bag,
            I'm fucking telling you, fuck and I done them for ages.
            You know, shite bags, you want to see the size of the
            bastarding things. In some of the ones I got, you
            know, there was calves inside of them ... (inaudible) ...
            Fuck, I was nearly sick. I didn't wanna fucking go
            back to work. You should've seen me, I just wanted to
            boke my ring up ... you wanna smell it. And the smell
            would've stayed there. It didn't go away or nothing.
            It just clung near, just around where I was standing.
            It just stayed there ...//... For fuck's sake, it's
            terrible.   (T)

Terrible it may have been, but Billy was seventeen, a married man
with one child and another on the way. Whether he wanted to or not,
he had little choice but to return to work if he wanted high wages.
It must be reiterated, however, that although money is the most
important factor in the Lads' decisions about jobs, it is not the
only one. They do distinguish between jobs using other criteria.

R.J.   Who are you working with?

Wilkey   Ach there's ... Bobby's scaffolding ...//... I wouldn't
            like it ... the way he works, you know ... me, well
            I'd be doing ... the likes of this room, it'd take me
            half a day to clean out, you know, all the auld rough
            mortar off the floor ... Well, he'd be working like
            hell, you know, and he's only getting an extra, what? ...
            four pound?

R.J.   So Bobby's getting paid more than you? For being up
           off the ground?

Wilkey   Aye ... more bonus and that, that's all. I wouldn't do
           it, it wouldn't be worth it.   (T)

There is a third aspect of the Lads' 'choices' and goals. For a
school-leaver with few or no qualifications, white-collar work may
be very difficult to find, although, as discussed earlier, some
unqualified young people to obtain white collar jobs. Furthermore,
in a labour market in which the number of skilled manual jobs is
declining, the competition for apprenticeships is fierce. There is
a limit, therefore, to the scope for choice in this context. Although
I cannot demonstrate it on the basis of the interview data, I would
suggest that some school-leavers with few or no qualifications may
not compete for apprenticeships or white-collar jobs, believing that
they will be unsuccessful if they do. Whether this decision is made
before leaving school, or after experiencing the frustration of the
unsuccessful job search, is a matter for further research. In this
economic climate the use of 'connections' to find one's children or
young relatives good jobs will probably be commonplace. (6)

The notion that some of the lads, for example, may opt out of
the competition for apprenticeships is difficult to establish using
retrospective data. It receives indirect support, however, from
the discussion of education in Chapter 5. If those at the bottom
of the educational hierarchy accept the identity 'stupid' with which
others label them, there seems no reason to suppose that they will
not do the same in the labour market, opting out of the search for
skilled jobs in much the same way that they avoid failing examinations. Further support for this suggestion comes in the shape of
the answers to the question, 'If you could go back and live your
life over again, what kind of job would you choose?' Eight of
the Lads (57 per cent) chose a trade, only 3 (21 per cent) electing
to remain in unskilled work. By comparison, of the 17 Citizens,
8 (47 per cent) were satisfied with their present occupations and
6 (35 per cent) opted for further study, 3 wanting to be teachers,
2 nurses and 1 a youth worker.

Clearly, these answers reflect different experiences of work. In
the main, the Citizens are either satisfied with their lot or
anxious to 'better themselves' and 'get on in the world'. By contrast,
the Lads are satisfied with their present occupational lot in only
three cases. There is more to the Lads' replies than a wistful
recognition of their own failure, however. Six of them explicitly
mentioned that what they would most like to do was either a job
that they at one stage failed to obtain, a job they once had and
lost, or a long-standing but unrealised ambition. There is, therefore,
good reason to suppose that in many cases their present unskilled
status reflects a failed goal, not a conscious choice of occupation
and career.

There is a second difficulty in using the notion of choice in
this context. Choice, such as it is, is not evenly distributed
through the labour market. For example, someone with good educational
qualifications who is looking for an apprenticeship or a white collar
job can mark time during their search by taking an unskilled job.
Similarly, for a 'time-served' tradesman there are two markets in
which to seek work, the skilled and the unskilled. This is a simpli-

fication but it does reflect the realities of the labour market for
the working class. A tradesman or a clerk can 'turn his hand' to
unskilled work; the reverse is not the case for the unskilled
worker, who is at the bottom of the market hierarchy of occupational
choice.

This raises the question of whether there is something about the
Lads' orientations to work in general which contributes to their
lack of continuity in the labour market. Returning to Table 6.7,
in 20 per cent of these cases the Lads left because they didn't like
the job. In a further 18 per cent of cases they left to go to
another job, a move which might indicate dissatisfaction with the
original job. Another reason for quitting a job which reflects the
individual's attitude to the job is dismissal due to misconduct and
30 per cent of their quits fell into this category. Taking the
three categories of quits together, as indicating the Lads' feelings
about work in general or the job in particular, 68 per cent of their
quits apparently reflect such feelings. Looking at the Ordinary
Kids, the equivalent percentage is similar, 66 per cent: 25 per
cent due to dissatisfaction with the job, 20 per cent moving to a
new job and 21 per cent sacked.

However, the Lads have a level of quits per individual which is
higher by a factor of 2.7 than the Ordinary Kids. Furthermore, a
higher proportion of the Lads' dismissals due to misconduct, 38 per
cent as against 26 per cent for the Ordinary Kids, were the result
of direct conflict with management or supervisory staff or a refusal
to accept informal supervision from their workmates. All three of
the incidents involving fights with workmates began with somebody
telling one of the Lads what to do, as did the following incident
reported by Alfie Wright.

I hit the foreman. I tried to cut his head off. He was a
reserve cop ... he told me to do a particular job and the boss
started shouting because it was wrong and he tried to say I done
it off my own bat.

Even if this is the case, however, and the Lads are more volatile
at work, it does not explain the higher incidence of all kinds of
quits for their sample. There are four possible explanations.
First, it may be due to differences in attitudes between the samples,
the Lads being more prone to voluntary job-changing. Second, it
may reflect the nature of the occupations which the Lads typically
enter, some occupations being organised in such a way that dismissals
and leavings are more common (cf. Ryrie and Weir, 1978, pp.159-79).
Third, employers and supervisors may respond to the Lads differently
than they would do to members of the other samples, treating them
with greater suspicion and being less prepared to give them the
benefit of the doubt. Finally, because they have had more jobs
than members of the other samples, their length of service in any
job will be shorter, leaving them more vulnerable to redundancy on
the 'last in first out' principle.

Since the Lads are disproportionately more prone to experience
all kinds of quits, all of these factors are probably involved.
However, it is clear that not all of these factors are important
to the same degree, as shown in Table 6.10, although it is impossible
to tease out the precise manner in which these factors are at work,
since factors (a), (b) and (d) in this Table are responsive to a

TABLE 6.10 Mean number of reasons for quitting work: Lads and Ordinary Kids

| | Mean number of reasons for quitting | | | |
	Personal dissatisfaction	To go to a new job	Redundant or paid off	Sacked for misconduct
Lads	1.14	1.00	1.29	1.71
Ordinary Kids	0.52	0.41	0.37	0.43
Difference	0.62	0.59	0.92	1.28

combination of the sample members' behaviour and the behaviour of employers and supervisors. It is clear, however, that there is an industrial or occupational component to the Lads' labour market discontinuity, which may, in turn, be related to managerial and supervisory practices.

An important reason for the differences between the Lads and the Ordinary Kids might be their different composition with respect to gender. The smaller number of job changes by the Ordinary Kids might be partly due to the different nature of participation in the labour market by young women. Closer examination of the data, however, does not support this idea. The number of jobs held by the male Ordinary Kids (97) is greater than the number held by the females (49) by a factor of 1.7. This must be set against the average number of years each has spent in the labour market since leaving school: (7) 3.8 years for the males and 2.3 for the females, the figure for the males being greater by a factor of 1.6. Thus any differences between the two samples with respect to the average number of jobs per individual are unlikely to be due to gender differences in the composition of the samples.

Having compared the Lads and the Ordinary Kids, I shall now turn to the Ordinary Kids and the Citizens. The differences between the Citizens and the Lads are so striking that further discussion is probably redundant. Most obviously, only 30 per cent of the Ordinary Kids' quits were voluntary, compared to 82 per cent of the Citizens', 64 per cent of whose quits were in order to take another job. This must be viewed alongside the two samples' quit rates: the mean number of quits for the Ordinary Kids is greater than that for the Citizens by a factor of 3.0. The Citizens appear to be less likely to leave their jobs, but when they do it is more probably for reasons related to finding another, presumably better, job. This finding supports the model of the ideal-typical Citizen as more interested in 'getting on' than members of the other life-styles. Their absence of dismissals due to misconduct suggests that the Citizens' relationships with management and supervisors make for a situation with little or no conflict and a consensus about acceptable behaviour at the workplace.

COURTSHIP AND MARRIAGE

Statistics concerning marriage in Ballyhightown were presented in
Table 4.1, which indicate that age at marriage has some relationship
to gender and occupational status. Women marry earlier than men as
a rule; 88 of the brides in this data are under 21 years but only
50 of the grooms. An important factor behind this pattern is the
economics of courtship; boys have to have a wage before they can
really compete for girls, whereas girls, who bear less of the direct
costs of courtship, can afford to 'go steady' earlier. In addition,
men and women in unskilled occupations tend to marry earlier than
those in skilled manual or white-collar occupations. Part of the
reason for this is the desire by apprentices to 'finish your time'
before marrying. More generally, the different ages at which the
adult wage is reached in different occupations has an affect also
(cf. Leonard, 1980, pp.47-8, 71-5).

   In this discussion of the differences between the samples with
respect to courtship and marriage, I shall rely heavily on participant
observation data. Correspondingly, the discussion of the Citizens
suffers from the relative absence of this kind of information. From
the interview material it is possible, however, to say something
about these topics. Bearing in mind the apparent relationship between
occupation and life-style, this data supports the picture derived
from the church records. The Citizens get engaged and marry later
than the Ordinary Kids or the Lads. In addition, it appears that
the Lads and the Ordinary Kids are more likely to become parents
quite soon after marriage (Table 6.11).

TABLE 6.11 Marriages and engagements: Lads, Ordinary Kids and
Citizens

	Lads (Male)	Ordinary Kids (Male)	(Female)	Citizens (Male)	(Female)
Average age (years)	20.7	19.3	18.1	19.2	18.7
Married, no children	2 (14%)(a)	–	–	–	1 (12%)
Married with children	3 (21%)	6 (21%)(a)	5 (20%)	–	–
Engaged	1 (7%)	5 (17%)	5 (20%)	1 (10%)	–
Uncommitted	8 (57%)	18 (62%)	15 (60%)	9 (90%)	7 (87%)
Total	14 (100%)	29 (100%)	25 (100%)	10 (100%)	8 (100%)

(a) Includes one legal separation in each case.

   The early arrival of children in the marriages of the Ordinary
Kids and the Lads reflects two factors. First, some of these were
'shotgun' weddings: four of the six married males in the Ordinary
Kids sample and two of the five married Lads 'had to get married'.
Looking at Jonty Bryans's network mentioned in Chapter 5, of the

eleven married men included, five married their pregnant girlfriends.

The other reason for the early birth of children is that it is expected, once an independent home has been established, that the wife should leave work and start having babies (cf. Hobson, 1981). For the lads and the ordinary kids, a woman's place is usually in the home. There are a few of the ordinary kids following a different strategy, saving for a home of their own and waiting to have children; we shall meet two of them, Carol and Davy, in the next chapter. This domestic strategy, however, is more characteristically adopted by citizens after marriage.

There are, therefore, two paths to the altar or the registry office in Ballyhightown, the planned and the precipitate. The first is the more 'respectable': a public courtship, leading to an engagement, leading, after a pre-determined period, to the wedding, which is still ideally in church. The symbolic public act of 'getting engaged', going into Belfast together to buy the ring and perhaps having an engagement party, is typically preceded by a period of 'going steady'. It is my impression that pre-marital sex within the framework of a 'steady' relationship is both accepted and widespread among the ordinary kids and the lads. This is not always the case, however. Some of the girls in the Youth Centre network place great store on their 'respectability'; virginity, for them, is to be saved for surrender on their wedding night. That such attitudes are more than window dressing is illustrated by the case of one couple, both members of the Ordinary Kids sample, who had been going steady for over two years in May 1979. He was seventeen and she had just celebrated her eighteenth birthday. Following a series of rows they split up by mutual agreement, both, separately and in private, blaming the break upon her sexual reticence.

The second path to marriage, a precipitate pregnancy, is not necessarily precluded by the above pattern. Marriage and engagement can always be hurried along by an 'accident'. There are, however, some marriages preceded by only a short or casual relationship resulting in a pregnancy. In such a case it is seen as the 'right thing' for the couple to marry, for the boy to 'do the right thing by her'. During my fieldwork I came across three cases, however, in which young mothers, or mothers-to-be, did not get married; these were all locally thought to be unusual. In two of the cases the mothers were notorious 'dirties', the consensus being that nobody knew for certain who the child's father was. In the third, the mother was an unusually resolute young woman who refused to marry the baby's father because she hardly knew him. The child had been conceived while she was drunk and she was supported in her decision by her parents, who disliked their putative son-in-law. (8)

While the planned marriage is not confined to any particular occupational group, there does seem to be a relationship between unskilled work (for males) and precipitate marriage, five of the six precipitate marriages among the Lads and the Ordinary Kids involving unskilled grooms. Were this, for example, to prove a general trend, it would indicate a model of social careers in which the unskilled occupational career is part of an unplanned experience of education, work and the status passage from adolescence to adulthood, in contrast to the more orderly and 'chosen' skilled manual and white collar careers.

Two things are largely responsible for the precipitate pattern.
First, there is alcohol, a central element in the social life of the
lads and many of the ordinary kids. Sexual encounters frequently
occur at the weekend, as the finale to a night's drinking when
discretion has long since ceased to be the better part of valour.
If the girl has not taken any precautions in advance and the boy
hasn't got any 'frenchies', caution is often thrown to the winds.
Second, local attitudes to contraception preclude many unmarried
girls from 'going on the pill'. The reasons vary from fear of
parental discovery to worries about 'turning into a wee whore',
although engaged girls are probably less wary of oral contraceptives.
Although there is a family planning clinic nearby, single girls are
reluctant to use it, even if they have decided to 'go on the pill'.

> After all, if you go the family planning clinic there's only one
> thing you could be there for, and I'd be affronted. If you're
> sitting waiting for the doctor you could be there for anything,
> nobody'd know you were on the pill.

Many girls, however, are equally loath to consult their family
doctors, being afraid that he or she will tell their parents. As
a result, for many couples contraception is either an inconsistent
attempt to remember to use a sheath or a token gesture in the
direction of 'pulling out in time'.

Marriage and engagement have important effects upon working
lives. In the case of a planned engagement and marriage, the
couple may begin to save for household goods and furnishings for
their own house well in advance of the proposed wedding day (cf.
Leonard, op.cit., pp.223-55). There is, therefore, pressure on
both to stay employed: marriage, either planned or precipitate,
is a strong push in the direction of 'settling down' in employment
for all but the most dedicated of the lads. After the birth of a
couple of children, however, there may seem to be persuasive
arguments in favour of not working, particularly in the, by now
relatively poorly paid, unskilled jobs they are 'qualified' for.
Peewee Stafford, whose wife worked 'cash in hand' part-time in a
local shop, explained to me why it wouldn't pay him to start work
once he started paying tax: 'I'd only be getting ten pounds a week
for myself and I get a fiver now, so where'd be the sense in it?'

That such arguments, and the brue-man ideology discussed in
Chapter 4, are rationalisations of their predicament by the lads,
despite the undoubted 'poverty trap' of low wages in Northern
Ireland, is suggested by Peewee's acceptance, a couple of months
later, of an unskilled job in a local engineering factory with whom
he had long had 'a form in'. Regardless of the growing realisation
in areas such as Ballyhightown that unemployment is now as much a
problem for protestants in Northern Ireland as catholics, the
pressures upon the individual to work remain strong.

For women, marriage changes things considerably. Marriage is
the framework within which to raise a family: most young women in
Ballyhightown want to have children soon after marriage and husbands
expect to become fathers. Masculinity has to be proved, even though
large families are no longer the norm, and with parenthood the final
steps across the threshold of adulthood are taken. There is also
the pressure from erstwhile grandparents, eager to spoil their
grandchildren in a way they never spoiled their own. This is, of

course, an ideal picture, and matters rarely run as harmoniously
as this. None the less, the truth of this model would be recognised
by the young people under discussion. A woman's work is minding her
children and keeping house for her husband; the man's work is bringing
home the wage. This pattern is changing, certainly for many citizens,
but nevertheless, marriage for the girls of the Youth Centre network
means leaving work sooner rather than later, even if only until the
kids start school.

For the husband, marriage (and engagement) has implications for
his working life. At a stroke he expands the scope and scale of his
personal network. In-laws, in their desire to ensure that their
daughter or sister is properly looked after, may be anxious to help
him find a new or better job and can be manipulated to this end.
When Chrissy and Tommy Brownleas 'had to get married', her sister-in-
law found Tommy a job in a local mill, cleaning up around the machines.
He left after a day: 'I didn't like it. You'd to clean all the dirt
up, so I left'. Three months later, another of her sister-in-laws,
who worked in a nearby factory, got him a job as a machine operator.
In December 1978 this factory, making cable gear, was closed by its
London headquarters and Tommy was redundant. Finally, in March 1979,
Chrissy's father got him started as a handyman at the hotel where
he worked. Chrissy's family were not doing Tommy a favour, however,
they were looking after the best interests of Chrissy and her
daughter.

In Chapter 4 a threefold model of the life-styles of the youth of
Ballyhightown was elaborated. In Chapters 5 and 6 I compared three
samples intended to represent these life-styles in order to discover
the differences between them with respect to family background,
education, criminal career, labour market experience and marriage.
It is apparent from these comparisons that there are obvious and
considerable differences between the life-styles, as reflected by
the samples, in these matters.

Life-styles do not simply reflect attitudes or 'cultural'
orientations, however. They are shared practical solutions to the
problem of making one's way in the world and it is clear that the
differences identified between life-styles are not all attributable
to 'subcultural' differences between the samples. The situation
is more complex than that. Every bit as important in the process
of growing up and coming of age in Ballyhightown are factors which
must be considered 'external' to the young people involved: the
behaviour of the adults with whom they must interact and the
organisational nature of the institutions they participate in. In
the next chapter I shall present detailed case-studies of eight kids
to flesh out the points which have been made in the discussion of
the interview data and to illustrate the salience of these 'external'
factors for the experience of particular individuals as they make
their way from youth into adulthood.

Chapter 7

EIGHT LIVES

The differences between the three life-styles have been examined at the level of overall patterns. In this chapter, detailed case-studies of members of those life-styles should allow some of the processes behind those patterns to be appreciated, illustrating the heterogeneity within life-styles as well as the differences between them.

Van Velsen has described this approach as 'situational analysis' or 'the extended-case method', the conscious attempt to go beyond general principles of social organisation to the practice of particular actors, sometimes reflecting those principles and sometimes not (Van Velsen, 1967). The preceding chapters have concentrated upon the life-styles as groups; in this chapter the emphasis is on individuals. Methodologically, my treatment of the data has much in common with Mark Holmström's discussion of the careers of Indian factory workers, in which he combines the merits of two approaches, autobiographical and questionnaire methods (1976, pp.86-7). Although using material from the structured interviews, advantage has also been taken of data from other sources: participant observation, school records and material written by kids themselves. (1) There are seven case-studies, covering two of the Lads, four of the Ordinary Kids and two Citizens, in that order.

JIM MITCHELL

'Mitch' left Ballyhightown Secondary School in June 1975 without taking any examinations. He had originally left a year earlier, to spend his final year at Craigaban Technical College, but returned at Easter 1975 after two terms there. The third child of four, he was brought up by his mother, his father having died two years after Jim's birth. At the time of the interview his eldest brother was a newly-enlisted member of the Royal Ulster Constabulary and the other a sheet-metal worker. His younger sister was attending the Technical College, studying for examinations in secretarial and commercial subjects which had not been taught at the grammar school where she had been a pupil for five years. Her ambition was to enter the Civil Service.

In October 1975 Mitch entered a Government Training Centre as an apprentice plasterer, a place which he got with the help of the school's careers master. He only accepted a plastering apprentice-ship because the courses he had wanted to join were both full: 'I wanted to be a joiner from before I left school, and bricklaying ... I just fancy the job.' Plastering was a second choice. In March 1976 one of the GTC staff used his contacts in the trade to find Jim an apprenticeship place with a building firm working on a local housing estate site. It was intended that he should finish 'serving his time' with them. This was not to be; in September 1976 he was sacked, 'for slabbering to an architect who tried to tell me my job'.

Help was at hand, however. His girlfriend's father found him a job with a business friend of his who ran a building firm. Mitch stayed there for three weeks before being paid off as 'unsuitable'; the builder hadn't really wanted an apprentice in the first place, he had been looking for a tradesman who could work unsupervised and possessed skills which were, as yet, poorly developed in Jim.

After a spell 'on the brue', the Careers Office found him work as a labourer in a nearby bottling factory, a job which also lasted for only three weeks. It was 'slave labour' and he got the sack for 'slabbering to a foreman'. Once more he was unemployed and he occupied himself by cleaning windows with a friend who was also unemployed at the time, 'doing a double', working and claiming benefit at the same time. In February 1977 he returned to plastering, as an apprentice with a small self-employed plastering squad, a job he found through a work-mate of a friend of his and which started out as another 'double'. In April the squad's contract ran out and he was unemployed again. At this time his occupational identity, in his own eyes, was still that of an apprentice plasterer.

He remained unemployed until November 1977, unsuccessfully seeking work in a depressed construction industry. Then he returned to work, although not as a plastering apprentice. One of the youth workers in the Youth Centre found Jim a job in his brother-in-law's car repairing company as a paint sprayer. But that was a 'boring type of work'; he left in April 1978 to go to a 'better job' with higher wages.

The 'better job' was labouring on a building site on the Shankill Road in Belfast which another friend, Tailor Burton, who was also working there, had tipped him off about. He started at the beginning of May 1978, earning a nominal 'top line' (gross pay) of £53 a week, in contrast to the £25 a week he had grossed in the garage. This, however, wasn't the job's only advantage; the foreman told him that 'after a while' he'd be started as a third-year plasterer. He had originally been introduced to the foreman as a plasterer by Billy Saunders, another acquaintance from Ballyhightown, who was also working on the site as a plasterer. Much to Billy's chagrin, however, Mitch admitted to the foreman that he wasn't 'out of his time' yet.

I mean to say, like ... how many plasterers or brickies or anything are really out of their time? They all say they're finished before they're done. So long as you can skim walls and do ceilings, you can bluff your way with the rest. Still ... I suppose I should've told him I told the gaffer he was a plasterer. I thought he'd realise, like.

The apprenticeship kept getting put off, and in mid-October 1978 he was paid off for 'carrying on' (acting the fool); according to Mitch, the foreman told him, 'I couldn't blame you. You were told you were going to be a plasterer and you were doing labourer's work. I'll fix it up so that it's all right with the dole.' At the time, there was some talk of his transferring, as a plasterer, to another site run by the same firm, but this came to nothing. A couple of weeks later Jim, Browner and I were sitting in a bar when the conversation turned to a discussion of his career to date: 'I just fucked about too much. Acted the lad and all.' The future looked bleak.

Within about a month he was back at work, labouring on another building site in the Shankill Road area, a job he had obtained via his next-door neighbour's brother, who 'put in a word for him'. This lasted until January 1979 when he was dismissed for bad time-keeping. He, along with three others, had in fact been dismissed the previous December for 'industrial misconduct' but the contractor had been pressured into taking them back by the trade union. Since that time, Jim claimed, the firm had been looking for 'any excuse' to get rid of them. A new girlfriend and late nights for a fortnight sufficiently affected his timekeeping that they readily found their excuse.

In May 1979, four years after he had originally left school, Jim was unemployed and nominally unskilled. Although he was still doing small plastering 'homers' he regarded himself as a labourer. All hope of ever finishing his plastering apprenticeship had long since receded. The only ray of hope he saw for his own future was that he had, with the encouragement of the staff in the Youth Centre, applied to work for a voluntary work organisation in England. The application had been accepted and, although he had no idea where in England he would be going or what he would be doing, he was looking forward to seeing Chelsea playing, even though they had just gone down to the Second Division. Mitch's general pessimism was shared by his mother.

> He's had the heart knocked out of him, so he has, Richard. And it's not through any real fault of his own ... I mean, I know that.... That's why I don't shout at him and all, to go out and get a job.... And I know he hasn't any money, so he hasn't, but I take money for his keep off him anyway. I'd be a-feared he'd only spend it in the bar if I didn't.

However, further disappointment lay ahead: the voluntary organisation didn't contact him again and he spent the next few months unemployed. In July 1980 he was back at work after nearly a year and a half unemployed, labouring on a building site again. He had also joined the part-time Ulster Defence Regiment, a move which finalised his effective withdrawal from the lads' network. By February 1982 he had become a full-time UDR soldier and was courting steadily. The transformation was complete.

BOBBY BOTHWELL

Born and brought up in the York Road area of Belfast, Bobby's family moved to Ballyhightown in 1969. His father, a joiner, works for a building contractor, his mother is a home-help. Bobby has a reputation among the other lads as a hard worker, someone who goes out and looks for a job until he finds one. Bobby himself is scathing in his criticism of many of the unemployed: 'there's a whole lot of people on the brue that don't want to work. That's why they're on the brue, they're getting enough on the brue'.

Bobby's time at Ballyhightown Secondary was punctuated by a succession of brushes with the law, escalating in seriousness as he grew up. In 1970, when he was eleven and still at primary school, he was conditionally discharged by the juvenile court for burglary. The following year he was found guilty on a similar charge and sent to Rathgael Approved School, where he spent fourteen months. Soon after his return to Ballyhightown, as a third-year pupil, he was back in court for breaking and entering; in March 1973, he was sentenced to 1-3 years in Rathgael. At this time one of his teachers summed him up as follows: 'Bobby has appointed himself as leader of the "rough element". No homework and little effort. Heading for trouble.' He returned to the estate at Easter 1974 and was soon back in court in the company of Tailor Burton, charged with breaking and entering. This time he got off with a fine.

At Easter 1975 he left school, having taken no examinations, to start work as a 'lorry boy' in a Belfast timber yard. He had worked there as part of the school's work experience scheme and so impressed them that they told him to come and see them when he left school. He was earning £14 a week 'in my hand'. Five weeks later he found himself another job, pool attendant at the Belfast Municipal Baths. The pay was better, £19 a week net: 'The only thing I didn't like was the shifts and the Sunday working'.

In June he changed jobs again to achieve what appears to have been his main occupational goal, going to sea. He signed on as a deck-hand on board a coal boat trading across the Irish Sea. His father and some of his uncles had all been to sea in their youth and 'they saw some men in the pool'. Bobby's maritime career was brought to an abrupt halt in July 1975, however, by the arrival on board of the police with a warrant for his arrest. He was in court that day, charged with assault, and before the day was out he was back in Rathgael. That December, an assault case which had been pending for some time was heard and he was put on borstal report. Shortly after Christmas, Bobby absconded from Rathgael; for the next three months he was 'on the run', mainly in Ballyhightown and Priorville.

Recaptured in March 1976, he was tried for various thefts committed whilst on the run and sent to Millisle Borstal where he remained until February 1977. Shortly after his release his father found him a job labouring on the building site he was working on. Bobby only stayed there for three days, however; immediately on his return to Ballyhightown he had 'put in a form' to the nearby cable factory and they wrote to him asking him to start as an unskilled general worker. He was there for four weeks. 'I hated it. Crap. It was just a wired-up job and I didn't fancy any of the people in it ... I was sacked, didn't get on with the forewoman. She wouldn't give me a pass out to go and look for another job.'

He was unemployed from April 1977 for seven months. In June in one of the local churches he married a girl from Priorville; five months later the baby was born. They moved into their own maisonette in Ballyhightown and by November Bobby was back at work, labouring

for Enterprise Ulster, a government public works agency, on their
site at Priorville. The pay was £30 a week net.

At this time the Careers Office in Belfast offered him a job on
a short-term engineering course at a Government Training Centre.
Bobby refused it.

> I don't see any sense in a six weeks or fourteen weeks course in
> engineering. You wouldn't learn anything about the job ...//...
> I would've learned more in seven months engineering in borstal,
> but it takes five years to learn a trade.

In February 1978 he was signing on at the local social security
office again, sacked this time for throwing stones. In May he found
a job labouring at a power station construction site outside Belfast,
a short-term job which came to an end in July. In September he was
working again, as a labourer in a Belfast factory: 'I tried all the
timber yards first and then I tried that place and I was lucky. I
got a job.' This lasted until February 1979 and when he was paid
off it was not particularly his doing; the company was bankrupt.

Bobby	They're going bust, so they say. They paid four of us off at the same time and put the rest on ninety days' notice, so they did.
R.J.	And what about Ernie? I heard he got paid off for chinning somebody.
Bobby	No he didn't, he got paid off at the same time. He never got fucking found out for that.... No, they're losing heaps of money. They say they owe over six million in debts ...//...
Tailor	That was after I left, so it was. There was a whole lot of 'Hightown fellas there ... Shorty and all. I really tore the fucking arse out of it, so I did... Do you remember, Bobby, I used to go in at eight in the morning and clock straight out again? It was wild.
Bobby	That's right. This cunt used to clock out again at three minutes past eight ... fucking eejit. He tore the arse out of it altogether. But the company made a very silly move, they put all the 'Hightown fellas in one place. They should've known we'd rake to fuck.

After seventeen days' unemployment he was in trouble again. He had
been going to appeal against a four-month sentence for assault -
like most of his assault cases resulting from a night's drinking
with the lads - but decided not to risk it. He had, after all, no
job to keep him outside. Ten weeks later he was released from Long
Kesh and he started work the next day; his father had put a word
in for him again. When I left the estate at the end of June he was
still in that job and, as far as I know, although he has been in
and out of work since he has managed to keep out of prison.

BRIAN McWILLIAMS

Brian started work as an apprentice butcher in a small shop in
Glasnacree in July 1977, six weeks after leaving Woodlands Secondary
School with CSE Woodwork and Art. His father, a labourer, had been
unemployed for some time and his elder brother was also a butcher.
Brian 'phoned the shop-keeper after a mate of his, Tommy Brownleas,

who had just been sacked for absenteeism, told him about the job and
suggested that he enquire about it. On doing so, Brian was asked to
come up and meet the butcher, who hired him on the spot. Things
progressed reasonably well at work for Brian, apart from an unofficial
week off at the end of December 1978 caused by an overdose of festive
spirits.

In September 1978 Brian married his 'steady girl', who had been at
school with him and worked as a clerk. Michelle was several months
pregnant and soon they were allocated a flat in Ballyhightown. In
May 1979 his employer took a fortnight's holiday and left his brother
in charge of the shop while his mother came in at the weekend to look
after the till, as usual. What follows is an abridged version of
Brian's account of the events which ensued.

On the Saturday before the boss returned, his brother told Brian
to go and serve at the counter. It was half past eight in the
morning and the girl who normally did the counter had not arrived
for work yet. Brian insisted that the boss's brother put him on
the counter 'for badness', because he knew that Brian didn't like
serving. In response, Brian said that he was busy making up an
order for a local hotel and couldn't the other apprentice, who
was doing nothing at the time, do it? The boss's brother said
that would be fine. Shortly afterwards, the boss's mother came
into the back of the shop and said to Brian, 'You were told to
put your coat on and go home.' Brian: 'I wasn't'. Boss's
mother: 'You were'. Brian: 'Very well, I'll go now then'.
Boss's mother: 'I'm very glad to hear it'. So Brian left. He
returned the following Monday morning to work his week's notice,
but the boss, who had by this time returned from holiday, told
him that since he had been so rude to his mother he would not
let him start again. What is more, he had no intention of giving
him any severance pay in lieu of notice.

Brian felt unfairly treated. With the encouragement of Michelle
and the Youth Centre staff he applied to the Labour Relations Agency
in Belfast for an Industrial Tribunal hearing. After separate
discussions with Brian and his ex-employers the Agency's officers
decided not to proceed to a Tribunal hearing, citing Article 24(1)(a)
of the Industrial Relations (N.I.) Order 1976: an employee cannot
appeal against unfair dismissal if he/she has not been in continuous
employment for twenty-six weeks or more. Brian's 'lost week' at
Christmas had been his downfall. The Agency's officers would
probably not have found in Brian's favour anyway, since they are
empowered, by Article 24(2) of the same order, to disregard the
qualifying period, 'if it is shown that the reason (or, if more
than one, the principal reason) for the dismissal was an inadmissable
reason'. Misconduct is an admissable reason within the definition
of the order; presumably this is how they were interpreting Brian's
behaviour since they invoked the qualifying period.

Brian had never wanted to return to his old employer and had
been busy looking for a new job. He 'phoned another butcher in
Glassnacree who had placed a situations vacant advertisement in the
'Belfast Telegraph'. The butcher said he would contact Brian if
no one else applied for the job but that was the last that Brian
heard.

A more concrete offer came via one of the Youth Centre staff,

whose neighbour had a butcher's shop in the Beechmount district of
the catholic Upper Falls area of Belfast. He offered Brian a job
and a lift to and from work. When Brian realised where the shop
was located he turned the offer down; Michelle was particularly
adamant that he wasn't going. About a fortnight later I met him
while we were both on our way down to the Youth Centre. He had
just been for an interview with a butcher in a town several miles
away, and he had seen another butcher's job advertised in that
night's 'Telegraph'. He was starting to consider the possibilities
outside butchery.

Brian   Anyway, sure maybe I'll no bother. I've put in a form
           for Grant's (a local engineering firm), so I have.

R.J.   Why did you do that? There's not a lot of future left
           in Grant's. And even if you only stayed in a butchers
           to finish your time, you'd always have your trade to
           fall back on.

Brian   Sure I don't care really ... what I want is a job
           where you don't have to work Saturdays.... Like that
           job in _____ wouldn't be so bad, you get Saturday
           off.... But you feel wick, so you do, stuck inside an
           auld shop all Saturday when your mates and all are
           away out. At least in Grant's I'd get Saturday morning
           to myself.

Nothing came of the interview. A week before I finally left the
estate he was contacted by a friend he had previously worked with
in the original shop in Glassnacree. He had left to work in the
butchery department of the local 'Co-op'. Now he was leaving to
start up his own business, he offered to put in a word on Brian's
behalf to the supermarket's manager. As a result, Brian saw the
manager and a couple of days later he received a letter telling him
that he had got the job. Six weeks after being sacked, he was back
at work.

RUTH SIMPSON

The eldest girl of five children, Ruth's schooldays were already
over when her family moved to Ballyhightown. Born and raised on
the Shankill Road, she attended secondary school there, leaving at
Easter 1971 without having taken any examinations. She was fifteen
and for the first four or five months she was busy around the house.
During this period she did not register as unemployed: 'I didn't
even know about the brue.'

In the late summer of 1971 the family 'flitted' to Ballyhightown,
glad to escape the tension of the city and the poor housing
conditions. Although Ruth remembers her childhood on the Shankhill
with affection, she is certain that she prefers Ballyhightown. In
November 1971 she started work as a yarn twister in 'the Mill', a
long-established textile factory a few miles from Ballyhightown:
'I went up and asked.' Her mother, who had worked in textile mills
in Belfast, started shortly after Ruth, and as her younger sisters
left school places in the Mill were found for them too. Ruth stayed
there until February 1973, earning £7 a week net. Then she left:
'My granny was sick and I had to stay at home to look after her.'

She looked after her granny for six months, and at this time she
started 'seeing' Billy Simpson on a regular basis. He was a third-
year apprentice fitter in Mackie's engineering works in Belfast and
a year older than Ruth. Ruth's younger sister was going out with
Billy's mate, Jacky, and the four of them became a familiar sight
around the estate. During her granny's illness she had sent in an
application form to TransInternational Electronics at Priorville
and in August 1973 she was called for interview. She started work
as a frame-wirer, a job requiring manual dexterity and continuous
concentration upon the correct placing of colour-coded wires. In
retrospect, she describes this as the best job she ever had: 'It
was clean and there was a good atmosphere ... you know, the people.'
At the time, however, it was a different story. Ruth was earning
£20 a week net, but she had to work for it.

> I liked it at the beginning, so I did, but it started to get on
> top of me towards the end, like. I couldn't do it fast enough,
> so I thought I'd leave before I got sacked.

She left TransInternational and signed on the dole for the first
time in February 1975. She can't remember how long she was unemployed,
but in 1976, at the beginning of the summer, she returned to the
Mill for about six weeks. Working as a twister once again, this
time she found that she couldn't stick it: 'The work piled up and
you were afraid of the foreman.' Anyway, there was always work to
be done in the house. Her mother was still in the Mill and, since
Ruth's father had left work because of ill-health, she was more than
happy to have Ruth at home to look after the house for her.

In 1976, Billy and Ruth got engaged and she started to look for
a job again. Although Billy was 'out of his time' and bringing
home good wages, extra money for their future home would come in
handy. At the beginning of 1977 the Employment Office offered her
a place on a catering training course but she turned it down: 'You
had to go to Portrush for sixteen weeks.' She didn't think she'd
like being away from home for so long and, besides, Billy wasn't
happy about it.

So in February 1977 it was back to the Mill, as a spinner this
time at a net weekly wage of £28; her mother had spoken to the
supervisor on her behalf. Although they needed the money, she still
found the pace of the machines too much. In June 1977 Billy and
Ruth got married and in September she handed in her notice again.
'Billy made me leave. The work was depressing me.'

Shortly afterwards, they moved into a maisonette in Ballyhightown
and Ruth and her sister, who had married Jacky, settled into their
new roles as housewives, visiting their parents and doing the
shopping together. Ruth didn't register as unemployed after leaving
the Mill and seemed not to be interested in working again. In
December 1978, she gave birth to a daughter, an event which appeared
to set the seal on her final withdrawal from the labour market.
However, by July 1980 the financial pressures of moving into another
house had taken their toll; Ruth was back in the Mill while Billy's
mother minded the child.

DAVY DOUGLAS AND CAROL MONTEITH (2)

The Douglas family moved to Ballyhightown when Davy was nine months
old; they have lived in the same house ever since. His father is
a driver, a hard worker who, in Davy's words, 'would work the three
minutes' silence'. Sometimes he feels a keen sense of disappointment
that not all his sons share the same work ethos.

> I always tried to instil in 'til them that they should take it
> when they could get it. If you want to eat you've got to work
> ...//... If you want the wage that's what you've got to do.
> You know what they say, must do is a good master ...//... They're
> settling down now, of course, but it's too late, so it is.

This case-study is largely concerned with the story of Davy's
'settling down'. He left Ballyhightown Secondary School in 1972
at the age of fourteen; his birthday fell during the summer holidays
and he was able to leave after only three years' secondary education.
As he explained, it wasn't that he didn't like school, when he was
there he enjoyed himself, but there were always better things to do
elsewhere: fishing, hunting with terriers and ferrets, petty
crime and, as he got older, chasing women. When he was thirteen
he was in the juvenile court twice, once charged with breaking and
entering, once with carrying an offensive weapon. His father had
to pay the fines on both occasions; on both occasions, Davy 'got a
hammering'.

A week after leaving school he started work as a sales assistant
in a large electrical wholesalers at Dunbeg.

> A fella told me about it and I went up that Monday morning and
> got started. I was supposed to get started in the saw-mills
> but this fella said he'd give me a lift up so I just went up
> and started.

The take home pay was £7.50 a week and shortly after he began work
he started training as a television engineer. He returned to sales
after six weeks: an apprentice's pay was too low. In December 1973
he handed in his notice; he and his best mate, Jim Smyth, had heard
that they could earn £30 a week as drivers' helpers with a dairy
in Glassnacree. Davy did not reach his decision without regret.

> It was brilliant. I was sorry the day I left. The week I left
> I was offered assistant manager of the tapes department, but the
> thought of the milk.... It sounded great like, £30 a week.

Three weeks later he started at the dairy: 'I went up with Smyth
and Duncer. The man says, "Which one of you can start now?" and I
said I could. And I was wearing a suit and all.' Smyth started a
few days later but at the end of May 1974 they left after a row
with the boss over Sunday working. From May to November 1974 Davy
was out of work: 'I didn't even sign on. I got money from my ma.
I just didn't fancy signing.'

That summer he acquired two more criminal convictions, for assault
and for malicious damage, resulting in a £20 fine and a six-month
prison sentence, suspended for two years, respectively. The first
offence concerned a fight at a house in Priorville. 'We were drunk
and we beat the door down. There'd been a fight at the house
earlier that night and we went up with the fella who got beat up.'
As for the second: 'I didn't even do it, the bastards.' During
this period Davy and his mates joined one of the junior paramilitary
organisations.

His next job was on a building site in Glencairn, near the
Shankill Road; his father was working for one of the sub-contractors
and he got Davy started in December 1974. He didn't enjoy it but
the pay wasn't bad, £24 a week net. At the end of February 1975 he
left; he didn't like working with his father, who put him under
pressure to work harder and not take time off. From March to mid-
April he was on the dole again, 'doing a double' to make up his
pocket-money, working as a handyman and helping to build a social
club in Priorville.

It was early in April 1975 that he met Carol Monteith at a dance
in the local Orange Hall. In spite of her parents' open disapproval -
they thought that Carol was too young (she was fourteen at the time)
and 'much too good for the likes of him' - the relationship developed
and soon they were seeing each other regularly.

The Monteith family lived in Ballysloe, a housing estate near
Ballyhightown. Her father had previously worked in Grant's, a
nearby factory, but had recently gone into business for himself.
Carol was in her third year at Ballyhightown Secondary. In her
second year she had begun to 'beak off' and one of her reports
remarks that she 'has unfortunately leanings towards less disciplined
friends. There are ominous signs that Carol is going downhill.'
In her third year, however, she was 'showing signs of sobering up
and has moved apart from her harmful associates. Long may it last.'
When Carol looks back on school some of the reasons for her transformation become apparent.

I liked it. I beaked a lot in the first few years but not after
that. I got caught and got a hiding from my da. I think I was
too scared then. Our Denise doesn't know how lucky she is - I
got hidings with a big stick and she hasn't got a thing.

Carol's parents saw Davy as a new threat to their daughter's future.
They wanted her to 'make something of herself'. Nevertheless, Davy
and Carol continued to see each other and by this time Jim Smyth
was going with a mate of Carol's from Ballysloe, Jenny Smith.

In the middle of April 1975 Davy walked over to the site of the
new Social Services offices in Ballyhightown and asked the site
foreman if they needed anyone. He was hired as a labourer at a net
weekly wage of £25. When he finally got around to handing his
National Insurance card to the timekeeper, it was discovered that
he wasn't eighteen yet and his pay dropped to £16. He left: 'It
was low money for real donkey work.' He was unemployed again.

This spell of unemployment didn't last very long. In June 1975
he was convicted of the armed robbery of a petrol station on the
edge of the estate. Sentenced to twenty-three months in prison, he
was sent to Magilligan, a prison-camp near Londonderry. Carol was
distraught; her parents' judgment had been publicly vindicated.
Despite their discouragement, she continued to write to Davy, kept
in contact with his family and planned to make irregular visits to
Magilligan. By September 1975, Jim Smyth was in borstal for
possession of a pistol and Carol and Jenny saw a lot more of each
other.

Carol continued to do reasonably well at school; the general tone
of her teachers' remarks during her fourth year could be summarised
as, 'Satisfactory. Could do better if she tried harder.' Early in
1976, towards the end of her fourth year, the family moved. Her

father had bought a house in the expensive Castleowen suburb of
Greensville. She stayed at Ballyhightown Secondary, however, and
her social life remained focussed on her school-friends.

Jim Smyth left borstal in August 1976 and Davy followed him out
of Magilligan at the end of October. Although they kept many of
their contacts and renewed old friendships, they were both determined
to keep out of trouble. At first Jim didn't try too hard to get a
job. He hung around the Youth Centre and the local social clubs,
enjoying the liberty to do so. Davy, however, got a job the Monday
after he came out; he walked up to the Mill and asked at the gate.
Just before Christmas, he left: 'It was appalling conditions. It
was like going back a hundred years. The foremen are all management
mad.' Ironically, when Jim did finally get a job, it was also in
the Mill. It only lasted two hours: 'The foreman told me to brush
the floor and I told him to stick the brush up his hole.' Davy
and Jim were to spend most of 1977 unemployed.

In the meantime, Carol had been studying for her 'O' levels and
CSE examinations. Her parents' attitude towards Davy had not
mellowed and, although they tacitly accepted the relationship, they
were no nearer to liking or publicly accepting the situation; for
most of 1977 an elaborate fiction was maintained. Carol's relationship with Davy was going through a bad patch at this time anyway.
With nothing to do all day but 'run around with Smyth' he was
missing dates, turning up drunk and, she suspected, 'two-timing'
her as well. In May and June she sat her exams, failing 'O' level
English Language and Literature and getting CSEs in Typing (grade 1),
Mathematics (grade 3), French (grade 3) and Home Economics (grade 4).
She was successful in the RSA Stage 1 typing examination and the
sixty words a minute shorthand paper.

Now that she had left school she wasn't sure what she wanted to
do. Since she had not done as well as she had hoped in her exams,
she eventually decided to go to the local Technical College to do
a secretarial course for a year. Although she'd had quite enough
of school and exams, pressure and persuasion from her parents, Davy
and the author (as a youth worker) helped her to make up her mind.
The fact that her father was prepared to subsidise her while she
was studying was no small incentive.

In August 1977, Davy started work as a fitter's helper on a
construction site about eight miles away. It meant travelling, but
he was getting a lift so that wasn't too much of a problem. His
father, whose employers were sub-contractors on the site, arranged
the job for him, but it was a big place and they worked in different
parts of it so they didn't have to work together. By now Davy was
living with his married sister, so there was even less opportunity
for conflict with his father. The pay was good too: the basic
rate, when I interviewed him in April 1978, was £59 a week gross.
Taking normal overtime into account, he took home between £60 and
£65 a week on average. All in all, Davy was very satisfied: 'It's
brilliant, for a start the wages, and you're not pressured too much.
You're more or less your own boss. You're given a job and left to
do it.' The only problem, and that not an immediate one, was that
no one seemed sure how long the job would last. 'It might be six
months, it might be two years. It might end next week, for fuck's
sake.'

Carol started her course in September. She didn't like it much, but it seemed the best option which was open to her. In November they got engaged, on the same day as Jenny and Jim. Having bought their rings in Belfast, the two couples went out for a meal together in a hotel. By now, her parents had accepted that she was going out with Davy, but still didn't know that they were engaged. She was also starting to acquire a new set of friends through the secretarial course, friends of whom her parents approved. At a party in Davy's sister's house to celebrate the engagement, the festivities were marred by a row which broke out between one of Davy's mates and the boyfriend of one of her friends from the Tech.

Carol and Davy told her parents about their engagement at a New Year's party in her house. With the affair completely out in the open now, relationships with her parents started to improve. Gradually they started to socialise, as a couple, with her relatives and Davy started to get on better with her father. That summer he went on holiday with the family and when he was laid off during an industrial dispute, Mr Monteith paid him to help build an extension onto the house.

They were still seeing a lot of Jim and Jenny and another couple, Andy and Wilma. Jim was working too now, in the dispatch department of TransInternational Electronics. Jenny's father, a foreman in the works, had got the job for him and already they were buying furniture and domestic appliances for their future home. Tensions between Davy's social world and the social world of Carol, her relatives and her friends, were fast becoming apparent, however. On the one hand, the local bar and the TransInternational Social Club on a Thursday night; on the other, the 'Greensville Inn' and the Boat Club. Carol and Davy were torn between conflicting loyalties. Her ambitions were different to those of Davy's friends; trying to live up to her parents' expectations, she wanted to save up and buy a house away from Ballyhightown. Jenny was aiming for a Housing Executive house in Ballysloe. It was a time of conflict and many hurtful things were said. Davy's mates, for example, were very critical of Carol.

Sure he can't even get up in the morning to go hunting up the hill ...//... See Carol, she's trying to make him something he's not, putting off the wedding for three years because his job's not secure enough and wanting him to buy her a house. She's making a mug out of him ...//... And all the time her mother's telling her he's not good enough for her ...//... he should give her a fucking good kicking. Knock the nonsense out of her.

Carol finished her course in June 1978 but did badly in the examinations. After three weeks' unemployment, however, she started work as a typist for one of the largest engineering firms in Belfast. Her grandfather worked there and he got her an application form which he took into the personnel office for her. She liked it, even though she did have to go back to College on a day release basis. Work gave her another circle of friends and, again, conflict developed, Davy feeling once more under threat. He was steadily undermining his own network of mates and in return was frequently made to feel inferior by some of Carol's friends. Compromise and their continuing affection for each other prevailed, however; they

solved the problem as best they could by mixing with both sets of
friends regularly, but less frequently.

In late 1978 Davy was allocated a one-bedroomed flat on the
estate and together they set about furnishing it. Their long-term
plan was still to purchase their own house, but this was to be their
first home when they eventually married. By the New Year they had
brought the marriage forward, although they didn't decide on a date.
Jenny and Jim were getting married in June, 'a big church affair',
and Davy was to be the best man. Carol had by this time been
promoted, she was now the secretary of one of the firm's managers.
In addition to a pay rise, the promotion brought new pressures with
it.

> I thought I was smart too. Some executive secretary I'd make.
> It was wild. I had this man on the 'phone from America and
> there was something wrong with the line and it kept cutting out.
> And when I got him a second time the girl on the switchboard
> says, 'And don't hang up this time.' And the managing director
> was in Mr Jones's office and you're not allowed to put calls
> through when he's in there so I had this American buddy on one
> side waiting to talk to Mr Jones and I'm trying to keep him
> talking and Mr Jones on the other side telling me to keep him
> hanging on, and I'm sitting in the middle going daft. It was
> wild.

In May they booked a week-long holiday in Spain at the beginning of
September and having paid for the holiday, they decided that they
might as well make it their honeymoon, so they booked the Registry
Office as well. Then they told Mr and Mrs Monteith. The idea was
frostily received at first but gradually they warmed to the idea
and her father agreed to pay for the reception. Davy asked Jim
to be his best man.

Then, August, disaster struck. As Davy had known would happen
someday, he was made redundant. They went ahead with their plans,
but by the time they boarded the 'plane to Spain he still hadn't
found a job. By the next Spring the situation hadn't materially
improved; Davy had had two jobs since the wedding, both of them
temporary. The present one wasn't expected to last beyond September
so he was no nearer to permanent employment, try as he might. Jenny
Smith had by now left work and was busy preparing for the birth of
her first child. This was one more taunt Davy had to put up with;
when was he going to prove he was a man?

In June 1980 Carol's grandad came up trumps again. He had been
trying to get Davy started in the factory where Carol worked and
eventually, towards the end of June, Davy was offered an unskilled
production job. At the time of writing they are both still working
there and are still in their flat. A home of their own, given
today's prices, seems as far away as ever. (3)

RHONDA THOMPSON

When I interviewed her in February 1979, Rhonda was eighteen, nearly
nineteen. An only child, she lived with her parents, her father
an electrician and her mother a machine-minder in a factory. The
family moved from Belfast in 1972. Before then, Rhonda attended an

all-girls secondary school in Belfast, a few miles away from her new home, and her parents saw no reason to move her. Rhonda has mixed views about Ballyhightown: 'The part I live in's all right, but it depends on the area and the people that get into it.'

Although she went to school outside the estate, she made friends locally through the church which she and her parents attended. She joined the Girls' Brigade company, of which she was still an enthusiastic member in 1979, and the badminton club.

Rhonda liked school, she says she never beaked. At the end of fifth year, in 1976, she sat CSE examinations in English Language, English Literature, Religious Education (all of which she passed at grade 1 level), History, Geography and Maths. In addition, she passed her RSA Stage 1 typing examination and her Pitman's 60 words a minute shorthand test. She decided to stay for an extra year to study for some 'O' levels.

She wasn't happy staying at school, however, and in January 1977 she applied for a job she saw advertised in the 'Belfast Telegraph'. She got it and left school immediately. That job was as a clerk/telephonist with a shipping and forwarding firm at the docks in Belfast, paying £21 a week gross. At the end of March she handed in her notice: 'I liked it but the location was unhelpful. It was down on the docks, away from the centre. You couldn't go out in your lunch break.'

She hadn't left before finding a new job, however. Next Monday she started work in a dental surgery near Ballyhightown as a trainee dental nurse. The starting pay was £25 a week before tax and by February 1979 this had risen to £30 a week: 'It's all right for me, but I don't think it's enough for the job.' Rhonda didn't now have any further occupational ambitions. Due to be married three weeks after I interviewed her, she and her fiancé had already been allocated a flat in one of the multi-storey blocks in Ballyhightown. This would do until they could afford something of their own.

THOMAS KIDD

Born in Ballyhightown in 1960, Thomas is the oldest of three children. His father drives a fork-lift in a factory in Belfast and his mother works in a city-centre shop. At the time of the interview he was single and evinced an enthusiastic desire to remain so. A staff-sergeant in the local Boys' Brigade company, he was a part-time youth leader in his church youth club and a member of the Youth Fellowship.

Having passed his eleven-plus qualifying examination, Thomas attended a grammar school in Belfast: 'I was a bit of a messer, I wasn't too fussy on school at the time. I just did the bare minimum.' He left school in 1976 with four 'O' levels, English Literature, History, Maths and Religious Education. In September 1976 he started an Ordinary National Diploma course in Business Management at the College of Business Studies in Belfast. He had, in the meantime, applied for an apprenticeship place at a Government Training Centre, but decided not to pursue this any further. The local Education and Library Board agreed to pay for his tuition fees and travelling expenses; the rest of his needs he met with a succession

of weekend jobs. Whilst at the College he acquired two more 'O'
levels, English Language and Accounting; unfortunately, however, he
failed one paper of his OND, Economics. He was studying for this
as a part-time student when I interviewed him.

Finished at College, he spent the summer of 1978 'signing on':
'I wanted my holidays. I was casting around for jobs.' At the
beginning of August he applied for a trainee manager's job which
was advertised in the 'Belfast Telegraph' by a scientific instruments
company on the other side of the city. In mid-August he started
work, earning £45 a week gross. He was only there for a month.

> I had asked the company if they would give me day release to
> finish my OND. At the interview, they said no day release. Then
> they said, OK - until the end of the year. I wanted further day
> release ... to do more qualifications. And then I was offered
> a new job offering more day release ...//... Although it was a
> trainee job, they really wanted someone who was qualified. They
> just had you doing different jobs here and there, they hadn't
> a proper training programme. They sort of treated you as a
> labourer to get you used to the job. I didn't think there was
> any future.

The new job was another trainee manager's post, this time in a timber
yard near the docks. Thomas had applied for it at the same time as
the first job, but they had taken longer to make him an offer. They
offered him the advertised pay of £35 a week, increasing this to
£40 because of the drop in pay involved in leaving the other job.
When I interviewed him, Thomas was still working there and he was
still dissatisfied.

> I don't like it. They don't give you enough responsibility in
> the work, they just treat the trainee managers like message
> boys. It all depends which manager you're put with. Some are
> better than others. It's better than _____ (his first
> employer) though, they put you over labourers and you have to
> work to get their respect ... to get authority. There's more
> responsibility in that way, controlling men.

Eighteen years old and already 'controlling men', Thomas wasn't
sure yet where his own future lay. Of one thing he was sure; he
had his feet firmly on the bottom of the ladder which leads out of
Ballyhightown.

Viewing these case-studies in the context of the data presented in
Chapters 5 and 6, it should be apparent how some of the patterns
I highlighted there are worked out in practice. Among the more
obvious threads running through these individual accounts are the
importance of gender differences in structuring the experience of
growing up, the significance of the power of adults to make decisions
about kids and make those decisions stick, the ubiquity of informal
networks in the labour market and the pervasive effect of the peer
group. More generally, these case-studies underline the differences
in the lived experience of the three life-styles; differences which
are as much the result of events and circumstances beyond their
control as of their own decisions and actions.

There are other patterns which can be seen in these case-studies,
of course, such as the difference between locally oriented conserva-

tism and the externally directed ambition of many of the citizens.
Similarly clear is the strength of individualism – about which more
will be said in Chapter 10 – as the ideological framework within
which all of these kids understand their social world. In the
account of Carol and Davy we have highlighted another process which
is common in Ballyhightown; rough lad meets girl and, in the process
of winning her heart, moves away from his mates and towards the
middle ground of greater respectability. This is something else
which I shall discuss further in Chapter 10, as an important link
between the reproduction of gender and the reproduction of life-
styles.

Finally, there is further evidence in the accounts of Ruth and
Carol to support the material presented in Chapter 6 about the nature
of work for some of these young people. For these kids, not a
majority but sufficient in numbers to be important, employment is
neither an avenue to self-fulfilment nor a source of tolerable self-
sufficiency. (4) At best it is experienced as an unwelcome inter-
ruption of the 'natural' routines of life; at worst it produces
the lived sense of contradiction which Marx, in the 'Economic and
Philosophic Manuscripts', glossed as 'alienation' (Marx, 1970 edn,
pp.106-19). Experienced as a burden which must be carried, work
becomes a potent cause of anxiety and misery which flies in the
face of the liberal ideology of self-realisation and upward mobility.

Chapter 8

EMPLOYERS, INDUSTRIES AND THE STATE

In earlier chapters I discussed the labour market as experienced by young workers. In addition to looking at the models of work held by members of the different life-styles, and their behaviour at work, I examined the importance of factors nominally extrinsic to the labour market, such as marriage strategies, in producing differences in the young worker's experience of work. That this discussion has been grounded in the ethnography of working-class youth in Ballyhightown accurately reflects the major focus of the fieldwork.

However, the discussion so far has concentrated upon the supply side of the economist's equation only. The demand side of the labour market - apart from factors governing the level of aggregate demand, as discussed in Chapter 3 - will be approached in three complementary fashions: by considering the practices of employers or their delegates, in an examination of industrial differences in the institutional procedures for hiring and firing workers, and through a discussion of the increasingly important role of state intervention in supplementing the demand for labour through a variety of employment schemes. In this manner I shall attempt to develop a processual model of the labour market as 'those institutions which mediate, effect, or determine the purchase and sale of labour power' (Edwards, Reich and Gordon, 1975, p.xi).

EMPLOYERS IN THE LABOUR MARKET

I have described the folk-models of young people current in Ballyhightown in Chapter 4; the three life-styles discussed there are located on a continuum from the 'rough' to the 'respectable'. I would suggest that similar folk classifications are used not only by the working class but also by the 'rest of society'. Castleowen's Mayor, a local businessman and employer, is clearly working with a model of the 'reputable' and the 'disreputable' (cf. Matza, 1967) in the statement below. (1)

> There are a lot of very decent people in Ballyhightown but they
> are suffering because of the actions of a small percentage of
> people who are only happy, it would appear, when they are beside
> filth and dirt.

If employers do distinguish between types of workers in this manner
then it is to be expected that such a model will be reflected in
their decisions and matched by their classification of jobs. Apart
from the mobilisation in selection of criteria such as formal trade
or educational qualifications, some jobs may be regarded as appropriate
for some workers and not for others. Furthermore, regardless of the
job, some potential employees may be preferred to others.
   Recent studies of the labour market bear this out. Blackburn and
Mann, in their examination of the market for unskilled male manual
labour in Peterborough, analysed the recruitment policies of local
employers and concluded that, 'Responsibility and discipline are ...
the qualities valued by management and thought to be in short supply'
(Blackburn and Mann, 1979, p.107). They go on to say:
   Yet even when accepted for employment, workers must still prove
   that they do possess responsibility and discipline.... The internal
   labour market is fundamentally an apprenticeship in cooperation.
   (Ibid., p. 108, emphasis in original)
The central thrust of their argument is that it is not ability which
matters, however that is defined in the market for unskilled labour.
Since all jobs at this level require similarly low levels of 'skill',
perceived attitudes, especially 'stability' and 'reasonableness',
have a major influence upon recruitment decisions.
   In their study of employers' strategies in the recruitment of
young employees, Ashton and Maguire distinguish between five separate
selection strategies, ranging from an almost complete reliance upon
educational criteria to a total disregard for such criteria (1980,
1981; Ashton, Maguire and Garland, 1982). For certain kinds of work,
educational qualifications are a disadvantage; employers recruiting
for dead-end jobs may regard qualifications as evidence of an
inappropriate ambition. Even in those recruitment strategies which
place the highest value upon academic criteria, 'non-academic
criteria are still very important in determining which of the
applicants with the minimum qualifications will succeed' (Ashton and
Maguire, 1980, pp.151-2). The two most important non-academic
criteria are the interviewee's attitude to work, as interpreted by
the interviewer from non-verbal cues and answers to questions, and
their 'self-presentation', the interviewer's assessment of the job-
seeker's personality, as indicated by punctuality, cleanliness and
general 'smartness'. Two other important criteria are 'interest
in the job' and 'family background'. The emphasis throughout is on
'reliability' and 'predictability'.
   The relative peripherality of educational qualifications in
effecting final recruitment outcomes has been illustrated by other
research into the market for young workers (Reid, 1980, 1981).
The Manpower Services Commission, in their report upon young people
and work, found that, 'Most firms emphasised ... that personality,
alertness and other qualities were more important than paper
qualifications' (Manpower Services Commission, 1978, p.47).
   Recent research by the author in the Midlands has further
expanded upon the selection criteria which employers bring to the
recruitment of manual and routine non-manual workers (Jenkins,
1982b). In this analysis, the distinction is drawn between
functionally specific criteria, such as qualifications or on-the-job
training (suitability) and functionally non-specific criteria, such

as 'attitude' (acceptability). The most important among the latter
are the interviewer's 'gut feeling', the candidates' 'general manner'
and 'attitude', their appearance and presentation, their employment
record, and their age and family situation, a married man with two
kids and a mortgage being regarded as a reliable and stable worker.
Looking at the use of 'word-of-mouth', recruitment through personal
contacts, there are several reasons why employers use this strategy:
the reputation of the person doing the recommending serves as a
guarantee for the new recruit, the mediator will, in order to protect
his/her reputation, help to keep the new recruit under control, and
it is part of a particular kind of 'family firm' industrial relations
policy. The recruitment process is centrally concerned with the
maintenance of organisational control and 'the search for the settled,
habituated worker who will be at his or her machine or desk as and
when he or she is required to be' (ibid., p.26).

Although there are dangers in extrapolating research fundings from
elsewhere, (2) it seems reasonable to suggest that if employers do
categorise potential workers on a continuum from the rough to the
respectable (or the disreputable to the reputable), this categorisa-
tion will influence their ascription of attributes such as 'responsibility' and 'reliability', both important components of the folk
model of respectability. On the basis of speech, dress and 'manner',
it is probable that the lads, for example, might often be regarded
as a 'bad bet', employment-wise, for all but those jobs in which
high labour turnover is accepted as inevitable or desirable.

We are now better placed to understand the earlier finding that,
although the Ordinary Kids did poorly in terms of formal education,
they experience much greater labour market continuity than the Lads
and are less likely to be in unskilled jobs. The explanation is
relatively simple: the Ordinary Kids are not much better off than
the Lads in terms of functionally specific (i.e. educational)
criteria, but they are preferred by employers on the basis of
functionally non-specific criteria of acceptability. Returning to
Figure 4.1, some of the visual cues which recruiters might use to
distinguish between job applicants - clothes, tattoos, etc. - are
immediately apparent. Other cues might include speech style, non-
verbal behaviour such as 'manner', criminal record and employment
history. The Citizens, in their turn, are better endowed in
employers' eyes with the attributes of suitability and acceptability.

That the Citizens use word-of-mouth recruitment channels more
than the Ordinary Kids, who themselves use them more than the Lads
(Table 6.6), can now also be explained. If personal recommendation
concerns both the reputation of the job-seeker and the recommender -
the mediator within or with access to the organisation - then this
is just what might be expected: the Citizens are more 'recommendable'
than the Ordinary Kids, who are, similarly, more reputable than the
Lads. The case study of recruitment into TransInternational
Electronics in the next chapter provides an illustration of these
processes at work; this case study also demonstrates clearly the
manner in which informal word-of-mouth information networks effectively
serve to extend the internal labour market outside the formal
boundaries of the organisation.

That employers in Northern Ireland are similar to their counterparts elsewhere is indicated by the results of a small survey of

employers in Castleowen which I carried out in Spring 1979. (3)
In response to the question, 'When you are interviewing somebody
about a job, how important, to you, are their general appearance
and manner of speaking?', thirty (64 per cent) of the forty-seven
employers who responded thought these factors were important for
all jobs. The remaining seventeen thought them important for
clerical work or jobs dealing with the general public. Some idea
of the relative importance of educational qualifications as selection
criteria for these employers can be gained from Table 8.1.

TABLE 8.1 Educational qualifications required by employers:
Castleowen employers sample

Educational standards required by employer	Clerical	Type of job Craft apprentice	Technician apprentice
GCE 'O' levels	18 (35%)	8 (24%)	14 (61%)
CSEs or RSA Typing	21 (41%)	9 (26%)	3 (13%)
Result in internal test	8 (16%)	11 (32%)	4 (17%)
No educational standard required	4 (8%)	6 (18%)	2 (9%)
Totals	51 (100%)	34 (100%)	23 (100%)

    Two things should be borne in mind in interpreting this table.
First, some employers who did not employ the relevant categories of
workers did not complete this part of the questionnaire. Other
employers specified more than one criterion for a particular kind
of job. Thus this table should not be read, for example, as meaning
that 41 per cent of these employers rely upon CSE or RSA (Royal
Society of Arts) examination results when recruiting clerical workers.
At best, Table 8.1 indicates approximately the relative weight
attached by these employers to educational criteria. Second, no
distinction was made between the grades possible for each qualifica-
tion; for example, a Grade 1 CSE is nominally equivalent to an 'O'
level pass, and a Grade 5 CSE is a 'below average' result. However,
there is reason to believe that local employers do not usually
differentiate between the finer points of examination grades,
regarding an 'O' level as superior to a CSE whatever the grade
(Holmes, 1979). Such a distinction in the questionnaire would,
therefore, have been meaningless.
    Bearing this in mind, my data supports Ashton and Maguire's
finding that there are wide variations in the educational standards
required by employers and that scope remains for the unqualified
school-leaver to find, for example, an apprenticeship (1980, p.150);
this is regardless of the weight which may be attached to qualifications by school-leavers themselves (i.e. Corrigan, 1979, pp.83-6).
Judging from the Castleowen employers' responses concerning 'general
appearance and manner of speaking', educational qualifications,
functionally specific criteria suitability, at best act as critical

parameters within which discretionary factors, functionally non-
specific criteria concerned with the prediction of acceptability,
come into play. (4)

In the absence of a detailed ethnography of the interview room,
I can only speculate about these discretionary factors in the case
of employers in Castleowen and Belfast. However, that local employers
do use criteria of acceptability similar to those of employers
elsewhere is borne out by the case study material in Chapter 9.
If the factors which employers look for in recruits are as much
related to attitude as to ability - although, given the concern with
control at the work place, it is doubtful whether these criteria are
really this distinct - it is likely that a job candidate's life-style
as interpreted by the interviewer on the basis, for example, of
dress, speech or employment history, will be a significant factor
in recruitment decisions. Recent research has shown that the
distinction drawn by managers and supervisors between the 'best' and
'worst' young workers, in terms of personal behaviour and attitudes,
influences not only recruitment decisions but also the young worker's
subsequent career development (Industrial Training Research Unit,
1979).

This is one of the senses in which the labour market can be
thought of as a social field within which social identities,
including occupational identities, are ascribed to individuals -
and, at the aggregate level, to distinct collectivities - in a
cumulative labelling process not dissimilar to that described by
some sociologists of deviancy in their accounts of the acquisition
of criminal identities and the production of crime statistics
(Downes and Rock, 1971; Kitsuse and Cicourel, 1963). It must, of
course, also be understood that respectable identities are no less
socially constructed than their deviant counterparts, and in a
similar fashion (Douglas, 1970).

The role of word-of-mouth recruitment and information networks
in the labour market in the reproduction of life-style differences
now becomes clearer. Since these transactions depend upon the
production and maintenance of social reputations, respectability
and reputability are at the very heart of the process. Although,
as suggested in Chapter 6, the use of word-of-mouth recruitment may
vary from industry to industry, this is another sense in which the
processes of the labour market are centrally implicated in the
ongoing practical differentiation of class and life-style.

From the discussion so far, it should be clear that distinctions
apart from those of life-style and class may be constructed in
this fashion. Age categories are explicit in, among other things,
the model of the ideal employee as the 'married man with two kids
and a mortgage', and there are many other common-sensical distinctions about where young workers should or should not be employed.
Gender distinctions are reproduced in this fashion, as is clear
from accounts of the allocation of work (and wages) as either
'masculine' or 'feminine' (Armstrong, 1982; Coyle, 1982; Pollert,
1981, pp.91-108), and ethnic categorisations are similarly made
manifest and invested with practical significance in the workplace
(Jenkins, 1982b). In all of these cases, the process is essentially
the same. What passes for 'social reality' in the workplace - and
the wider labour market - is put together in the routine production

of social interaction in a variety of strategic situations, in this
case recruitment into employment. Although the process of the job-
search is important, given the effective control of recruitment
decisions exercised by employers, and, to a lesser degree, trade
unions, they effectively have the power to make their models of
reality count as the major reality. This is one illustration that
the reproduction of the social order is a contingent product of
competent social interaction (cf. Giddens, 1981b, pp.64-8).

INDUSTRIES IN THE LABOUR MARKET

Another aspect of the demand side of the market is the institutional
procedures for hiring and firing workers in different industries or
organisations, some of which I have touched upon in the first section.
Organisational differences existing between industries and enterprises may be reflected in their hiring, firing and other employment
practices. If so, young workers in different industrial and
organisational settings should have different experiences of the
labour market and employment. The nature of some of these
differences for apprentices may be seen in Table 8.2, and for manual
workers in Tables 8.3 and 8.4. (5) These figures indicate (although

TABLE 8.2 Apprenticeship experience by industry: Lads, Ordinary
Kids and Citizens

Industry	Terminated before completion	Apprenticeship experience Completed or under way with original employer	Completed or under way having changed employers (a)	Totals
Construction	8 (42%)	8 (42%)	3 (16%)	19 (100%)
Engineering	3 (27%)	8 (73%)	–	11 (100%)
All others (b)	3 (27%)	5 (45%)	3 (27%)	11 (100%)
Totals	14 (34%)	21 (51%)	6 (15%)	41 (100%)

(a) This excludes transfers from a GTC apprenticeship to an
    employer: these are enumerated under 'with original employer'.
(b) The following trades: book-folder, butcher, baker, printer and
    wood machinist.

due to the small number of cases the data must be interpreted with
caution) that there are differences between industries with respect
to the way in which young workers experience employment.
     For example, it appears that apprentices in the construction
industry are more likely to fail to finish their apprenticeship or
change employers before completion of their training than their
peers in engineering. Similarly, young manual workers of all grades
in the construction industry appear to be more vulnerable to
dismissal due to misconduct than those in engineering (Table 8.3)
and their jobs, on average, tend to be shorter in duration (Table 8.4).

TABLE 8.3 Manual workers' reasons for quitting employment by
industry: Lads, Ordinary Kids and Citizens

Reason for quitting job	Construction	Engineering	Other manufacturing
Personal dissatisfaction	12 (28%)	8 (31%)	13 (23%)
To take up a new job	8 (18%)	5 (19%)	11 (19%)
Redundant or 'paid off'	7 (16%)	7 (27%)	11 (19%)
Sacked for misconduct	14 (33%)	3 (12%)	14 (26%)
Other reasons (a)	1 (2%)	3 (12%)	8 (14%)
Not known	1 (2%)	-	-
Totals	43 (100%)	26 (100%)	57 (100%)

(a) Includes medical reasons.

The data in Table 8.4 indicate that, in the industries under
discussion, two kinds of employment experience are evident.   Those
sample members who were working in these industries in June 1979
had, on average, been working longer in their jobs than those whose
experience in each industry lay in the past or who were unemployed
at the time.   This may indicate either a pattern of occupational
stratification within each industry, between those jobs which are
established and long-term, protected by union-management agreements
or their centrality in the production process, and those jobs which
are short-term, unprotected and peripheral, (6) or differences in
the behaviour of workers within each industry, between the 'stable',
'responsible' or 'steady' workers, and those who are 'unreliable'
and 'badly motivated'.

TABLE 8.4 Mean job length for manual workers by industry: Lads,
Citizens and Ordinary Kids (a)

	Construction	Engineering	Other manufacturing	Combined mean
Previous jobs (weeks)	34.0	39.4	28.3	33.7
Present jobs (weeks)	65.8	156.9	53.6	92.1

(a) This table excludes short-term YOP and GTC courses.

Which interpretation is more correct is not immediately apparent.
While there is an apparent tendency for longer-lasting manual jobs
to be in skilled manual occupations (Table 8.5), the manual jobs
lasting a year or more held by the Lads and the Ordinary Kids are

TABLE 8.5 Manual jobs lasting 52 weeks or more by industry and occupation: Lads, Ordinary Kids and Citizens

Type of job	Construction	Engineering	Other manufacturing
Unskilled manual	2 (20%)	8 (44%)	8 (57%)
Skilled manual	8 (80%)	10 (56%)	6 (43%)
Totals	10 (100%)	18 (100%)	14 (100%)

evenly distributed between skilled and unskilled occupations for each sample. The difference between skilled manual and unskilled jobs is wholly attributable to the six skilled manual jobs held by Citizens. That none of the long-term manual jobs held by the Citizens are unskilled is unsurprising, given their low number of unskilled jobs: of the twenty-eight jobs held by the Citizens, only five were unskilled, four of these being temporary jobs.

TABLE 8.6 Manual jobs lasting 26 weeks or less by industry and occupation: Lads, Ordinary Kids and Citizens (a)

Type of job	Construction	Engineering	Other manufacturing
Unskilled manual	23 (70%)	14 (87%)	39 (97%)
Skilled manual	10 (30%)	2 (12%)	1 (2%)
Totals	33 (100%)	16 (100%)	40 (100%)

(a) Excludes short-term YOP and GTC courses.

A less ambiguous picture emerges from the data on jobs lasting six months or less, which are concentrated in the unskilled occupations and, bearing in mind the differences in sample size, among the Lads (Tables 8.6 and 8.7). This data does not, however, allow us to judge between the two possible explanations outlined above. The Lads may be in unskilled occupations because of their 'unreliability'; it is just as possible that their 'unreliability', as manifest in frequent job-changing, is the result of a predilection for, or tendency to obtain, unskilled jobs, many of which are short-term or unstable. Referring back to the discussion in Chapter 6, it seems likely that both factors, occupational organisational differences and differences between the life-styles, combine to produce this situation and only serve to reinforce each other. In Liebow's words, 'The job fails the man and the man fails the job' (1967, p.63). Furthermore, given the importance of employment history as an indicator of 'stability', there may be a vicious

circle in which workers with a history of job-changing are more
likely to be recruited to volatile or short-lived jobs. (7)

TABLE 8.7 Manual jobs lasting 26 weeks or less by sample and
occupation: Lads, Ordinary Kids and Citizens (a)

Type of job	Lads	Ordinary Kids	Citizens
Unskilled manual	44 (92%)	31 (77%)	1 (100%)
Skilled manual	4 (8%)	9 (22%)	-
Totals	48 (100%)	40 (100%)	1 (100%)

(a) Excludes short-term YOP and GTC courses.

Returning to my original point of departure, it is apparent that
there are important differences in the labour market experiences of
workers in the industries under discussion. The data are misleading
in some respects, however. In Table 8.5 in particular, the pattern
of distribution of jobs lasting over a year is more complex than is
apparent at first sight. First, of the unskilled manual jobs in the
engineering industry, five out of a total of eight are accounted for
by one factory, TransInternational Electronics. Second, in the
'other manufacturing' column in that Table, three of the six skilled
jobs and two of the eight unskilled jobs are in printing, 35 per
cent of the total. Nevertheless, the three industrial categories
may be said to exhibit differences in the experience of employment
they offer to the worker. Engineering, for example, offers the
likelihood of more long-term and fewer short-term jobs. In this
respect, construction and 'other manufacturing' are apparently
equivalent, although jobs in construction are apparently slightly
longer on average (Table 8.3). The differences between industries
for the sample members may be summarised thus: 33 (58 per cent)
of jobs in construction lasted six months or less, compared to 16
(41 per cent) in engineering and 40 (57 per cent) in 'other
manufacturing'. By contrast, 10 (18 per cent) of their jobs in
construction lasted a year or more, as against 18 (46 per cent) in
engineering and 14 (20 per cent) in 'other manufacturing'.

I have argued that labour market continuity is to some extent a
product of industrial organisational differences. Although the
data does not permit the specification of what the relevant
institutional factors and their significance might be, this argument
is in broad agreement with other studies which stress the important
effect of organisational differences upon the young person's
experience of work (Bazalgette, 1978; Ryrie and Weir, 1978; Venables,
1967). In the case studies in the next chapter the topic will be
explored in greater detail.

In the first section of this chapter I discussed another factor
which combines to produce labour market continuity, i.e. the
selection decisions of employers. In the next section, I shall
examine the role of recruitment decisions and institutional arrange-
ments in defining the impact for young workers of state intervention
in the labour market.

THE STATE IN THE LABOUR MARKET: YOUTH OPPORTUNITIES?

As youth unemployment became ever more a publically acknowledged
'problem' in the mid-1970s, state intervention in this area of the
labour market increased, and, in its nature, became more direct. (8)
Following the Holland Report (Manpower Services Commission, 1977)
these interventions were centralised and expanded to form the Youth
Opportunities Programme (YOP). (9)
   A similar policy initiative occurred in Northern Ireland, with
the local Youth Opportunities Programme being developed by the
Northern Ireland Department of Manpower Services at about the same
time as YOP in Great Britain.   In 1982 the Youth Training Programme
(YTP) replaced YOP, once again Northern Irish initiatives closely
following British developments.   This chapter will restrict its
comments to YOP and remain in the present tense; it seems unlikely
that the basic nature of the Programme has altered much.
   In certain respects the two Youth Opportunities Programmes are
different.   Building as it does upon a longer established pattern
of state job creation and training policies, YOP in Northern Ireland
is more concerned with off-the-job training and places less emphasis
upon work experience on employers' premises (Rees, 1980, p.59;
Study Group, 1978, p.44).   As a result of the greater emphasis on
training, the Department of Education for Northern Ireland is
centrally involved in YOP and some of the schemes it is responsible
for, such as Youthways, (10) have no immediate equivalent in the
rest of the UK.   In other respects, however, particularly in the
importance placed on the motivation of the youth workforce and the
hierarchical organisation of YOP provision, the two Programmes have
much in common (cf. Centre for Contemporary Cultural Studies, 1981,
pp.228-40; Cohen, 1982; Davies, 1981, pp.7-8; Frith, 1980).   In
this section I shall briefly describe the organisation of YOP
provision in Northern Ireland during the period 1977 to 1979 and
sketch out the availability of YOP schemes for the young people of
Ballyhightown.
   According to the Department of Manpower Services, (11) the Youth
Opportunities Programme in Northern Ireland can be divided into
three levels: first, at the 'top', are training schemes (apprenticeships and Attachment Training), work experience/training schemes
come next (Enterprise Ulster, Young Help, Work Experience and Work
Preparation Units), and at the 'bottom' are work participation
training schemes (Youthways and Young Persons' Training Schemes in
Government Training Centres).   There are two things to note about
the programme as a whole before going on to consider individual
schemes within it.   First, the Programme descends from those courses
which are concerned with straightforward vocational training to
those which are oriented towards accustoming or habituating the
young person to participation in waged employment.   Second, the
official view is that the 'various scheme elements should be seen
as a hierarchy of opportunities providing for an upwards progression
which allows the acquisition of additional knowledge and skills'
(DMS YOP Unit, 1978, p.2).   It should, therefore, be possible for
the school-leaver to start off at the bottom level of the Programme
and work his/her way up.   Before discussing the realities of this
possible progression it is necessary to describe the Programme's
constituent schemes in greater detail.

Apprenticeship training constitutes the bulk of the straightforward training schemes. It falls into two major types of provision:
grants to employers for their own in-house training, and apprenticeship training programmes in Government Training Centres (GTCs). I
shall concern myself primarily with the latter. In GTCs apprenticeships can be served in engineering, construction or motor vehicle
repair trades. The latter are sponsored by the Road Transport
Industry Training Board; in the engineering and construction trades,
apprentices sponsored by firms through the Industrial Training
Boards get priority, followed by those recruited through the Careers
Service. Recruitment to these unsponsored places is the responsibility of an interview panel representing the GTC Management, the
Careers Service, local employers and trade unions. After the course,
which can vary from six months to a year, is completed, those
apprentices who are not sponsored by an employer are placed in
employment, usually by the GTC Management or the Careers Service.
Ideally, no one leaves a GTC Apprenticeship Course without a job
to go to, unless at their own request; unplaced apprentices are
kept on until a place has been found for them.

Coming to Attachment Training Schemes, these are twelve-month
courses in specific skills, either on an employer's premises, or in
a College of Further Education, for adults or young people. The
nature of the training and recruitment to individual schemes is a
matter of agreement between the employer and the Department of
Manpower Services.

Of the work experience/training schemes, I do not intend to say
very much about Enterprise Ulster, a direct labour job creation
organisation engaged in construction and public works, which employs
both adults and young people, or Work Experience on Employers'
Premises (WEEP). The latter is very similar to its counterpart in
Great Britain and, one presumes, similarly variable in the nature
and quality of its constituent schemes.

The Young Help Scheme has no counterpart elsewhere. In co-
operation with organisations in the social services field, this
scheme provides work experience for a period of up to twelve months
in the broad area of 'caring', for example assisting in day centres
for the elderly or play groups. In common with Enterprise Ulster
this scheme pays union-agreed wages which are considerably higher
than the standard YOP allowance. Recruitment to the scheme is via
the Careers Service and the local Young Help team leader.

Work Preparation Units (Rees, 1980, pp.62-79) are designed to
offer basic training in an environment which resembles a 'real'
workplace as closely as possible. The training period lasts up
to twelve months. WPUs vary in their organisation, managerial
style and specific goals inasmuch as they are set up and managed
by local, community-based management committees. Once again
recruitment to these Units, whilst based on referrals by the Careers
Service, is the responsibility of the local organisers or staff.

Finally, there are the work participation training schemes:
Youthways and Young Person's Training Courses. The latter are
thirteen week courses in Government Training Centres, which aim to
provide trainees with a basic familiarity with the 'practices and
disciplines of working life' (12) in construction, engineering or
textile work (such as stitching). The Youthways schemes are

organised by the Department of Education and run by local Colleges
of Further Education. Lasting fourteen weeks, and including brief
residential periods, these courses have 'the primary aim of meeting
the needs of unemployed young people who are unqualified, untrained
and unmotivated ... to give young people a more realistic assessment
of their aptitudes and abilities, enhance their self-confidence and
prepare them for the day when they may get the chance of a job'
(Department of Education, 1979, p.3). There are two things to note
about the Youthways courses: first, the stress which is placed upon
motivation, and second, the importance which the Department ascribes
to the need to modify the unrealistic models which the target
population of young workers have of their abilities. Part of the
latter objective, presumably, is preparation for unemployment,
'showing the young people that even at a time of high unemployment
there are many useful things to be done in personal leisure pursuits'
(ibid., p.17). In pursuing both of these goals, the courses are
concerned less with skill training than relatively unsophisticated
behaviour modification. Finally, the point is worth making that,
if the young people concerned are 'apathetic', without 'all
motivation for finding employment' and 'unattractive as prospective
employees' (ibid., p.1), then there is a real danger that interventions of this nature may only serve to stigmatise them in their
own minds and hence further limit their horizons. (13)

In this context it is worth recalling an incident which took
place in Ballyhightown Youth Centre. The local Youthways scheme
were using the building, on this occasion for a roller-skating
session, and I was standing watching and talking to two of the
course staff, a woman who had previously worked part-time in the
Centre and a woman I had been at school with. A number of the kids
were also standing with us. During a discussion of the course's
general objectives - and in full earshot of the kids - one of the
workers informed me that the course handbook specified that it was
for 'the lowest strata only'! And this on a course that is
'designed to give young people some idea of the world of work and
to improve their self-confidence' (Study Group, op.cit., p.44, my
emphasis).

Thus we can see the manner in which the Northern Ireland YOP
system is hierarchically structured, ascending from those courses
which are concerned with the functionally non-specific criteria of
acceptability (motivation) to the courses which impart the
functionally specific attributes of suitability (skill). However,
as has already been noted, the Programme is nominally organised in
such a way that progression up through this hierarchy is both
possible and desirable.

On closer examination, this official model of YOP turns out to
be something of a fiction. Looking at the document in which the
possibilities for progression are most clearly spelled out (DMS
YOP Unit, 1978), it is clear that, for example, recruitment into
the 'top level' apprenticeship schemes is unlikely to occur either
after the initial intakes of each year or after the candidate is
older than about sixteen-and-a-half. Interviews with careers
officers, the Industrial Liaison Officer at the local FE College
and GTC staff indicate quite unambiguously that this is the case.
(14) There is, therefore, little likelihood that an individual

will be able to progress to apprenticeship training via other YOP courses; furthermore, due to the high proportion of apprenticeship places which are taken up by sponsored apprentices, the number of places available to YOP candidates is strictly limited anyway. Thus, although there is progression possible between the work participation training and work experience/training levels of YOP, progression into the training level from within YOP is more unlikely. In this respect the Youth Opportunities Programme in Northern Ireland is even more hierarchically organised than might at first appear to be the case.

Looking at the availability of YOP schemes for the young people of Ballyhightown, we find the whole of the Programme represented. The local Government Training Centre runs apprenticeship courses and Young Person's courses in engineering and construction, the Further Education College has a Youthways course and puts on Work Preparation courses (although these are not a part of YOP inasmuch as no training allowance is paid) and there is a local Young Help team in Castleowen. In addition, Attachment Training and Work Experience placements are available. The only form of YOP provision which is not represented in Castleowen is a Work Preparation Unit. As the local employment scene contracts, YOP - or YTP as it is now - is becoming ever more important as a source of pseudo-employment for local school-leavers. (15)

In this section I have sought to describe the hierarchical structuration of the Youth Opportunities Programme and the manner in which the notions of suitability (skill) and acceptability (motivation) are built in to the institutional organisation of state intervention in the labour market. Recruitment decisions are also important, although constraints upon space demand that they have not been given the attention they deserve. For example, although careers officers may operationalise models of 'need' and 'deprivation' in their selection decisions, this tendency is more than counter-balanced by the fact that employers' models of acceptability and suitability influence, either directly or indirectly, final recruitment to many YOP places. In the case of Work Experience schemes, the choice is actually made by the employer, on the basis of the criteria which I have discussed earlier in this chapter. Less obviously perhaps, recruitment to places on GTC schemes is mainly influenced by the fact that GTC managers and instructors have their own informal placement networks which spread throughout the local labour market. They are not easily going to accept recruits who may be difficult to place or who may become an embarrassment to them once they have been placed. Their reputation as providers of labour to local employers is at stake here and the emphasis once again is on the search for the 'stable', 'reliable' young worker. (16) As one member of the local GTC staff told me, 'If a boy's not managing we try to terminate his course. We try to only send out good boys.' Thus are the routine allocation procedures and patterns of the capitalist labour market reproduced within the institutions of state intervention in that market.

In this chapter I have not approached the labour market as a more or less mechanical system which regulates wage rates and allocates workers to jobs, as in the conventional models of neo-classical

economics. Instead I have tried to demonstrate some of the ways in
which the processes by which the market is routinely socially
constructed might contribute to the production and reproduction of
life-style, and hence class, differences. In particular, I have
highlighted the importance of decision-making by recruiters, and
the significance of organisational differences within and between
industries. Both of these factors, selection decisions and
institutional organisation, are, for example, central to any understanding of state intervention in the market for youth labour.
In the next chapter case study material will be used in a more
detailed discussion of the issues raised here with respect to three
specific industries.

Chapter 9

'IT'S NOT WHAT YOU KNOW...'

In the previous chapters, I have argued that the differences between
the life-styles, as represented by the three samples, with respect
to their experience of the labour market and work, are not simply a
reflection of their own cultural orientations. Three other factors
have been implicated in the production and reproduction of life-
style differences: organisational differences between occupations,
the institutional patterns of particular industries and the practice
of employers in the recruitment process.

In order to reach a more detailed understanding of the manner in
which these factors arise from, and feed back upon, the routine
production of day-to-day interaction, I shall present case studies
from each of the three industrial sectors discussed in the previous
chapter: the building industry (construction), the printing
industry ('other manufacturing') and a light engineering factory.
I am examining a single organisation within engineering because
much of the industry is made up of fairly large units in which the
internal labour market is important. This makes anything but the
most superficial examination of any section of engineering impractical.
As it is, the priorities and practical constraints of fieldwork
necessitated that these case studies be less detailed than I would
have liked.

The case studies also illustrate the salience of different
organisational features: small firms with low levels of unionisation
(building), small firms with high levels of unionisation (printing),
and medium to large firms with high levels of unionisation
(engineering). In the language of labour market economics they can
be classified as examples of different types of labour market. The
building industry is intermediate between an enterprise market,
where 'the criteria governing entry to an establishment are fairly
responsive to external market conditions' and a competitive market
in which 'some jobs are not contained within well-defined
administrative units and for which the process of allocating and
pricing occurs in a more or less competitive fashion' (Doeringer and
Piore, 1971, pp. 3, 4). The printing industry, however, approximates
to a craft market, in which 'the major problems of internal allocation
are those of preparing apprentices or trainees to be journeymen and
of moving groups of workers of roughly equal skill and rank among

jobs of short duration' (ibid., p.4), while the light engineering
factory I shall discuss exhibits many of the features of an internal
labour market, 'an administrative unit such as a manufacturing plant,
within which the pricing and allocation of labour is governed by a
set of administrative rules and procedures' (ibid., pp.1-2). (1)
As the case studies unfold, however, it should be apparent that, at
best, these are very imprecise categories with which to organise
the material.

CONSTRUCTION: THE BUILDING INDUSTRY

In the previous chapter, construction was characterised as typified
by less stable apprenticeships, shorter than average jobs, and a
greater likelihood of dismissal for misconduct than the other
industries considered. The Northern Irish construction industry is
predominantly a small-firm industry; in 1976, 5 per cent of those
active in the industry as a whole were classified as 'working
principals'. In the building sector (i.e. 'house construction',
'other building' and 'repair and maintenance – houses and buildings')
small firms are more common than in civil engineering: 7 per cent
as opposed to 2 per cent of the work force are 'working principals'
(Department of Manpower Services, 1978, p.17). In August 1977,
63 per cent of firms in the construction industry in Norther Ireland
employed under twenty-five people: a further 30 per cent employed
between 25 and 99 workers (ibid., p.15). (2) In September 1976,
84 per cent of those employed in construction were employed in the
building sector (ibid., p.15).
     The distribution of labour within each sector, building and
civil engineering, is also different. The figures for 1976 are as
follows: civil engineering, 28 per cent craftsmen and 50 per cent
labourers; building, 47 per cent craftsmen and 29 per cent labourers
(ibid., p.17). In this section I concentrate upon apprenticeships
in the building industry, an industry with many small businesses
under the immediate control of owner-managers employing a high
percentage of tradesmen.
     Concerning unionisation, it is difficult to provide a quantified
picture of the industry. However, in the words of one union official,
'There's very poor unionisation in the industry in general ... the
smaller the company the worse it is. It's a problem, with workers
always moving about the place and not enough union organisers.'
As we have seen in the case studies in Chapter 7, there is much
word-of-mouth recruitment in the building trade. However, due to
the organisational looseness and geographic dispersal of building
sites, many jobs result from casual inquiries by job-seekers
'walking around and asking'.
     When asked about apprenticeships, those working in the industry
to whom I spoke cited the following reasons for the insecurity of
apprenticeships, although the weight accorded to each factor varied
from person to person. First, in an industry with a high level of
geographic mobility there may be problems for employees in an area
such as Belfast, with well-defined ethnic territories. As an
official of the Construction Industry Training Board said,
     What you've got to realise is that we're a gypsy industry, a

romany industry.... Maybe a firm starts an apprentice and he's
working, for example, on the power station at Kilroot, and then
two years later that contract ends and the apprentice is maybe
expected to move to another site.... It might be up the Falls or
on the Shankill Road. (3) Well, given the state of affairs in
Northern Ireland at the present time he mightn't want to go, what
with the security situation and the like. So you see, unfortunately
in the present situation in Northern Ireland we've got instead of
horses for courses, horses for particular sites.

Second, the economy of the building industry is important. Many
firms live from contract to contract and their vulnerability in
recession is heightened by cash-flow difficulties. In many respects,
construction may be described as a 'debt economy', the contractor
being obliged to purchase materials and labour before interim payments
are made, a system which can result in the accumulation of severe
debts. However, it is not clear in what way construction differs
from many manufacturing industries, whose apprenticeships appear to
be more secure, in this respect.

Next, there are the fluctuations in demand for labour due to the
developmental cycle of each contract and site: first of all,
labourers dig and pour the foundations and bricklayers erect the
shell of the building, following which joiners do the joists, window-
frames and roof-frame. Then the roof-tilers, plasterers, floor-
tilers and -layers, electricians and plumbers all add their respective
touches. Finally, the joiners, glaziers and painters do the
finishing off. Unless a company has a lot of work in hand, it may
have a substantial percentage of its labour force idle at any
particular moment. This is an encouragement for sub-contracting
and a possible disincentive to employers to hire apprentices: 'It's
cheaper for the contractor not to employ people.' These routine
fluctuations in demand for labour are compounded by the seasonal
nature of much building work; both help to encourage a casual
employment relationship.

Fourth, the absence of formal or informal institutional procedures
specifying the rights and duties of employers and apprentices is
important. In this respect, the most highly organised sections of
the building industry are electrical contracting and plumbing, both
of which are organised through their respective Joint Industry
Boards. These are national organisations set up by employers and
trade unions to regulate the industry and do away with ad hoc site
agreements about pay and holidays. Each JIB has a number of regional
boards, with one for Northern Ireland. According to an official of
the EEPTU, (4) in this, the most organised area of the building
industry, only about 50 electrical contractors in the province (out
of a probable total of about 300 firms) are affiliated to the JIB
for the electrical contracting industry: 'They won't join ... they
won't even spend the money on the Electrical Contractor's Association,
their own employers' association.'

The JIB is also the registration body for apprentices in electrical
contracting. There is no statutory requirement for an employer to
register an apprentice and the apprentice cannot do so himself; it
must be via his employer. The registration of an apprentice imposes,
through a deed of apprenticeship, obligations upon both parties and
the apprentice's parents. Lack of work, for example, is not regarded

as sufficient cause for paying an apprentice off; similarly, if the
employer is bankrupt, the JIB's regional Apprentice Secretary will
attempt to place the apprentice elsewhere.

However, given the large number of unaffiliated contractors, there
is the problem described by this union official as the 'bucket shop'.
He claims to deal with at least one apprentice a week who has been
paid off before the end of his time, wanting to join the union to
get some belated protection. The EEPTU has on two occasions taken
large advertisements in the 'Belfast Telegraph' warning school-
leavers and their parents of the pitfalls of unregulated apprenticeships. Although, in law, 'cowboy' employers cannot prevent their
apprentices from joining a union, there are, of course, many ways
in which they can discourage them.

The casual organisation of building apprenticeships is matched
by a low level of participation in vocational education. The union
official and Training Board officer who are quoted above agreed that
electrical contracting is the most comprehensively organised sector
in this respect, about 50 per cent of its apprentices taking City
and Guilds courses. At the other extreme, apparently only about
5 per cent of joinery apprentices take examinations.

Another factor affecting apprenticeships is that in the 'wet
trades', plastering, bricklaying and painting, much work is done
on a labour-only sub-contracting (LOSC) basis, also known as 'the
lump', 'the grip' and 'priced work'. The main contractor hires a
LOSC gang to do a job for a pre-arranged price, regardless of the
labour time involved, the contractor supplying the materials.
Without wishing myself to enter the argument surrounding this
practice, i.e. its effect on the quality of the work done, the
undermining of the workers' legal rights at work or the effect on
trade unions, (5) many people in the industry see it as a highly-
paid distraction for second- and third-year apprentices, who are
usually capable of doing the work demanded of them (see, for example,
Jim Mitchell's case study in Chapter 7). Some employers blame
this system for a shortage of skilled 'suitable' men (Schofield
and Carlisle, 1978, p.10). Many of these gangs work illegally,
paid 'cash-in-hand' while in receipt of supplementary or unemployment
benefit, evading income tax and National Insurance contributions.
Apprentices lose any guarantee of ever formally finishing their
training and all protection against redundancy or industrial injury.
There is evidence to implicate employers of collusion in and
encouragement of this practice (P.A. Management Consultants, 1977).
One civil servant, who declined to be identified, diagnosed first-
year apprentices leaving Government Training Centres, as particularly
vulnerable: 'You see, one of the problems is that the training
they're getting in the GTCs is so good it makes other apprenticeships look a bit of a farce. They're nearly as good as tradesmen
after one year in the GTC.'

Finally, many employers vocally bemoan the poor quality of
apprentices, many of whom are apparently 'unfit' to complete their
training (Schofield and Carlisle, op.cit., p.13). I am sceptical
about the level of their concern about this; in the words of the
'Bulletin' of the Federation of Building and Civil Engineering
Contractors (N.I.),

From time to time members complain about the quality of boys

coming out of Government Training Centres to be placed in the
Industry to complete their apprenticeship.... Unfortunately,
however, over recent months it has become increasingly difficult
to obtain sufficient employers' representatives who are prepared
to devote their time to attending Apprentice Selection Panels.
It is not unreasonable to suggest, therefore, that employers are
hardly in a position to grumble about the quality of the boys
offered to them, if they are not prepared at the outset to
devote a little time to selecting suitable boys. ('Federation
Bulletin', 1978, No.1, p.2)

Examining the experience of the Lads, the Ordinary Kids and the
Citizens in the light of the above, of the 8 apprentices who did
not complete their training, 4 were in electrical contracting,
2 were plumbers and 2 plasterers. One of the latter was Jim Mitchell
(see Chapter 7); his apprenticeship foundered through a series of
rows with his bosses. Three of the others left their apprenticeships
for similar reasons; one because his employer wouldn't send him to
day-release classes and he thought he'd be better off making more
money 'at the labouring', one was 'under pressure from the boss
himself' and left because he couldn't put up with it any longer,
and the last was paid off while out 'on the sick' with asthma.

It was terrible. The management was bad ...//... I phoned them
up and the fella asked how long I'd be on the sick. I said I
didn't know and he said that he didn't know whether or not he
could keep the place open for me. I lost the head and said,
'All right, I'll come up and get my cards.'

Of the other four, one was 'doing a double', signing on as unemployed
while working as an electrician's apprentice, a job which eventually
petered out. Two of the other apprenticeships were terminated
because of bad timekeeping and the other apprentice left work due
to domestic reasons.

Looking back at the reasons for quitting employment of our
sample members (Table 8.3), all of whom were in building, in possible
contradiction to the above reasons for apprenticeship instability
in this industry, only 15 per cent of these quits were due to
redundancy or lack of work. Taking the three factors, 'personal
dissatisfaction', 'to take up a new job' and 'sacked for misconduct',
as indicators of difficulties experienced by the young worker at
work, in that they imply some problem in the work situation, then
79 per cent of the sample members who left jobs in building did so
for these reasons. Seven were dismissed or left because of personal
difficulties with management or supervisory staff, 16 per cent of
the total number of quits. In small firms, the role of senior
management in these confrontations may be very personal.

I was sacked. I'd had a couple of days off. There was a mistake
on the sick line, it wasn't back-dated or something. The boss,
the owner himself, sacked me. 'Take yourself off', he said
...//... I hated it.... The foreman called the tradesmen by
their first names but the labourers by their surnames.

Thus, for these young workers, confrontations with authority are as
important a cause of job-loss in building as the economic uncertainties
of the trade. Weak trade unionism seems to be another factor. In
only one of the cases of dismissal or redundancy was there, to my
knowledge, union involvement.

The point is not, however, that relationships between employer and worker in building involve more conflict than in other industries.   That may be the case, but to demonstrate this requires more detailed research than was possible in this study. (6)   What I am arguing is that, in addition to factors intrinsic to the economic cycles of the building industry, the lack of recourse to institutional dispute procedures and, more important, the casual nature of the contract between management and worker, even for apprentices, makes disputes and difficulties more likely to lead to dismissal or voluntary quits.

THE PRINTING TRADE IN BELFAST (7)

The printing industry in the Belfast urban area is mainly made up of small businesses relying on a variety of kinds of labour, from the highly-skilled and expensive-to-train journeyman in the printing sector (characteristically male), to the 'semi-skilled' or unskilled machine operators in the box-making sector (typically female). For printers, compositors, linotype operators, etc., a union card, obtainable only after an apprenticeship, is a prerequisite of employment.   In a study dating from 1974, eight characteristics of the local industry were identified: the large number of small, family-owned firms, an increasing use of new technology, increasing specialisation by firms in particular areas of the trade, the industry's concentration in or around Belfast, management's confidence in the continuing expansion of their markets, the relatively high numbers of employers' and employees' groups and associations, a high degree of local ownership and control and the importance of trade unions in employment and manning decisions, including the level of apprentice intakes (Department of Manpower Services, 1974, p.6; Industrial Training Services, 1974, p.5).   A further characteristic of the industry mentioned in these reports is the high turnover of workers in certain sectors, particularly 'semi-skilled' or unskilled (women) operatives in packaging firms and companies specialising in books and magazines, and skilled (male) workers in the jobbing printing sector.   Since these are the areas of the trade in which the sample members working in printing are active, I shall confine my attention to them.

Recruitment to most printing apprenticeships in the area is co-ordinated by the Joint Apprenticeship Panel, set up by the employers' organisation, the Belfast Printing Industry Association, and the two major trade unions involved, the National Graphical Association (NGA) and the Society of Graphical and Allied Trades (SOGAT).   Apprenticeship levels for the coming year are decided in accordance with national agreements on journeymen-apprentice ratios and in consultation with local firms.   After written tests, candidates for which are attracted through school careers talks and newspaper advertisements and which all applicants sit, those youngsters who reach the required standard complete application forms and are informally matched up with particular employers.

Female applicants for printing apprenticeships are, as a Panel member told me, 'on a hiding to nothing, the employer's point of view being that it's expensive to train an apprentice just so that

when she's twenty-two or twenty-three she can up and get married and
that'll be the last thing they see of her.' (8) Printing is still
regarded as a 'man's trade' by most school-leavers anyway; in 1979
there were only four girls out of 79 applicants to the Panel.
Although the assessment procedure is formalised, once the papers
have been marked criteria of geographic location and ties of family
and friendship come into play to determine the actual recruitment
outcome.

Not all local firms belong to the employers' association, however;
52 of an estimated total of 80 firms were members in 1979, approximately 65 per cent. This leads to a significant amount of completely
informal recruitment. Some of these firms do approach the Panel for
the names of those who have passed the test, but the most frequent
recruitment channels are friends-of-friends, family ties and, more
rarely, newspaper advertisements.

There are very few 'black shops' or 'rat shops' (i.e. non-
unionised firms) in the industry, however. Once apprentices are
recruited, their training is relatively uniform, involving both
on-the-job training and further education at the local Art College,
leading to the relevant City and Guilds certificates.

In the finishing sector, predominantly book-binding, organised
by SOGAT and regarded as less skilled than the NGA-dominated
printing sector, recruitment is less formalised, relying on
recommendations by relatives and friends and newspaper advertisements.
There is less formal training and many women are employed; a
distinction is drawn between male book-binders, frequently recruited
through the Panel, and the nominally less skilled book-folders,
usually women. The work is in many respects the same, the men
taking more responsibility for setting up the machines. It is
only recently that there has been limited agreement that book-folding
be preceded by an apprenticeship, instead of a 'learnership' as
previously. This sector of printing is also strongly unionised,
SOGAT acting as an informal employment agency, mediating between
employers and job-seekers in the same way as the NGA does in its
sphere. Due to the important role of the unions in the printing
labour market there is a close fit between numbers of union members
and jobs, particularly in printing and finishing.

At the 'bottom' of the industry, packaging and box-making, the
situation is quite different. Unionisation is lower than elsewhere
and more unskilled labour is involved in the production process.
Unions play only a limited role in hiring and firing; female machine
operators are frequently recruited through the state employment
services, widely regarded as sources of cheap, unskilled workers.
(9)

Turning to the young workers I have been discussing, there are
nine individuals and ten jobs. One is a printer and male, two
girls are apprentice book-folders, and the remainder, five females
and a male, work, or have worked, in box-making. All six box-makers
worked or work for one of two firms, both notorious 'black shops'.
Five of the six found their jobs through the Careers Office; the
other girl started after one of the others 'put in a word' for her.
Only one of the six is still working in the industry. Two were
paid off by the same firm: 'They said the machines was broke.
They said they would send for us when the machines were fixed and

I'm still waiting for word.' One was sacked after nine weeks for bad
timekeeping, one girl left to go to another job, and the last girl
had an argument with the firm's owner because she was feeling sick
one day and he wouldn't let her go home. When she got home at the
end of the day, her father told her she wasn't going back to 'a
place like that'.

Of the two book-folders, one was recruited via a newspaper
advertisement, and one via her aunt, an ex-book-folder who used her
contacts in SOGAT to get her a job. The printer, who had finished
his apprenticeship by the time I interviewed him, was recruited
through the Apprenticeship Panel. All three were still in the
industry in June 1979; in the middle of July the printer, Johnny
McAndrew, left Belfast for a printing job in Holland. While this
information cannot confirm or deny the general picture outlined
above – the numbers are too small for that – its close agreement
with it does underline the significance of organisational differences
within printing for the work experience of manual workers in that
industry.

In order to flesh out my necessarily superficial account of the
printing industry, I shall now present a case study of one of the
book-folders. Susan Steenson, one of the Ordinary Kids, is
remembered by those who taught her at Ballyhightown Secondary School
as bright but something of a handful. Having spent an unhappy first
year at the local grammar school, she eventually left secondary
school with four '0' levels, four CSEs and some secretarial qualifications. On the Monday after her sixteenth birthday, in August
1977, she started work as an apprentice book-folder with a firm in
a town about sixteen miles away. Her aunt, an ex-mother-of-chapel,
(10) had had a word with one of the local SOGAT officials and he
found Susan an apprenticeship. The next sixteen months were
miserable; she was always finding excuses not to go into work.

> I hate it. The foreman lives with the forewoman and you have
> to lick the forewoman to keep in with the foreman, and he's
> a wee yuck and she imagines everyone fancies him so you get
> intimidated and picked on by both of them.... Didn't we nearly
> get the sack? The work itself is really boring, it's not my
> scene. There's bound to be something better than that to life.
> It doesn't take any brains, any half-wit cuckoo could do what
> I do ... you have to be really daft.

The incident mentioned next, when Susan and another girl were
sacked and reinstated, typifies the trivial but incessant difficulties
she felt herself subject to.

> The foreman told me to make a cup of tea, with Hazel, she's
> another apprentice. And you only do it as a favour, you don't
> have to. Well we refused, because you see whenever you do?
> You only get called a stupid bitch and bastard for cooking it
> wrong. They never even thank you. So he lost the head and told
> us to fuck away off home.... Anyway the union sorted it all
> out ...//... I'm on the sick now with a sore arm. That's because
> the auld bastard put me on another machine, it's a lot heavier
> like, for badness, after I wouldn't make the tea ...//... If I
> don't leave soon I'll crack up, so I will.

Susan asked the union official to find her a new job, closer to
home, but he refused, arguing that that would be 'giving in'. By

September 1978 she had started to search in earnest for jobs outside
printing, by and large looking for clerical jobs but prepared to
take anything she could get. She started to call in to the Careers
Office in Belfast.

They gave me this form for a newsagents' shop in Craigabann and
they said to go down any time. So we just went in and the woman
there said that they were on their break and I said that the
Careers Office said to come down any time and then she said that,
anyway, the vacancy was filled, so I just said, 'Aye, all right',
and walked out again.

In December 1978 she found a job in a shop in Glasnacree and
handed her notice in. Within a week the union official got to hear
of it through Susan's aunt and found her a place in another printing
firm, also in Glasnacree. In June 1979 she was still working there,
no more impressed by the demands that book-folding made upon her
but happy with her new employer and work-mates, many of whom she
knew from Ballyhightown. Once she had finished her training, she
intended, through SOGAT, to find a job in England. (11)

This discussion of the printing industry indicates that, for
our purposes, the main difference between building and printing
does not lie in a more rewarding experience of work for the employee
or better relationships between management and workers. The
difference lies in the institutional frameworks for hiring, training
and firing workers. These differences, I would suggest, reflect
the nature of the labour processes involved and the different
history of each industry. (12)

LIGHT ENGINEERING: TRANSINTERNATIONAL ELECTRONICS

Part of a large multi-national corporation, TransInternational's
factory at Priorville is a mile and a half from Ballyhightown.
The firm has a large personnel department with formal recruitment
procedures. Production, the assembly of electrical machinery of
a variety of kinds, relies upon a large workforce in the ambiguous
category of the 'semi-skilled', for example, wirers and assemblers.
In February 1979 their labour force consisted of approximately 120
craftsmen in the tool-room and the maintenance section, 160 to 180
technicians and engineers, 400 white collar workers and 1900
production workers and supervisory staff. The majority of the
firm's recruitment needs are for unskilled workers who can be cheaply
and quickly trained on site. In reflection, probably, of the notion
that women are better at detail and intricate work, most of the
assembly workers are women. As the case study of Ruth Simpson
illustrates (Chapter 7), the pressures of this kind of work may
be considerable. The recruitment procedures are, as we shall see,
more an attempt to recruit a stable, habituated workforce which
will present no supervisory problems than a response to the need
for workers with specific technical skills or knowledge.

The recruitment procedure, as explained to me by the plant's
Personnel Officer and Training Manager in February 1979, is as
follows. Decisions concerning projected manning levels and manpower
needs are taken by the local Manpower Controller. These decisions
are made in the light of the company's order books, orders which

originate in the first place from group headquarters in England,
and ultimately from higher corporate levels in Europe and the USA.
The Manpower Controller requisitions, in much the same way that
line managers requisition other factors of production, the required
workers from the Personnel Office, after the internal plant managers,
in consultation with foremen, section heads and supervisors, decide
what they need to fulfil production targets. This decision-making
process can, of course, work in reverse to shed workers, as happened
several years ago when other plants in the province closed down and
several hundred workers at Priorville were made redundant. (13)

If recruitment is authorised, Personnel posts internal advertisements for the job or jobs, for which any worker with more than six
months service may apply. If the job is not filled internally, the
Personnel Officer then goes through the files of current completed
application forms and sends for several people to interview. The
firm receives a steady stream of completed application forms for
employment in general, many delivered by hand with the name of a
relative, neighbour or friend currently employed by the firm included
in the personal details given on the form. The Personnel Officer
admitted that discrimination in favour of those with a contact
inside the factory gates might be exercised in deciding who to
interview. After this, however, she stressed that selection was
an impersonal and formal procedure: an interview, a medical examination (since much of the work is 'fiddly' and involves colour-coded
components, minimal eyesight standards are required) and a visit
to the shop-floor to allow the applicants to see what the job
entails. The final selection is made once the Personnel Officer
'has a chat' with the relevant foreman or supervisor.

This is the formal recruitment procedure at TransInternational.
However, of the eight sample members (14) who work or have worked
for the company, seven insist that somebody 'got them started'.
On re-examination of the official model of the procedure, there are
two strategic points at which informal, non-procedural factors
intervene to determine who actually gets hired: at the initial
stage of short-listing candidates and when the Personnel Officer
has her 'chat' with the foreman or supervisor. At both junctures,
informal connections, 'getting a word put in' or 'having someone
to speak for you', are important:

John Black (15)	International's the same as most places round here ... ninety per cent of it's through who you know. It's not what you know it's who you know and don't let anybody tell you anything else. I got hundreds started.
R.J.	But what about all the paper work? Interview panels and the rest?
John	D'you see all of that? It's just a big smoke-screen, that's all. You see, what happens is this. A requisition'll come down ...//... that comes from Personnel. At least it did when I was there, I don't know what it's like now but I don't think it has changed much. Anyway, say a requisition comes for six operators, well that goes up on the noticeboard - they have them all over the factory - and there's a lot

of wheeling and dealing goes on between foremen. One
foreman mightn't want Jimmy Brown to go to another
department because he's a good man, but maybe Jimmy Brown's
a bad timekeeper and had been giving me a lot of problems
so I'll bum him up and say he's a real cracker. So if
someone comes up to you and says what a good worker this
fella is, you begin to wonder, like.

R.J.   Well, that's recruitment from inside the factory. What
about, say, if you wanted to get your neighbour's lad
started, for example?

John   Well, that works the same way.... Now, I don't know if
I should be telling you this.... Why not? Sure I don't
care. A lot of the senior foremen would keep piles of
application forms in their office and they would go through
them and decide those that were suitable for an interview.... What you have to realise is that when International's
first came here, they wanted to make it a family affair.
And they succeeded ... it was all cousins and brothers and
uncles.... Another good one was, sometimes the manager
would want someone started and he'd come up to you and
say, 'D'you see so-and-so? He's a good man ... but it's
up to you now, whether you start him or not.' And that
way it was your fault if he turned out to be a dummy.
But most jobs you could train people for and besides, to
be honest, they didn't demand that much skill anyway, like.
It was in a few of the skilled jobs, where you needed men
with experience of that machine or something, that you'd
see a few strange faces creeping in.

This account has been denied by the company's representatives.
However, from the official account, and many accounts of past and
present employees, (16) there seems good reason to suspect that it
has some substance. One consequence of this informal recruitment
procedure is that, since it is situated in a predominantly protestant
area, the factory remains a mainly protestant institution. First,
most relatives and 'friends of friends' will be protestant, and
second, most catholics would think twice about applying for a job
anyway, certainly on the shopfloor. The firm is anxious to maintain
its existing good relationship with its workforce and the unions –
disputes are rare, productivity high and wage-round bargaining
usually smooth. Allowing its workforce to participate in recruitment
is a strategy for ensuring continued good labour relations. Any
large-scale recruitment of catholics would probably present problems.
(17)

The internal labour market is also important; of the eight sample
members, three were promoted after their initial recruitment. 'Who
you know' is important here as well. However, the manipulation of
personal contacts is never enough, in itself, to guarantee the
job-seeker success. Witness the three conversations with Tailor
Burton, recorded below.

(a) 13 February 1979:

Tailor Burton   'I'm starting in Internationals on Monday, so I
am.'

Denis Anderson 'How the fuck did you manage that? I have about
six forms in, so I have.'

Tailor	'But sure I've been putting in forms ever since I came out of borstal, so I have.'
Bobby Bothwell	'Are you starting though ... right enough?'
R.J.	'Did you have an interview then Tailor?'
Tailor	'No, sure I don't have to.... They put it through the Senior Foreman instead, it didn't go through the offices. You see, the brother's the secretary of the Social Club, so he is, and he spoke to the manager of the football team and he's the manager of the place, you know.... Anyway, he said I'd be all right.'
R.J.	'I don't see how that works. You have to go for an interview, so you do.'
Tailor	'Well they started two yesterday, so they did, and the brother, he said they were starting six fellas next week and that they'd probably send for me.'
Bobby	'You have to go for an interview but Tailor ... it's only a fucking formality though.'

(b) 19 February 1979:

Tailor	'I went for my interview in International's today, so I did.'
R.J.	'Well ... how did it go then?'
Tailor	'Well you see, there was four of us put in for the job and two of them already works there.'
R.J.	'They'd applied internally then?'
Tailor	'Aye ... I think it's all right because the fella that, you know ... took the interview, like, was the fella that took the form for me and he's over the football team, so he is, and I play for them, so I think it's all right. He said he'd send out word to me next week.... For fuck's sake, I had to go for a medical and all, so I did'.
R.J.	'What kind of job is it then?'
Tailor	'It's working right next to my brother ... I don't know exactly. It's sort of semi-skilled, working on a machine ... making plates or something.'

(c) 1 May 1979

R.J.	'How're you doing then, Tailor? Did you get that job in Internationals?'
Tailor	'I did not.... Someone from the darts team got it. I never got started after all ... it was some auld fella that used to work in the machine shop, he got it.'

These conversations, and John Black's account, provide further clues as to the function of recruitment by patronage for the company. Although apparently relying upon criteria irrelevant to the firm's labour requirements, i.e. 'who you know', the process remains one of selection. From the employer's point of view, the procedure achieves two important things cheaply and, we may suppose, relatively efficiently: first, it provides information, through the network of present employees, as to each applicant's acceptability, in terms of their reputation for 'reliability', and second, it places upon the worker thus hired an obligation to the person who 'put a word in'.

The recruit must ensure that the mediator will not be embarrassed. Furthermore, the mediator is obliged, if necessary, to enforce the new recruit's good behaviour. (18) As John Black said, 'it was your fault if he turned out to be a dummy'. Thus this case study bears out the brief analysis of word-of-mouth recruitment in Chapter 8. Informal recruitment methods may, of course, also form part of shop-floor struggles for greater influence over managerial decision-making. In Tailor's case, his long prison record and poor employment history (only 15 per cent of his time between leaving borstal in January 1978 and June 1979 was spent working), combined with his local notoriety as a 'tea leaf' (thief), might have seemed good reason not to risk employing him. His brother might very well not have wished to compromise his own position and reputation within the plant by seriously recommending Tailor. This, of course, is probably not how he represented his actions within the family. On the other hand, however, the particular job might already have had 'somebody else's name on it'.

That 'reliability' and co-operation are important to Trans-International is apparent if we look at two specific areas of recruitment. First, concerning young workers, the Personnel Officer told me, 'I fought a battle to get more school-leavers employed, against the opposition of the shop-floor and the foremen. I took in groups of school-leavers and learned by my mistakes. A block of school-leavers admitted all at once are more difficult to train and harder to discipline. It's youthful high spirits'. Seen as presenting a problem for supervision, young workers are now acceptable only in small numbers, taken on in ones and twos.

Second, the plant sometimes experiences temporary peaks in demand, to which 'housewives' shifts' or 'twilight shifts' are the solution. In February 1979 there were about fifty women, all ex-full-time workers, temporarily employed to work four evenings a week, from five to ten o'clock. The Training Manager explained the usefulness of this arrangement:

> From the management's point of view it's a godsend. They come in at five o'clock and work until ten and don't require any supervision from the foreman. They come in and they've had the kids all day and maybe want a break, and it gets them some pin money of their own.

The fact that these women work twenty hours a week, after a day's housework, belies the view that they work for 'pin money'. Although I do not doubt that many of these women do enjoy the chance to get out of the house, and that this may enhance their 'attitude to work', economic necessity is also a significant component of their 'reliability'. Both of these situations illustrate the management's underlying concern with control on the shop-floor.

Coming finally to disciplinary and firing procedures, those I spoke to in management were proud of the fact that, 'No one ever gets sacked from TransInternational.' The eight sample members bear this out: four were still employed by the firm in June 1979, having been there an average of 79 weeks; the other four, having worked there an average of 77 weeks, had quit for a variety of reasons. One, a fitter, was made redundant, (19) two young women left because they were pregnant and a third (Ruth Simpson) left because she didn't like the work. This happy state of affairs is rooted in two related areas of the organisation. First, informal recruitment acts as a screening device, ensuring that most recruits will 'fit in', and as an informal system of social control on the shop-floor. Second, the formal disciplinary procedure, with its hierarchy of verbal and written warnings, suspension and appeal, involving management and trade union representatives, is, apparently, little used. Given the existence of informal alternative channels of control it is probably little needed.

This case-study illustrates that although the printing industry and a factory such as TransInternational are, on the face of things, different, in many respects they have much in common. For example, they both rely on informal recruitment and screening procedures in which management, workers and trade unionists collude. In printing this is largely in order to maintain the supply of skilled workers in a carefully fostered situation of near scarcity, in TransInternational Electronics, this strategy is adopted in order to maintain smooth industrial relations and prevent the disruption of production. At the end of the day, regardless of the illusions of 'human relations' such as worker fulfilment, the goals of the capitalist organisation must be achieved.

In Chapters 8 and 9 I have examined aspects of the relationships between members of one class, employers – and, in mediation, their delegates (20) – and members of another class, workers. As such, the discussion has been about power and the social construction of capitalism and class society. In the labour market and the workplace it remains true that to all intents and purposes the 'balance of power', predicated upon a taken for granted relationship between labourer and capitalist, lies with the employer. This is particularly true in Northern Ireland, with its conservative working class and basically reformist trade union movement. (21) However, as these case studies have shown, the true exercise of this power lies in its never having to be demonstrated; this principle lies at the heart of the search for the relatively autonomous, habituated worker. Conformity to the demands of capitalism may, like virtue, be its own punishment; the reward of minor personal resistance, however, particularly in an area of high unemployment, may be a place in the dole queue. The material in these chapters underlines the need, in any discussion of the labour market and employment, to acknowledge that relationships predicated upon power and resistance, collective or individual, are never more than just below the surface of routine social interaction. The source of this power lies, in the first instance, in the axiomatic legitimation of a system of hierarchical and differentiating social practices and notions of property extending throughout the social field of social democratic capitalist society.

Thus the young worker's experience of work is a reflection not only of his or her personal characteristics. The outcome is also the product of the practices of employers or their delegates, and the organisational characteristics, both formal and informal, of specific industries, occupations and state institutions. In the labour market, the young person's experience is crucially bound up with the capitalist wage relationship and the fact that he or she

must seek work. From this stems the need for self-presentation in
the market place. It is in this ritual of self-presentation,
fundamentally imbalanced with respect to the comparative power of
the parties to the transaction, that the personal characteristics
of the job seeker intersect with the practices of recruiters and
the role-system of institutions in the social construction and
reproduction of life-styles and class. (22)

Chapter 10

DIFFERENT KINDS OF PEOPLE

In Chapter 1 I asked the question, 'What are the patterned differences within the young working class, and how are those distinctions produced and maintained?' In attempting to answer that question I have been concerned with the categories which classify and differentiate between young people in modern capitalist society, and the manner in which that differentiation is challenged or upheld in routine social interaction. The patterns of differences resulting from that process I refer to as life-styles. It is in the social construction of life-styles that the class system is conjured up as the contingent product of the mundane practices of 'everyday life'.

In Chapter 4 I described the way in which young people classify themselves in Ballyhightown as the lads, the ordinary kids and the citizens. This classification may be located along a moral continuum stretching from the 'rough' to the 'respectable' which has wide currency in the larger society outside the estate. In Chapters 5 and 6 I developed an analytical model of the differences between the life-styles which I shall now summarise.

The lads are the most likely to have come from a single-parent household, have a criminal record, possess few or no educational qualifications, be in unskilled work or unemployed and marry relatively early. Although the ordinary kids do not do much 'better' than the lads at school, they are less likely to have unskilled jobs, be unemployed or have been in trouble with the law; some of them at least may marry later. In complete contrast, the citizens marry comparatively late, are typically in skilled manual or white-collar occupations and do not have criminal records. In Chapter 7 I used case-studies to highlight the lived differences in individual experience which are the meaning of the life-styles for the kids themselves.

This tells us what the differences between the life-styles are, differences which are less than straightforward in some respects. The lads are comparable to the ordinary kids in the educational sphere, for example, while the family backgrounds of the ordinary kids and the citizens are not dissimilar. The reasons for these differences may be correspondingly complex.

How are these differences produced and reproduced? There are,

in fact,   three dimensions to this process: first, that which reflects
the practices of the young people themselves, second, that which is
located in the practices of significant others, and third, that which
relates to the organisation of the institutional context within which
both sets of practices are located.   However, these three aspects of
the production and reproduction of life-styles are only analytically
distinct; in the practice of day-to-day life each is chronically
implicated in the other two.

Looking at the young people concerned, it is readily apparent that
life-styles are, from this point of view, very much the creations of
their members, reflecting the working-class milieu in which they
arise.   Parents, siblings and the peer group are a fount of conventional wisdom about the world which contributes to the constitution
of that world in practice.   The earlier discussions of the value
attached to apprenticeships, or the norms of courtship and marriage,
illustrate the vitality of the local view of the world.   It is
partly in the fragmentation of that world view through the contrast
between the 'rough' and the 'respectable', the pub and the church,
that differences between the life-styles are generated.

However, there is more to it than this.   There are many senses
in which the young people's actions and views of the world are in
contradiction of their actual outcomes.   For example, as argued in
Chapter 6, the number of kids in unskilled jobs does not reflect a
conscious choice on their part, nor even a less specific orientation
towards unskilled work.   As I have argued elsewhere (Jenkins, 1983),
the surest route to an unskilled job - or, indeed, unemployment -
is the absence of a clearly formulated occupational goal in a labour
market which is predicated on the establishment of specific
occupational identities.

There are many examples in the preceding chapters of the
importance of significant other people who, although 'external' to
the local social world in terms of their own life-styles or class
identity, are heavily implicated in the production of that world.
In this analysis I have drawn attention to the role of housing
officials, the police and teachers in this process, and in Chapters
8 and 9 I concentrated on employment recruiters as agents in the
differentiation of life-style experiences.   These are all people
who, occupying positions within particular institutions, are able
to allocate identities to those with whom they deal and to then
make those identities count as reality through the process of
allocating resources (or penalties).   The cumulative outcome of
decisions being made across a wide range of institutions (1) on the
basis of a broadly agreed-upon set of folk models categorising
different kinds of people is the partial constitution in terms of
those models of the lived experience of the people about whom those
decisions are made.   Inasmuch as members of the working class also
share these classificatory models, some of this allocatory work
can, in effect, be 'sub-contracted', as happens with supervisors in
industry or policemen.

It is in the similarity between institutional allocatory
procedures that the third aspect of the production and reproduction
of life-style differences is found.   There are two senses in which
the structuration of public and private organisations is significant.
First, as an institutionalised hierarchy of positions and careers

in the labour market, they constitute the taken-for-granted backcloth of life-style differences. Indeed, in a very immediate sense, institutional positions, typically jobs or occupations, are one of the mediums through which the differentiation of class and life-style is achieved, in recruitment and selection procedures. Furthermore, the way in which such positions are organised and allocated means that the manner and level of entry into employment may have important consequences for eventual career outcomes (Stewart, Prandy and Blackburn, 1980).

Second, the fact that those positions within organisations which bestow upon their incumbents allocatory functions and the authority to label others are typically filled by recruitment from certain class positions or life-styles, helps to ensure the continuity of the institutional similarities with which I am concerned. Recruitment at this level is essentially a similar process to recruitment to positions further down the organisational hierarchy (Salaman and Thompson, 1978; Silverman and Jones, 1973). It is in one sense a reflection of a hierarchical class system; in another sense, however, it is a medium of that system's reproduction and constitution in practice.

The above discussion has been predicated upon the overall legitimacy of existing systems of power and authority, a legitimacy which is firmly embedded in a set of axiomatic notions concerning property relationships. The axiomatic legitimation of relationships of property and power is reciprocally implicated in the production and reproduction of class and life-style. This is epitomised, for example in the historical process by which models of skilled and unskilled labour were developed and mobilised in the labour market. Similarly, although there may be working-class struggle and resistance centring around the allocation of jobs and their rewards, the basic capitalist wage relationship itself has all too rarely been questioned.

The ideology of the working class contributes, of course, to the legitimation of working-class subordination. This contribution, however, is less straightforward than Bourdieu (1977a; 1977b) or Willis (1977) have suggested. One of the central ideological strands in the thinking of the young people of Ballyhightown is their individualism, a world view which explains social events in terms of the nature or psychology of the individuals engaged in those events. Whatever the situation, there is usually somebody who can be held to be responsible or accountable. This individualism is deeply rooted in the collective knowledge of the working class, reflecting the inescapable reality that people are not automata. However, the individualist theme is constantly reinforced by school and the media; it is, in fact, one of the dominant cultural principles of our society, as unavoidable as the language in which it finds expression.

Why then, if individualism is such a dominant theme, understood and shared across the class system, is it a political handicap for the working class in particular? To answer this question we must reconsider institutions and power relationships. There are two important elements to the answer: power and the inexperience of inequality, on the one hand, and restricted spatial horizons, which I shall call localism, on the other.

The meeting of working-class individualism and an unequal system of power relationships has certain consequences. If life depends primarily upon 'what you make of it', it seems probable that what you have 'made' of it already will have some impact both upon your interpretation of your present experiences and your formulation of plans for the future. An important political effect of the individualist world view is that those who wield power or authority, or who occupy privileged positions, may be thought to do so either because they have a natural entitlement ('a better class of person'), or as a result of their individual hard work or personal abilities. Power and inequality become transformed, as a result, into the expression and reflection of real differences in the qualities of individuals. As Wilkey put it, 'There's bad 'uns and there's good 'uns.... It's the way of the world, so it is.' As 'the way of the world', the possibility of interfering with it is rarely broached; when it is, its very taken-for-grantedness makes the proposal appear utopian. Thus is inequality axiomatically legitimated.

This is, of course, an over-simplified picture. As is quite clear from the ethnography, the young people of Ballyhightown do not simply accept all the responsibility for the situations in which they find themselves. The routine oppressions of industrial capitalism and the bureaucratic inefficiencies of the modern state are personally experienced too often to be ignored. These experiences lead to criticism and minor resistance. However, due to their individualism, this criticism, cast as it is within a fragmented world view, frequently seeks solutions in an exploration of alternatives within the local taken-for-granted world, rather than of alternatives to that world.

The forms which this criticism takes highlights the importance of localism as part of their world view. Reflecting the comparatively limited geographical mobility of the working class, something which is not peculiar to Belfast (Goldthorpe et al., 1980, pp.147-74), the socially mapped area within which responsibility can be allocated is correspondingly restricted. The frustration or anger which arise from their experiences and encounters with inequality are either vented against those immediately available to shoulder the blame - bad neighbours, the foreman, 'them pigs up at the brue', 'the fenian bastards from Ballyfee', or whatever - or directed towards external figures who are easily available as scapegoats through their media stereotypes: 'blacks', 'the unions', 'republicans' or 'fucking politicians', for example. The coming together of individualism and localism in working-class ideology leads to a sectional and perhaps even a conspiratorial view of society, and away from the appreciation of the wider dimensions and patterns of society which is surely the prerequisite for successful working-class collective political organisation. (2)

These are two important facets of the ideological framework within which the young workers of Ballyhightown grow up and come of age. The fact that there are distinct class life-styles within a cultural or ideological framework which is shared to some extent across the boundaries of class has, as should be clear, great significance for the reproduction of class divisions. (3)

There are also gender divisions to be taken into account, however. As we have seen, there is an intimate connection between life-style

differences and gender. In particular, it is important to understand
the central role which notions of 'respectability' have in both the
reproduction of acceptably socialised women, on the one hand, and
of acceptable habituated workers, on the other. The ways in which
the two processes are linked are many; three of the most conspicuous
and important areas in which this connection can be seen are as
follows.

First, there is the role of young women during courtship, in
'settling down' the lads or the 'rougher' members of the ordinary
kids network.   This can be seen to good effect in the case study
of Davy and Carol in Chapter 7.   Second, and as the logical extension
of the first, there is the role of women as wives, as the consumers
of wages and household managers. In this sense households are an
important means of locking workers – both male and female – into
waged labour. In a two-parent household the needs of the household
may serve as an encouragement for acceptable behaviour at the
workplace; that this is so is recognised by employers (see Chapter
8). In a single-parent or low-wage household, the economic needs
of the domestic economy may have a similar effect. Particularly
in the first case, however, the 'needs' of the household are
frequently expressed as the maintenance of 'respectable' standards
in the eyes of the local world, something which most girls learn
early – from their mothers and aunts, in domestic science classes
and from women's magazines. The role of the wife as home-maker
can, in this respect, be seen to have important consequences for
the nature of the labour market as an arena in which class and
class life-styles are reproduced.

Third, and leading on from the above, there is the role of the
woman as mother and/or wife in the initial socialisation of children,
particularly, given the above analysis, female children. If the
habituation of male labour is at least partly achieved through the
pressures of female 'respectability', the production of fully
socialised female children, themselves committed to the pursuit of
'respectability', is important.

This is, of course, too simple to adequately depict the reality.
A major empirical weakness of this book has been in the area of the
family; as a result, the discussion raises more questions than it
answers. Two areas which suggest themselves immediately as worthy
of more research are the role of women and notions of gender in the
reproduction of what I have called the lads' and the citizens' life-
styles. Looking at the lads, it is obvious that, as Willis argues
(1977), notions of masculinity are central in their lives. However,
what is not so obvious is the role of wives and sweethearts in the
reproduction of 'rough' male life-styles. How families contribute
to this process is something which is not immediately apparent.
Similarly, while it may be easy to imagine the contribution of
mothers, girlfriends and 'respectability' to the life-style espoused
by the citizens, the place of ideologies of masculinity is less
clear.

What is relatively certain, however, is the centrality of gender
to any discussion of class or life-style, and vice versa. Each
is chronically implicated in the other through a set of notions
concerning the public and the private, the waged and the domestic,
the active and the passive, the producer and the reproducer, the

skilled and the unskilled, and the 'rough' and the 'respectable' (not to mention, of course, the male and the female!). I am uncomfortably aware of the inadequacies of the present work in this area, having done not much more than explore the topic at a necessarily superficial level, given that my concern was primarily with the nature of class life-styles. Hopefully, however, this is an aspect of the problem which further research will help to clarify.

Coming in closing to the differences between social reproduction, the patterned historical process whereby the institutions of the state are maintained, and cultural reproduction, the manner in which cultural forms and social practices are continuous with or legitimate the relations of domination in capitalist society, I am no longer certain that the distinction is a useful one. Given the direction in which the analysis of the reproduction of life-styles in Belfast has unfolded, and the degree to which different 'levels' of that analysis have been shown to be reciprocally interlinked, it becomes clear that distinguishing between these two aspects of the social construction of reality is, at best, only of narrow theoretical utility. When it comes down to the detailed analysis of actual social situations, or, indeed, the formulation of political strategies, the 'cultural' and the 'social' (or the 'interactional' and the 'institutional') dissolve into a more or less unified field of human practice. It is this practice, the mundane everyday activities of men and women, which is the site of the production and reproduction of capitalist society or its alternatives. It is with this practice that we must concern ourselves in any genuinely politically active social science.

THE SAMPLES: FURTHER DETAILS

The most important information about the samples which has not been given in the main text concerns the distribution of ages within each group. This is indicated in the table below.

Sample		Age						n	Mean age (years)
		16	17	18	19	20	21-25		
Lads	(m)	-	-	-	2	5	7	14	20.7
Ordinary Kids	(m)	-	7	7	5	1	9	29	19.3
	(f)	1	6	9	7	1	1	25	18.1
Citizens	(m)	1	1	2	2	-	4	10	19.2
	(f)	1	-	2	2	3	-	8	18.7

Throughout the text many individual young people have been mentioned. The list below should enable the reader to identify the life-style 'identity' of these kids. Those names marked with an asterisk (*) were not formally interviewed and are therefore not part of the samples.

LADS
Bobby Bothwell
Billy Bradshaw*
Browner
Jonty Bryans*
Tailor Burton
Ivan Green

Whippet McIlwaine*
Jim Mitchell (Mitch)
Billy Robinson (Robbo)
Billy Saunders*
Peewee Stafford*

Eddy Stewart
Mac Sutherland*
Tinker
Wilkey
Alfie Wright

CITIZENS
Thomas Kidd
Wilma McCullough*
Rhonda Thompson

135

ORDINARY KIDS

Denis Anderson	Audrey Duff	Carol Monteith
Tania Barr	Mackers	Jenny Smith
Blacko	Johnny McAndrew	Jim Smyth
Gary Brown	Mandy McAuley	Billy Simpson
Chrissy Brownleas	Craig McComb	Ruth Simpson
Tommy Brownleas	Brian McWilliams	Susan Steenson
Davy Douglas	Michelle McWilliams	Billy Turner

CLASSIFYING OCCUPATIONS

Throughout the book I have been using a four-fold classification of occupations which is intended to reflect the local folk models of jobs and work. As such it is partly a scale, with unskilled jobs being unambiguously at the bottom, status wise. The relationship between the skilled manual and the white collar occupations is more ambiguous; the white collar jobs are, however, probably correctly viewed as being seen as in some senses superior to all manual occupations by a majority of the young people.

UNSKILLED: bread salesman, box-maker, building worker, cashier, crane-driver, flour-mill worker, fork-lift driver, gardener, groundsman-driver, labourer, lorry driver, machine operator, machinist, medical orderly, milkman, nursing auxiliary, packer, postman, process worker, seaman, shop assistant, slaughterman, spinner, stitcher, storekeeper, waitress, wirer, yarn inspector.

SKILLED MANUAL: baker, book-binder, book-folder, bricklayer, butcher, coachbuilder, dental nurse, electrician, fitter, hairdresser, joiner, machine setter, nurse (SEN and SRN), plasterer, plumber, printer, tailor, technician, tiler, turner.

WHITE-COLLAR: bank official, civil servant, clerk, clerk/typist, data processor, foreman, forewoman, garage manager, insurance inspector, management trainee, programmer, punch-tape operator, receptionist, salesman, secretary, shorthand typist, supervisor, tax officer, telephonist.

OTHER: Armed services, police, teacher, Ulster Defence Regiment.

As can be seen from this, 'other' is very much a residual category. The absence of a 'semi-skilled' category reflects the fact that such a term appears not to have much meaning in Ballyhightown: in a manual occupation, you're either skilled or you're not. It is reassuring to note that this very rough and ready exercise in mapping the local Ballyhightown models of occupations appears to be approximately in line with the results of the more sophisticated methodology of Coxon and Jones (1979, pp.56-92).

NOTES

CHAPTER 1 INTRODUCTION

1 A fuller version of this critique of Bourdieu can be found in Jenkins, 1982a.
2 Not everybody views Bourdieu's work in this light; see Rachel Sharp's attack on his work as Weberian, 'liberal theory in disguise' (1980, pp.66-76).
3 My distinction between social reproduction and cultural reproduction follows Willis (1981, pp.48-51).
4 For a detailed discussion of my conception of models see Jenkins, 1981a.
5 For example: Bew, Gibbon and Patterson, 1979; Burton, 1978; Darby, 1976; Darby and Williamson, 1978; Easthope, 1976; Fraser, 1974; Harbison and Harbison, 1980; Harris, 1972; Leyton, 1974; Nelson, 1975; O'Dowd and Tomlinson, 1980; O'Dowd, Rolston and Tomlinson, 1980; Osborne, 1980; Probert, 1978. This is a very incomplete list; for a more comprehensive coverage of recent work in particular, see Darby, Dodge and Hepburn, 1981.
6 Notable exceptions are research reports on poverty and low pay in Northern Ireland (i.e. Black, Ditch, Morrissey and Steele, 1980; Evason, 1976, 1978, 1980), David Byrne's research into deindustrialisation (1981), Weiner's classic study of urban planning in Belfast (1975) and the tradition of educational research sponsored by the Northern Ireland Council for Educational Research (e.g. Bill, Trew and Wilson, 1974; Spelman, 1979). Bill Rolston, in a discussion of trade unionism in Ulster, highlights the problems attaching to the attempt to separate sectarianism or ethnicity from class issues (1980).
7 These remarks should not, however, be read as supporting Moore's poorly documented contention that ethnic conflict in Northern Ireland is a 'race relations' situation (Moore, 1972), an idea which has, unfortunately, recently been resurrected (McKernan, 1982). See Nelson (1975) for a convincing critique of this model of the Irish conflict.

CHAPTER 2 AN ANTHROPOLOGIST COMES HOME

1 One of the most serious problems of participant observation and other kinds of field research lies in deciding when one is 'off duty' (Barnes, 1979, pp.77–8).
2 For good accounts of participant observation in 'sensitive' localities, with its attendant difficulties, see Burton, 1978, pp.164–79; Polsky, 1971, pp.115–47; Whyte, 1955, pp.279–358.
3 For a discussion of the role conflict involved in this kind of research situation, see Hargreaves, 1967, pp.193–205.
4 To distinguish the three life-style samples from the more general usage of the life-style categories, the samples are denoted by the use of capital letters, i.e. Lads, Citizens and Ordinary Kids.
5 For good discussions of the participant method, see McCall and Simmons, 1969; Burgess, 1982.

CHAPTER 3 BALLYHIGHTOWN

1 In addition to the works cited in the text this section draws extensively on Darby, 1976; Deutsch and Magowan, 1973–5.
2 In addition to fieldnotes, local newspaper files and the sources cited in the text, the following were consulted in writing this section: Byrne, 1979; Government of Northern Ireland, 1945; Ministry of Health and Local Government, 1963; Mathew, 1961; the 1966 and 1971 Northern Ireland Census reports. Several other publications cannot be cited by their actual titles, in order to preserve the estate's anonymity: the 'Souvenir Handbook' of Castleowen Urban District Council (1958), the 'Castleowen District Guide' (1978), and the unpublished reports of local community workers, Clem and Rowan, whose help I gratefully acknowledge. The collection of ephemera relating to the 'troubles' in the Linenhall Library, Belfast, was also invaluable.
3 A description of Ballyhightown in Castleowen UDC's 'Souvenir Handbook' (1958).
4 In interpreting Table 3.4 it should also be borne in mind that, in comparing figures for employment in construction for April 1971 and June 1978 the seasonal fluctuations of this industry should be recognised.

CHAPTER 4 LIFE-STYLES

1 In this sense, the Kai is something like Glasgow's 'Maryhill Fleet', an umbrella term for the subsumption of small 'teams' within a larger, local identity (Patrick, 1973, p.36).
2 This material compares well with the ethnography on black unemployment in the United States (Hannerz, 1969; Liebow, 1967).
3 It is stating the obvious to recognise that the relationship between the sexes described here is neither peculiarly Northern Irish, protestant or working-class.
4 It is likely that skilled manual occupations are over-represented

in Table 4.1, for two reasons. First, spouses may have recorded their occupations in such a way that, although they are unskilled or 'semi-skilled', it appears that they are in a skilled job. For example, 'machinist' might either mean a time-served turner, or a machine minder. Second, it is possible that the absence of those couples who married in the registry office may have distorted the picture somewhat.

5   For a discussion of juvenile crime in Ballyhightown, see 'Hightown Rules' (Jenkins, 1982c), particularly the chapter on 'The Outlaws'.

6   Northern Ireland has yet to change to a comprehensive secondary education system.

CHAPTER 5   GROWING UP

1   For further details of the composition of the samples, age-wise, see Appendix 1.

2   For more detailed material on the Outlaws, see the chapter devoted to them in 'Hightown Rules' (Jenkins, 1982c).

3   For an example of this interview schedule, see Jenkins, 1981b, pp.292-5.

4   This is an extract from an essay entitled, 'What I want to be when I leave school', written by a girl in the first-year remedial class at Ballyhightown Secondary School.

5   For other 'labelling' approaches to educational success and failure, see Cicourel and Kitsuse, 1963; Rist, 1977.

6   See Caven and Harbinson, 1980; Department of Education, 1977.

7   Blacko's evidence points out at least one reason why the official truancy figures are underestimations!

8   This ethnography is evocative of other accounts of working-class conservatism produced by the fear of failure (i.e. Liebow, 1967, pp.210-11; Whyte, 1955, pp.37-40).

9   'Getting a death' means being subjected to public ridicule.

10 The distinction between detention of all kinds and custodial sentences is important in Northern Ireland: one of the Lads spent nine months in prison on remand, only to be eventually found not guilty.

11 The only book I know of concerned with adolescent female crime is by Anne Campbell (1981).

CHAPTER 6   COMING OF AGE

1   See footnote 4, Chapter 4, above.

2   My notion of 'labour market continuity' is essentially a less arbitrary, broader version of the notion of 'sub-employment' proposed by Norris (1978).

3   This is discussed in much greater depth in Chapters 8 and 9.

4   It is interesting that Blackburn and Mann report that one of the few significant orientations towards work exhibited by their subjects concerned outdoor work: 'a collection of rewards, including autonomy - especially from supervision' (1979, p.149).

5   This conflicts with Willis's view that working-class boys 'are not choosing careers or particular jobs, they are committing

themselves to a future of generalised labour' (1977, pp.99-100, my emphasis).
6 Research in Great Britain also points to the increased use of informal networks in a time of recession (Bryman et al., 1982).
7 'Time in the labour market' is calculated here as time spent since leaving school minus periods spent in prison and withdrawals from the labour market by young women due to maternity.
8 During the fieldwork I only heard of two abortions, both involving schoolgirls below the legal age of consent.

CHAPTER 7   EIGHT LIVES

1 I have made further use of the kids' autobiographical writings in 'Hightown Rules' (Jenkins, 1982c).
2 Carol Monteith's own view of her life may be found in Chapter 4 of 'Hightown Rules' (Jenkins, 1982c).
3 By July 1982 this possibility had become even more remote: in February 1982 Davy was made redundant and Carol only avoided redundancy by the skin of her teeth.
4 For other evidence on the quality of the work experience for many young workers, see Blackburn and Mann, 1979, p.280; Carter, 1966, p.167; Maizels, 1970, pp.275-8.

CHAPTER 8   EMPLOYERS, INDUSTRIES AND THE STATE

1 Quoted from an interview in the Castleowen local paper.
2 Rees (1966) provides comparable material from the United States; Hunt and Small (1981) do the same for Scotland. Salaman and Thompson (1978) and Silverman and Jones (1973) provide evidence that the same factors are at work in selection interviewing for higher status jobs. Beynon and Nicholls (1977, pp.97, 199) have also documented the 'married-man-with-a-mortgage-and-two-kids' stereotype.
3 I extracted from the Northern Ireland yellow pages telephone directory all of the entries for Castleowen falling into the categories manufacturing, construction, distribution and services, as in the Standard Industrial Classification (Central Statistical Office, 1968). Within these groups I stratified the organisations in a very crude fashion into 'large', 'medium to large', 'small to medium' and 'small' on the basis of my own local knowledge. I then selected 25 firms in each industrial group: 3 'large', 6 'medium to large', 8 'small to medium', and 8 'small'. Forty-seven employers responded, as shown below.

Number of employees	Manufacturing	Construction	Distribution	Services
1-15	2	5	6	7
16-50	3	2	3	1
51-250	7	4	1	1
251+	1	1	3	-

The questionnaire used in the postal survey is reproduced in Jenkins, 1981b, pp.298-301.

4   The importance of the ability to present oneself as 'acceptable' in an interview is stressed in popular guides on 'how to be interviewed', i.e. Fletcher, 1981; Higham, 1982.

5   White-collar workers are excluded from this discussion; differences between 'shop-floor' and 'staff' may be as important as differences between industries.

6   This is the dual labour-market hypothesis; see Bosanquet and Doeringer, 1973; Gordon, 1972, pp.43-52; Piore, 1971.

7   This is another aspect of labelling in the labour market; this may, however, depend very much on labour market conditions. Job-changing does not appear to disadvantage the job-seeker in a period of full employment (Cherry, 1976).

8   See Casson, 1979, pp.9-29, 61-87; Rees and Atkinson, 1982.

9   For further details of the Youth Opportunities Scheme, see the 'Annual Reports' of the Manpower Services Commission.

10 For further information on the Youthways scheme, see the 'Times Educational Supplement', 29 February 1980, p.10.

11 DMS YOP Unit, 1978.

12 Ibid., Appendix 1, p.1.

13 Cf. A. Stafford, 1981; however, another piece of research (E.M. Stafford, 1982) has argued that participation in YOP has a positive and beneficial effect on young workers.

14 The importance of the time factor in limiting access to apprentice-ships has been highlighted by Lee and Wrench, 1983.

15 Some idea of how important YOP schemes are locally can be gauged from a study I made of 1978 school-leavers from Ballyhightown Secondary School which is reported elsewhere (Jenkins, 1983).

16 In addition, ethnic factors come in. The Manager of the local GTC told me that employers would come to him and say, 'He's got a fine pair of hands, but what about his feet?' This refers to 'which foot he digs with', i.e. is he a protestant or a catholic? Ethnicity here is another dimension of accepta-bility.

CHAPTER 9   'IT'S NOT WHAT YOU KNOW ...'

1   For a different labour-market classification, see Kerr, 1977, pp.21-37.

2   These figures are based on the levy payable to the Construction Industry Training Board and due to the way in which the levy is calculated very small firms may be under-represented.

3   The Falls Road is a catholic district in Belfast, the Shankill Road protestant.

4   Electrical, Electronic, Telecommunications and Plumbing Union.

5   For two contrasting socialist analyses of this practice, see Direct Labour Collective, 1978, pp.39-52; Lamb, 1974.

6   In this context, Sykes's interpretation of navvies' relation-ships with their bosses is interesting (1969a, 1969b). Other useful comparative accounts of the construction industry are Austrin, 1976; Clegg, 1975; Foster, 1978; Lumley, 1980; Marsh, Hendy and Matheson, 1981; Moore, 1981.

7   For a comparative perspective on the printing industry, see
    Blauner, 1964, pp.35-57; Child, 1967; Curran and Stanworth, 1979,
    1981; Sykes, 1960a, 1960b.
8   I suspect that this is a rather disingenuous justification of
    their behaviour by these employers, inasmuch as the jobbing
    printing sector as a whole is characterised by the rapid turnover
    of skilled workers.
9   A similar view of official job placement agencies has been
    reported from England: Carter, 1966, p.147; Keil, 1976, pp.17-19.
10 Mother- and father-of-chapel refers to shop stewards in the
    printing industry.
11 By 1982 Susan, having completed her apprenticeship, was serving
    full-time in the Ulster Defence Regiment.
12 See notes 6 and 7, above.
13 Since I finished the research TransInternational has declared
    further redundancies.
14 In order to raise the numbers, I have included white-collar
    workers here. The organisational structure of the plant affects
    both manual and non-manual workers in much the same fashion.
15 John Black is an ex-senior foreman.
16 Including an ex-member of the personnel function.
17 Since the appointment of a new (catholic) General Manager, there
    is some anecdotal evidence that more catholics have been recruited.
    However, given the low level of recruitment the numbers involved
    are likely to be small.
18 For discussions of recruitment through informal networks which
    raise some of the same issues, see Brookes and Singh, 1979;
    Jenkins, 1982b; Rees, 1966.
19 He has since been re-employed, once again, he insists, because
    'somebody spoke for me'.
20 This glosses over, rather glibly I am aware, the complex debate
    surrounding the notion of the 'professional-managerial class':
    see Walker, 1979; Zimbalist, 1979.
21 See Rolston, 1980. Another good discussion of Northern Ireland
    trade unionism may be found in issue number 7, Summer 1979, of
    the Belfast Workers' Research Unit's 'Belfast Bulletin'.
22 After writing this, I came across the following passage which
    says something similar: 'at the crucial intersection of labour
    market and organisation, "class" is produced and used as a
    device for reproducing class structure' (Clegg and Dunkerley,
    1980, p.431). Norris (1978) appears to say much the same sort
    of thing concerning the manner in which unemployment is socially
    allocated through the processes of recruitment and severance,
    and Kreckel's model of labour market segmentation (1980) is
    also comparable in some respects. Offe's discussion of 'ability'
    as a source of achievement in work organisations is also
    pertinent to this discussion (Offe, 1976).

CHAPTER 10   DIFFERENT KINDS OF PEOPLE

1   For example, in the allocation of welfare benefits (Lipsky, 1981;
    Marsden and Duff, 1975, pp.26-32, 133-49) and of public housing
    (Flett, 1979).

2   By comparing this passage with my distinction between analytical
    and folk models (Chapter 1) the possibility for a politically
    radical social science should become apparent.
3   With respect to this kind of analysis of class society, see
    Touraine's model of workers' consciousness as made up of a
    principle of unity, a principle of opposition and a principle
    of totality, all of which find expression in social action
    (Touraine, 1977, pp.313-17).

BIBLIOGRAPHY

ALTHUSSER, L. (1971), 'Lenin and Philosophy and Other Essays', New Left Books, London.

ARMSTRONG, P. (1982), If It's Only Women It Doesn't Matter So Much, in West, J. (ed.), 'Work, Women and the Labour Market', Routledge & Kegan Paul, London.

ASHTON, D.N. and FIELD, D. (1976), 'Young Workers', Hutchinson, London.

ASHTON, D.N. and MAGUIRE, M.J. (1980), The Function of Academic and Non-Academic Criteria in Employers' Selection Strategies, 'British Journal of Guidance and Counselling', vol.8, pp.146-57.

ASHTON, D.N. and MAGUIRE, M.J. (1981), 'Employers' Demand for Young Workers', University of Leicester, Leicester.

ASHTON, D.N., MAGUIRE, M.J. and GARLAND, V. (1982), Youth in the Labour-market, 'Research Paper No. 34', Department of Employment, London.

AUSTRIN, T. (1976), A Divided Workforce: Casual Workers in the Building Trade and Union Membership, 'New Society', 15 July 1976, pp.115-16.

BAKER, S.E. (1973), Orange and Green: Belfast, 1832-1912, in Dyos, H.J. and Wolff, M. (eds), 'The Victorian City: Images and Realities', Routledge & Kegan Paul, London.

BALDWIN, J. and BOTTOMS, A.E. (1976), 'The Urban Criminal', Tavistock, London.

BARNES, J.A. (1976), 'Who Should know What? Social Science, Privacy and Ethics', Penguin, Harmondsworth.

BAZALGETTE, J. (1978), 'School Life and Work Life', Hutchinson, London.

BECKER, H.S. (1963), 'Outsiders: Studies in the Sociology of Deviance', Free Press, New York.

BECKETT, J.C. (1966), 'The Making of Modern Ireland', Faber & Faber, London.

BELL, C. and NEWBY, H. (1971), 'Community Studies', Allen & Unwin, London.

BEW, P., GIBBON, P. and PATTERSON, H. (1979), 'The State in Northern Ireland 1921-72', Manchester University Press, Manchester.

BILL, J.M., TREW, K.J. and WILSON, J.A. (1974), 'Early Leaving in Northern Ireland', Northern Ireland Council for Educational Research, Belfast.

BLACK, B., DITCH, J., MORRISSEY, M. and STEELE, R. (1980), Low Pay
in Northern Ireland, 'Low Pay Pamphlet No.12', Low Pay Unit, London.
BLACK, W. (1977), Industrial Development and Regional Policy, in
Gibson, N.J. and Spencer, J.E. (eds) 'Economic Activity in Ireland',
Gill & Macmillan, Dublin.
BLACKBURN, R.M. and MANN, M. (1979), 'The Working Class in the Labour
Market', Macmillan, London.
BLAUNER, R. (1964), 'Alienation and Freedom', University of Chicago
Press, Chicago.
BOAL, F.W. (1981), Ethnic Residential Segregation, Ethnic Mixing and
Resource Conflict: A Study in Belfast, Northern Ireland, in Peach, C.,
Robinson, V. and Smith, S. (eds), 'Ethnic Segregation in Cities',
Croom Helm, London.
BOISSEVAIN, J. (1975), Introduction, in Boissevain, J. and Friedl, J.
(eds), 'Beyond the Community: Social Process in Europe', Ministry
of Education and Science, The Hague.
BOSANQUET, N. and DOERINGER, P.B. (1973), Is there a Dual Labour
Market in Great Britain?, 'Economic Journal', vol.83, pp.421-35.
BOURDIEU, P. (1977a), 'Outline of a Theory of Practice', Cambridge
University Press, Cambridge.
BOURDIEU, P. (1977b), Cultural Reproduction and Social Reproduction,
in Karabel, J. and Halsey, A.H. (eds), 'Power and Ideology in
Education', Oxford University Press, New York.
BOURDIEU, P. (1979), 'Algeria 1960', Cambridge University Press and
Editions de la Maison des Science de l'Homme, Cambridge and Paris.
BOURDIEU, P. (1980), A Diagram of Social Position and Life-style,
'Media, Culture and Society', vol.2, pp.255-9.
BOURDIEU, P. and PASSERON, J.-C. (1977), 'Reproduction in Education,
Society and Culture', Sage, London and Beverley Hills.
BOURDIEU, P. and PASSERON, J.-C. (1979), 'The Inheritors: French
Students and their Relation to Culture', University of Chicago Press,
Chicago.
BOWLES, S. and GINTIS, H. (1976), 'Schooling in Capitalist America',
Routledge & Kegan Paul, London.
BRAKE, M. (1980), 'The Sociology of Youth Cultures and Youth Sub-
cultures', Routledge & Kegan Paul, London.
BROOKS, D. and SINGH, K. (1979), Pivots and Presents: Asian Brokers
in British Foundries, in Wallman, S. (ed.), 'Ethnicity at Work',
Macmillan, London.
BRYMAN, A., JENKINS, R., et al. (1982), 'The Management of the
Recession', mimeo, University of Aston/Loughborough University.
BULMER, M. (ed.) (1975), 'Working-class Images of Society', Routledge
& Kegan Paul, London.
BURGESS, R.G. (ed.) (1982), 'Field Research: A Sourcebook and Field
Manual', Allen & Unwin, London.
BURTON, F. (1978), 'The Politics of Legitimacy: Struggles in a
Belfast Community', Routledge & Kegan Paul, London.
BYRNE, D. (1979), 'Housing in Belfast: Reproductive Politics and
Class Politics in a Different Place', mimeo, Ulster College,
Newtownabbey.
BYRNE, D. (1981), The Deindustrialization of Northern Ireland,
'Antipode', vol.12, pp.87-97.
CAMPBELL, A. (1981), 'Girl Delinquents', Basil Blackwell, Oxford.
CARTER, M. (1966), 'Into Work', Pelican, Harmondsworth.

CASSON, M. (1979), 'Youth Unemployment', Macmillan London.
CAVEN, N. and HARBISON, J.J.M. (1980), Persistent School non-attendance, in Harbison, J. and Harbison, J. (eds), 'A Society Under Stress', Open Books, Shepton Mallet.
CENTRAL STATISTICAL OFFICE (1968), 'Standard Industrial Classification', 3rd edn, HMSO, London.
CENTRE FOR CONTEMPORARY CULTURAL STUDIES (1981), 'Unpopular Education: Schooling and Social Democracy in England since 1944', Hutchinson, London.
CHERRY, N. (1976), Persistent Job Changing - Is it a Problem?, 'Journal of Occupational Psychology', vol.49, pp.203-21.
CHILD, J. (1967), 'Industrial Relations in the British Printing Industry, The Quest for Security', Allen & Unwin, London.
CICOUREL, A.V. and KITSUSE, J.I. (1963), 'The Educational Decision-Makers', Bobbs-Merrill, Indianapolis.
CLARKE, J., HALL, S., JEFFERSON, T. and ROBERTS, B. (1976), Sub-cultures, Cultures and Class: A Theoretical Overview, in Hall, S. and Jefferson, T. (eds), 'Resistance through Rituals', Hutchinson, London.
CLEGG, S. (1975), 'Power, Rule and Domination: a Critical and Empirical Understanding of Power in Sociological Theory and Organisational Life', Routledge & Kegan Paul, London.
CLEGG, S. and DUNKERLEY, D. (1980), 'Organisation, Class and Control', Routledge & Kegan Paul, London.
COE, W.E. (1969), 'The Engineering Industry of the North of Ireland', David & Charles, Newton Abbot.
COHEN, P. (1980), Subcultural Conflict and Working Class Community, in Hall, S., Hobson, D., Lowe, A. and Willis, P. (eds), 'Culture, Media, Language', Hutchinson, London.
COHEN, P. (1982), School for Dole, 'New Socialist', no.3, pp.43-7.
CORMACK, R.J., OSBORNE, R.D. and THOMPSON, W.T. (1980), 'Into Work? Young School-leavers and the Structure of Opportunity in Belfast', Fair Employment Agency, Belfast.
CORRIGAN, P. (1979), 'Schooling the Smash Street Kids', Macmillan, London.
CORRIGAN, P. and WILLIS, P. (1980), Cultural Forms and Class Mediations, 'Media, Culture and Society', vol.2, pp.297-312.
COWIE, C. and LEES, S. (1981), Slags or Drags, 'Feminist Review', no.9, pp.17-31.
COXON, A.P.M. and JONES, C.L. (1979), 'Class and Hierarchy: The Social Meaning of Occupations', Macmillan, London.
COYLE, A. (1982), Sex and Skill in the Organisation of the Clothing Industry, in West, J. (ed.), 'Work, Women and the Labour Market', Routledge & Kegan Paul, London.
CRAWFORD, W.H. (1972), 'Domestic Industry in Ireland: The Experience of the Linen Industry', Gill & Macmillan, Dublin.
CULLEN, L.M. (1969), The Irish Economy in the Eighteenth Century, in Cullen, L.M. (ed.), 'The Formation of the Irish Economy', Mercier Press, Cork.
CURRAN, J. and STANWORTH, J. (1979), Self-selection and the Small Firm Worker, 'Sociology', vol.13, pp.427-44.
CURRAN, J. and STANWORTH, J. (1981), Size of Workplace and Attitudes to Industrial Relations in the Printing and Electronics Industries, 'British Journal of Industrial Relations', vol.19, pp.14-25.
DARBY, J. (1976), 'Conflict in Northern Ireland', Gill & Macmillan, Dublin.

DARBY, J., DODGE, N. and HEPBURN, A.C. (1981), 'Register of Research into the Irish Conflict, 1981', New University of Ulster, Coleraine.
DARBY, J. and MORRIS, G. (1974), 'Intimidation in Housing', NI Community Relations Commission, Belfast.
DARBY, J. and WILLIAMSON, A. (eds) (1978), 'Violence and the Social Services in Northern Ireland', Heinemann, London.
DAVIES, B. (1981), Restructuring Youth Policies: The State We're In, 'NYB Occasional Paper 21', National Youth Bureau, Leicester.
DAVIS, H.H. (1979), 'Beyond Class Images', Croom Helm, London.
DAVIS, J. (1975), Beyond the Hyphen: Some Notes and Documents on Community-State Relations in South Italy, in Boissevain, J. and Friedl, J. (eds), 'Beyond the Community', Ministry of Education and Science, The Hague.
DEEM, R. (1980), Women, Work and Schooling, in Deem, R. (ed.), 'Schooling for Women's Work', Routledge & Kegan Paul, London.
DEPARTMENT OF EDUCATION (1977), 'Persistent School Absenteeism in Northern Ireland', Department of Education (NI), Bangor.
DEPARTMENT OF EDUCATION (1979), 'Youthways – Courses for the Young Unemployed. A Report of the Pilot Projects, January 1977–July 1978', Department of Education (NI), Bangor.
DEPARTMENT OF MANPOWER SERVICES (1974), 'Survey of Recruitment and Employment in the Printing and Publishing Industry in Northern Ireland', Unpublished report, DMS, Belfast.
DEPARTMENT OF MANPOWER SERVICES (1978), 'Northern Ireland Construction Industry Training Board, Report and Statement of Accounts for the Period 1 April 1976 to 31 March 1977', HMSO, Belfast.
DEUTSCH, R. and MAGOWAN, V. (1973-5), 'Northern Ireland 1968-74: A Chronology of Events', 3 vols, Blackstaff Press, Belfast.
DIRECT LABOUR COLLECTIVE (1978), 'Building with Direct Labour', Conference of Socialist Economists, London.
DITTON, J. (1979), 'Controlology: Beyond the New Criminology', Macmillan, London.
DMS YOP UNIT (1978), 'Recruitment/Selection Criteria for YOP Schemes', unpublished paper, Department of Manpower Services, Belfast.
DOERINGER, P.B. and PIORE, M.J. (1971), 'Internal Labour Markets and Manpower Analysis', Heath Lexington Books, Lexington.
DOUGLAS, J.D. (1970), Deviance and Respectability: The Social Construction of Moral Meanings, in Douglas, J.D. (ed.), 'Deviance and Respectability: The Social Construction of Moral Meanings', Basic Books, New York.
DOWNES, D. (1966), 'The Delinquent Solution', Routledge & Kegan Paul, London.
DOWNES, D. and ROCK, P. (1971), Social Reaction to Deviance and its Effects on Crime and Criminal Careers, 'British Journal of Sociology', vol.22, pp.351-64.
EASTHOPE, G. (1976), Religious War in Northern Ireland, 'Sociology', vol.10, pp.427-50.
EDWARDS, R.C., REICH, M. and GORDON, D.M. (1975), Introduction, in Edwards, R.C., Reich, M. and Gordon, D.M. (eds), 'Labor Market Segmentation', Lexington Books, Lexington.
ENNEW, J. (1980), 'The Western Isles Today', Cambridge University Press, Cambridge.
EVASON, E. (1976), 'Poverty: the Facts in Northern Ireland', Child Poverty Action Group, London.

EVASON, E. (1978), 'Family Poverty in Northern Ireland', Child Poverty Action Group, London.

EVASON, E. (1980), 'Ends that Won't Meet', Child Poverty Action Group, London.

FAIR EMPLOYMENT AGENCY (1978), 'An Industrial and Occupational Profile of the Two Sections of the Population in Northern Ireland', FEA, Belfast.

FARRELL, M. (1976), 'Northern Ireland: The Orange State', Pluto Press, London.

FLETCHER, C. (1981), 'Facing the Interview', Allen & Unwin, London.

FLETT, H. (1979), Bureaucracy and Ethnicity: Notions of Eligibility to Public Housing, in Wallman, S. (ed.), 'Ethnicity at Work', Macmillan, London.

FOSTER, M.G. (1978), Industrial Relations in Construction, 1970-77, 'Industrial Relations', vol.17, pp.18-31.

FRANKENBERG, R. (1966), 'Communities in Britain', Pelican, Harmondsworth.

FRASER, M. (1974), 'Children in Conflict', Pelican, Harmondsworth.

FRIEDMAN, A.L. (1977), 'Industry and Labour', Macmillan, London.

FRITH, S. (1978), 'The Sociology of Rock', Constable, London.

FRITH, S. (1980), Education, Training and the Labour Process, in Cole, M. and Skelton, B. (eds), 'Blind Alley: Youth in a Crisis of Capital', G.W. and A. Hesketh, Ormskirk.

GARNSEY, E. (1978), Women's Work and Theories of Class Stratification, 'Sociology', vol.12, pp.223-44.

GIBBON, P. (1975), 'The Origins of Ulster Unionism', Manchester University Press, Manchester.

GIDDENS, A. (1976), 'New Rules of the Sociological Method', Hutchinson, London.

GIDDENS, A. (1979), 'Central Problems in Social Theory', Macmillan, London.

GIDDENS, A. (1981a), 'The Class Structure of the Advanced Societies', 2nd edn, Hutchinson, London.

GIDDENS, A. (1981b), 'A Contemporary Critique of Historical Materialism', Macmillan, London.

GILL, O. (1977), 'Luke Street: Housing Policy, Conflict and the Creation of the Delinquent Area', Macmillan, London.

GINZBERG, E., GINSBURG, S.W., AXELRAD, S., and HERMA, J.L. (1951), 'Occupational Choice', Columbia University Press, New York.

GOLDTHORPE, J.H., LLEWELLYN, C. and PAYNE, C. (1980), 'Social Mobility and Class Structure in Modern Britain', Clarendon Press, Oxford.

GORDON, D.M. (1972), 'Theories of Poverty and Under-employment', D.C. Heath, Lexington.

GOVERNMENT OF NORTHERN IRELAND (1945), 'Planning Proposals for the Belfast Area', Cmnd 227, HMSO, Belfast.

HAKIM, C. (1979), Occupational Segregation, 'Research Paper No.9', Department of Employment, London.

HALL, S. (1980), Cultural Studies and the Centre: some Problematics and Problems, in Hall, S., Hobson, D., Lowe, A. and Willis, P. (eds), 'Culture, Media, Language', Hutchinson, London.

HANNERZ, U. (1969), 'Soulside', Columbia University Press, New York.

HARBISON, J. and HARBISON, J. (eds) (1980), 'A Society Under Stress', Open Books, Shepton Mallet.

HARGREAVES, D.H. (1967), 'Social Relations in a Secondary School', Routledge & Kegan Paul, London.
HARRIS, M. (1968), 'The Rise of Anthropological Theory', Routledge & Kegan Paul, London.
HARRIS, R. (1972), 'Prejudice and Tolerance in Ulster', Manchester University Press, Manchester.
HEBDIGE, D. (1979), 'Subculture: The Meaning of Style', Methuen, London.
HIGHAM, M. (1982), 'Coping with Interviews', New Opportunity Press, London.
HOBSON, D. (1981), 'Now that I'm married ...', in McRobbie, A. and McCabe, T. (eds), 'Feminism for Girls', Routledge & Kegan Paul, London.
HOLMES, R.M. (1979), 'An Investigation into the Evaluation of Examination Grades with Special Reference to CSE', unpublished dissertation, Stranmillis College, Belfast.
HOLMSTRÖM, M. (1976), 'South Indian Factory Workers', Cambridge University Press, Cambridge.
HUNT, J. and SMALL, P. (1981), 'Employing Young People: A Study of Employers' Attitudes, Policies and Practices', Scottish Council for Research in Education, Edinburgh.
IMRAY, L. and MIDDLETON, A. (1982), 'Public and Private: Marking the Boundaries', paper presented at the annual conference of the British Sociological Association, Manchester, April 1982.
INDUSTRIAL TRAINING RESEARCH UNIT (1979), 'The A-Z Study: Differences Between Improvers and Non-Improvers Among Young Unskilled Workers', ITRU, Cambridge.
INDUSTRIAL TRAINING SERVICES (1974), 'Survey of the Training and Manpower Needs in the Printing and Publishing Industry in Northern Ireland', unpublished report, ITS, Belfast.
JENKINS, R. (1981a), Thinking and Doing: Towards a Model of Cognitive Practice, in Holy, L. and Stuchlik, M. (eds), 'The Structure of Folk Models', Academic Press, London.
JENKINS, R. (1981b), 'Young People, Education and Work in a Belfast Housing Estate', PhD thesis, University of Cambridge.
JENKINS, R. (1982a), Pierre Bourdieu and the Reproduction of Determinism, 'Sociology', vol.16, pp.270-81.
JENKINS, R. (1982b), Managers, Recruitment Procedures and Black Workers, 'Working Papers on Ethnic Relations No.18', Research Unit on Ethnic Relations, Birmingham.
JENKINS, R. (1982c), 'Hightown Rules: Growing Up in a Belfast Housing Estate', National Youth Bureau, Leicester.
JENKINS, R. (1983), Goals, Constraints and Occupational Choice: the First Twelve Months in the Belfast Labour Market, 'British Journal of Guidance and Counselling', vol.11.
JOHNSON, R. (1979), Three Problematics: Elements of a Theory of Working-class Culture, in Clarke, J., Critcher, C. and Johnson, R. (eds), 'Working Class Culture', Hutchinson, London.
KEIL, E.T. (1976), 'Becoming a Worker', Leicestershire Committee for Education and Training/TSA, Leicester.
KERR, C. (1977), 'Labor Markets and Wage Determination', University of California Press, Berkeley.
KITSUSE, J.I. and CICOUREL, A.V. (1963), A Note on the Uses of Official Statistics, 'Social Problems', vol.11, pp.131-9.

KRECKEL, R. (1980), Unequal Opportunity Structure and Labour Market
Segmentation, 'Sociology', vol.14, pp.525-50.
LACEY, C. (1970), 'Hightown Grammar', Manchester University Press,
Manchester.
LAMB, D. (1974), 'The Lump: an Heretical Analysis', Solidarity,
Lancaster.
LEE, G. and WRENCH, J. (1983), 'Skill Seekers: The Quiet Disadvantage
of Black Youth', National Youth Bureau, Leicester.
LEMERT, E.M. (1967), 'Human Deviance, Social Problems and Social
Control', Prentice-Hall, Englewood Cliffs.
LEONARD, D. (1980), 'Sex and Generation: A Study of Courtship and
Weddings', Tavistock, London.
LEWIS, I.M. (1976), 'Social Anthropology in Perspective', Pelican,
Harmondsworth.
LEYTON, E. (1974), 'The One Blood: Kinship and Class in an Irish
Village', Institute of Social and Economic Research, Newfoundland.
LIEBOW, E. (1967), 'Tally's Corner', Little Brown, Boston.
LIPSKY, M. (1981), 'Street Level Bureaucracy: Dilemmas of the
Individual in Public Services', Russell Sage Foundation, New York.
LUMLEY, R. (1980), Industrial Relations on a Large Industrial
Construction Site, 'Journal of Management Studies', vol.17, pp.68-81.
LYONS, F.S.L. (1973), 'Ireland since the Famine', Fontana, London.
McCABE, T. (1981), Schools and Careers: for Girls who do want to
wear the Trousers, in McRobbie, A. and McCabe, T. (eds), 'Feminism
for Girls', Routledge & Kegan Paul, London.
McCALL, G.J. and SIMMONS, J.L. (eds) (1969), 'Issues in Participant
Observation: a Text and Reader', Addison-Wesley, Reading, Mass.
McKERNAN, J. (1982), Value Systems and Race Relations in Northern
Ireland and America, 'Ethnic and Racial Studies', vol.5, pp.156-74.
McKERNAN, J. and RUSSELL, J.L. (1980), Differences of Religion and
Sex in the Value Systems of Northern Ireland Adolescents, 'British
Journal of Social and Clinical Psychology', vol.19, pp.115-18.
McROBBIE, A. (1978), Working Class Girls and the Culture of
Femininity, in Women's Studies Group, 'Women Take Issue', Hutchinson,
London.
McROBBIE, A. (1980), Settling Accounts with Subcultures: a Feminist
Critique, 'Screen Education', no.34, pp.37-49.
McROBBIE, A. and GARBER, J. (1976), Girls and Subcultures, in
Hall, S. and Jefferson, T. (eds), 'Resistance through Rituals',
Hutchinson, London.
MAIZELS, J. (1970), 'Adolescent Needs and the Transition from School
to Work', Athlone Press, London.
MANPOWER SERVICES COMMISSION (1977), 'Young People and Work', ('The
Holland Report'), MSC, London.
MANPOWER SERVICES COMMISSION (1978), Young People and Work, 'Manpower
Studies No.19781', MSC, London.
MARSDEN, D. and DUFF, E. (1975), 'Workless: Some Unemployed Men
and their Families', Pelican, Harmondsworth.
MARSH, A., HENDY, P. and MATHESON, J. (1981), 'Labour Mobility in
the Construction Industry', OPCS, London.
MARX, K. (1970 edn), 'The Economic and Philosophic Manuscripts of
1844', Lawrence & Wishart, London.
MATHEW, R.H. (1961), 'Belfast Regional Survey and Plan', ('The
Mathew Plan'), HMSO, Belfast.

MATZA, D. (1967), The Disreputable Poor, in Bendix, R. and Lipset, S.M. (eds), 'Class, Status and Power', 2nd edn, Routledge & Kegan Paul, London.
MILLER, R. (1978), 'Attitudes to Work in Northern Ireland', Fair Employment Agency, Belfast.
MILROY, L. (1980), 'Language and Social Networks', Basil Blackwell, Oxford.
MINISTRY OF HEALTH AND LOCAL GOVERNMENT (1963), 'Belfast Regional Survey and Plan: Recommendations and Conclusions', Cmnd 451, HMSO, Belfast.
MITCHELL, J.C. (1967), On Quantification in Social Anthropology, in Epstein, A.L. (ed.), 'The Craft of Social Anthropology', Tavistock, London.
MOORE, R. (1972), Race Relations in the Six Counties: Colonialism Industrialization and Stratification in Ireland, 'Race', vol.14, pp.21-42.
MOORE, R. (1981), Aspects of Segmentation in the United Kingdom Building Industry Labour Market, in Wilkinson, F. (ed.) 'The Dynamics of Labour Market Segmentation', Academic Press, London.
MURDOCK, G. and McCRON, R. (1976), Youth and Class: The Career of a Confusion, in Mungham, G. and Pearson, G. (eds), 'Working Class Youth Culture', Routledge & Kegan Paul, London.
NADEL, S.F. (1957), 'The Theory of Social Structure', Cohen & West, London.
NELSON, S. (1975), Protestant 'Ideology' Considered: the Case of 'Discrimination', 'British Political Sociology Yearbook', vol.2, pp.155-87.
NEW ULSTER POLITICAL RESEARCH GROUP (1979), 'Beyond the Religious Divide', NUPRG, Belfast.
NICHOLS, T. and BEYNON, H. (1977), 'Living with Capitalism: Class Relations and the Modern Factory', Routledge & Kegan Paul, London.
NORRIS, G.M. (1978), Unemployment, Subemployment and Personal Characteristics, 'Sociological Review', vol.26, pp.89-108, 327-47.
O'DOWD, L., ROLSTON, B. and TOMLINSON, M. (1980), 'Northern Ireland: Between Civil Rights and Civil War', CSE Books, London.
O'DOWD, L. and TOMLINSON, M. (1980), Urban Politics in Belfast: Two Case Studies, 'International Journal of Urban and Regional Research', vol.4, pp.72-95.
OFFE, C. (1976), 'Industry and Inequality: the Achievement Principle in Work and Social Status', Edward Arnold, London.
OSBORNE, R. (1980), Religious Discrimination in the Northern Ireland Labour Market, 'International Journal of Social Economics', vol.7, pp.206-23.
PA MANAGEMENT CONSULTANTS (1977), 'Survey of Employment Problems and Practices in the Northern Ireland Construction Industry', unpublished report, The Federation of Building and Civil Engineering Contractors (NI) Ltd, Belfast.
PARKER, H. (1974), 'A View from the Boys', David & Charles, Newton Abbot.
PATRICK, J. (1973), 'A Glasgow Gang Observed', Eyre Methuen, London.
PIORE, M.J. (1971), The Dual Labour Market: Theory and Implications, in Gordon, D.M. (ed.), 'Problems in Political Economy: an Urban Perspective', D.C. Heath, Lexington.
PITT-RIVERS, J. (1971), 'The People of the Sierra', 2nd edn, University of Chicago Press, Chicago.

POLLERT, A. (1981), 'Girls, Wives, Factory Lives', Macmillan, London.
POLSKY, N. (1971), 'Hustlers, Beats and Others', Pelican, Harmondsworth.
PROBERT, B. (1978), 'Beyond Orange and Green', Academy Press, Dublin.
PROJECT TEAM (1976), 'Belfast Areas of Special Social Needs', HMSO, Belfast.
PRYCE, K. (1979), 'Endless Pressure', Penguin, Harmondsworth.
REES, T.L. (1980), 'Studies of Direct Job Creation in Northern Ireland', Study No. 790140, Commission of the European Communities, Brussels.
REES, T.L. and ATKINSON, P. (1982), 'Youth Unemployment and State Intervention', Routledge & Kegan Paul, London.
REID, E. (1980), Young People and Employment (i): Employers' Use of Educational Qualifications, 'Educational Policy Bulletin', vol.8, pp.46-64.
REID, E. (1981), Managers and Young Employees, 'Policy Studies', vol.1, pp.173-95.
REVIEW TEAM (1975), 'Economic and Industrial Strategy for Northern Ireland', ('The Quigley Report'), HMSO, Belfast.
RIST, R.C. (1977), On Understanding the Processes of Schooling: the Contributions of Labelling Theory, in Karabel, J. and Halsey, A.H. (eds), 'Power and Ideology in Education', Oxford University Press, New York.
ROBINS, D. and COHEN, P. (1978), 'Knuckle Sandwich', Pelican, Harmondsworth.
ROLSTON, B. (1980), Reformism and Class Politics in Northern Ireland, 'Insurgent Sociologist', vol.10, no.2, pp.73-83.
ROSSER, C. and HARRIS, C. (1965), 'The Family and Social Change', Routledge & Kegan Paul, London.
RYRIE, A.C. and WEIR, A.D. (1978), 'Getting a Trade', Hodder & Stoughton for the Scottish Council for Research in Education, London.
SALAMAN, G. and THOMPSON, K. (1978), Class Culture and the Persistence of an Elite, 'Sociological Review', vol.26, pp.283-304.
SAWDON, A., PELICAN, J. and TUCKER, S. (1981), 'Study of the Transition from School to Working Life', vol.3, Youthaid, London.
SCHOFIELD, R.B. and CARLISLE, J. (1978), 'Final Report on a Pilot Study of Apprentice Training in the Construction Industry', unpublished report, NI Construction Industry Training Board, Newtownabbey.
SHARMA, U. (1980), 'Women, Work and Property in North-West India', Tavistock, London.
SHARP, R. (1980), 'Knowledge, Ideology and the Politics of Schooling', Routledge & Kegan Paul, London.
SILVERMAN, D. and JONES, J. (1973), Getting In: the Managed Accomplishment of Correct Selection Outcomes, in Child, J. (ed.) 'Man and Organization', Allen & Unwin, London.
SINFIELD, A. (1981), Unemployment in an Unequal Society, in Showler, B. and Sinfield, A. (eds), 'The Workless State', Martin Robertson, Oxford.
SPELMAN, B.J. (1979), 'Pupil Adaptation to Secondary School', Northern Ireland Council for Educational Research, Belfast.
SPENDER, D. (1982), 'Invisible Women: The Schooling Scandal', Writers and Readers Publishing Cooperative, London.
STAFFORD, A. (1981), Learning not to Labour, 'Capital & Class', no.15, pp.55-77.

STAFFORD, E.M. (1982), The Impact of the Youth Opportunities Programme on Young People's Employment Prospects and Psychological Well-being, 'British Journal of Guidance and Counselling', vol.10, pp.12-21.
STEWART, A., PRANDY, K. and BLACKBURN, R.M. (1980), 'Social Stratification and Occupations', Macmillan, London.
STUCHLIK, M. (1976), Whose Knowledge?, in Holy, L. (ed.), Knowledge and Behaviour. 'The Queen's University Papers in Social Anthropology', vol.1, The Queen's University of Belfast, Belfast.
STUDY GROUP (1978), 'Opportunities at Sixteen', ('The Birley Report'), HMSO, Belfast.
SUPER, D. (1953), A Theory of Vocational Development, 'American Psychologist', vol.8, pp.185-90.
SYKES, A.J.M. (1960a), Unity and Restrictive Practices in the British Printing Industry, 'Sociological Review', vol.8, pp.239-54.
SYKES, A.J.M. (1960b), Trade Union Workshop Organisation in the Printing Industry: the Chapel, 'Human Relations', vol.13, pp.49-65.
SYKES, A.J.M. (1969a), Navvies: Their Work Attitudes, 'Sociology', vol.3, pp.21-35.
SYKES, A.J.M. (1969b), Navvies: Their Social Relations, 'Sociology', vol.3, pp.157-72.
TOURAINE, A. (1977), 'The Self-Production of Society', University of Chicago Press, Chicago.
TOWNSEND, P. (1979), 'Poverty in the United Kingdom', Pelican, Harmondsworth.
TREWSDALE, J.M. and TRAINOR, M. (1979), 'Womanpower No.1: A Statistical Survey of Women and Work in Northern Ireland', Equal Opportunities Commission for Northern Ireland, Belfast.
VAN VELSEN, J. (1967), The Extended-Case Method and Situational Analysis, in Epstein, A.L. (ed.), 'The Craft of Social Anthropology', Tavistock, London.
VENABLES, E. (1967), 'The Young Worker at College - A Study of a Local Tech.', Faber & Faber, London.
WALKER, P. (ed.) (1979), 'Between Labour and Capital', Harvester Press, Brighton.
WEBER, M. (1968), 'Economy and Society', New York, Bedminster Press.
WEINER, R. (1975), 'The Rape and Plunder of the Shankill', Notaems Press, Belfast.
WHYTE, W.F. (1955), 'Street Corner Society', 2nd edn, University of Chicago Press, Chicago.
WILLIS, P. (1977), 'Learning to Labour', Saxon House, Farnborough.
WILLIS, P. (1979), Shop Floor Culture, Masculinity and the Wage Form, in Clarke, J., Critcher, C. and Johnson, R. (eds), 'Working Class Culture', Hutchinson, London.
WILLIS, P. (1981), Cultural Production is Different from Cultural Reproduction is Different from Social Reproduction is Different from Reproduction, 'Interchange', vol.12, nos.2-3, pp.48-67.
WILLMOTT, P. (1969), 'Adolescent Boys of East London', Pelican, Harmondsworth.
WORKERS' RESEARCH UNIT (1978), Women in Northern Ireland, 'Belfast Workers' Research Bulletin 5', WRU, Belfast.
ZIMBALIST, A. (ed.) (1979), 'Case Studies on the Labour Process', Monthly Review Press, New York.

INDEX